Other True Crime Accounts by

DIANE FANNING

The Pastor's Wife

Out There

Under the Knife

Baby Be Mine

Gone Forever

Through the Window

Into the Water

Written in Blood

Available from the True Crime Library of
St. Martin's Paperbacks

A POISONED PASSION

A Young Mother, Her War Hero Husband,
and the Marriage that Ended in Murder

Diane Fanning

St. Martin's Paperbacks

A POISONED PASSION

Copyright © 2009 by Diane Fanning.

For information address St. Martin's Press, 175 Fifth Avenue, New York, NY 10010.

EAN: 978-0-312-94507-7

Printed in the United States of America

St. Martin's Paperbacks edition / September 2009

St. Martin's Paperbacks are published by St. Martin's Press, 175 Fifth Avenue, New York, NY 10010.

10 9 8 7 6 5 4 3 2 1

To Shane and Tristan—
May you build the strength you need
to face and conquer your past

ACKNOWLEDGMENTS

This book was possible because of the help and cooperation of many public employees across a broad swath of Texas. Thanks to Barbara McNichols at the Third Court of Appeals of Texas, Jason Clark, Texas Department of Criminal Justice, Loris Jones and Investigator Michael Miller at the Texas Board of Veterinary Medical Examiners and Linda Sherwood and Kaye Schulz at Texas Parks and Wildlife in Austin; the folks at Justice of the Peace Offices in San Angelo, including Tom Green County Judge Eddie Howard and Janet McEntyre in Precinct 4 and Judge Fred Buck in Precinct 3; Wendy Hind at the Tom Green County Sheriff's Office; Lieutenant Curtis Milbourn and Carla Davis of the San Angelo Police Department; Leandra Turley, Tom Green County District Court Clerk's Office and, last but definitely not least, someone many of you will recognize from *Gone Forever*, Texas Ranger Lieutenant Shawn Palmer.

Other Texans providing invaluable assistance were Attorney Thomas Goff, Artist Jimmy Don Cox, Buda Howell, Donald Baker at Blaine's Pub, retired Water Valley vocational agricultural teacher Charlie Fleming, Dr. Jay Jones, Dr. Larry Ellis, Realtor Joe Stephens, J.D. Gould, Frank Langley, Ruth Marshall, Jason Geron, Dr. Murl Bailey, veterinary medicine professor at Texas A&M, the best university in the state of Texas, and right here in New Braunfels, Dan Phillips of Mission Investigations, Michael Devers of Lone Star Music, and my very own veterinarian Dr. Michael Dougherty at Creekview Veterinary Clinic.

For life in rural Maine, my thanks to Bruce Lindberg, headmaster of Lee Academy, and a special thanks to those people who now share a place in my heart: Shirley Harvey, Aunt Lenore, Brinda and Nicole Spinney and Les Severance—thank you for sharing your memories of Michael Severance.

As with every true crime book I've written, there were a handful of folks who were willing to talk to me, but who didn't want anyone else to know about it. To all of you, I kept my promise of your anonymity and take this opportunity to acknowledge your contribution to this book—thank you.

As always, I appreciate my agent Jane Dystel for her faith in me, Charles Spicer for his support of my writing and Yaniv Soha for his brilliant editing. I can't thank any of you enough.

And thanks to my good friend Kathryn Casey, who was always willing to listen as I worried over problems and struggled for solutions; and to the wonderful man in my life, Wayne, who listens, reads, suggests, consoles and cheers from the sidelines.

ONE

On his long weekend off, in early March 2005, Game Warden Marshall Davidson drove four hundred miles from Zapata in south Texas up to the west Texas town of San Angelo to visit with his parents at the family home. It was a tumultuous time for the Davidson clan. Marshall's brother-in-law Michael Severance had disappeared without a trace in January. Wendi, Marshall's veterinarian sister, was running a new business and caring for her infant and 3-year-old sons with help from her parents. Marshall's grandmother, Jessie Mae Eggemeyer, was suffering through the terminal stages of lung cancer. The family agonized as they watched her waste away and become progressively more uncommunicative.

Marshall sat down to dinner with his mother and father, Judy and Lloyd Davidson and his 3-year-old nephew, Wendi's son Tristan, on Saturday, March 5. They'd barely taken a bite when the telephone rang. Judy answered. When she returned to the dining table, Marshall saw distress wrinkling his mother's face. "What's wrong?" he asked.

"I don't know," she said, shaking her head.

"Who was on the phone?"

"Wendi."

"What did she want?" Marshall prodded.

"She said somebody's chasing her and she's going to keep driving and go to the cemetery."

"Well, who's chasing her?"

"She doesn't know."

Marshall strapped on his pistol and drove a couple of miles, turning in at the sign that read "GRAPE CREEK CEMETERY—Founded 1895." He entered a gate surrounded by scrubby trees and tall weeds, and went up the narrow dirt lane into the small graveyard. It was a patchwork of old worn gravestones and newer flat plaques, amidst clumps of grass, dirt and rocks. The whole thing could have fit inside the twenty-yard line of a football field. The hum of the nearby highway traffic filled the air.

He saw his sister's 2001 red Chevrolet Camaro first, then he saw her standing by the grave of their grandfather. Wendi was obviously agitated as she paced over a tiny circular patch of ground like a high-strung race horse.

He walked toward her, looking around for any sign of another person or vehicle, but none was in sight. "Who's following you? What's up?"

"No. Nobody's following me. It's just that, you know, I mean, I got something that I need to say, but I'm going to wait till Mom and Dad are here."

"No," Marshall said, a bit irritated at being put off by Wendi after he'd raced over to come to her aid. "Something's bothering you this much, so what is it?"

"Look, nobody's going to believe me . . ." Wendi began.

Marshall shifted his weight from one foot to the other waiting for her to continue.

"I didn't kill Mike, but, you know, I did find him dead, and I moved his body to the tank."

"You did what?"

"I took him to the tank at Terrell's. I was just, like, freaking out."

"Why?" Marshall asked. "Why, why would you do something like that?"

"I don't know," she wailed. "I just found him dead there, and, you know, it's— One of the doors, normally you have to use a key—or, you know, it locks from the inside, so you use a key to get it— You know, check it to see if it's unlocked anyways. I went in there, and all the doors were locked up and he was—you know, he was laying there in the bed, and, you know, dead or whatever. And I freaked out, and the first thing that came to my mind is, somebody I know had to do it, you know? How did they get in the clinic if they didn't?"

"The door was locked?"

"I assumed it was," Wendi answered.

"Why?"

"I didn't really check. I just put my key in and turned it. They had to have a key. Maybe it was Nanny," she said referring to their dying grandmother. "She had a key."

"Nanny? You think Nanny killed Mike?" Marshall thought of his dying grandmother and knew the suggestion was absurd.

"I don't know who did it, but I didn't," she snapped. "Nobody liked him, you know?"

"That's no reason to kill somebody."

"I didn't kill him. They're going to think I did. That's why I moved the body."

Lloyd and Judy's pick-up truck pulled into the cemetery with the Davidsons seated in the front seats and young Tristan in a child's seat in the back. Wendi, sobbing, rushed over to them with Marshall on her heels. Both started telling the story at the same time. The 4-and-a-half-month-old infant in the Camaro chose that moment to wake up and add his cries to the cacophony.

Marshall shouted to be heard over the din. "Wendi, you know, the best thing for you to do is just keep your mouth shut." He stalked off and flipped open his cell. He dialed the San Angelo Police Department and asked for Detective Dennis McGuire. The investigator wasn't in the office. Marshall said it was an emergency and left the number to his cell phone. They told him that they'd have McGuire return the call.

When Marshall walked back to the Davidsons' pick-up, Wendi was in the back seat of the truck next to Tristan, comforting the child. Judy was babbling, Wendi was crying. Marshall tried to settle everyone down, but failed. Three minutes after his first call, Marshall redialed the police department and was told that McGuire hadn't answered his cell. "Give me his number," Marshall demanded.

"We're not authorized to give his number."

Marshall identified himself as law enforcement and insisted, "Somebody better give me his number. I need him to meet me at Grape Creek Cemetery."

"Hold on. We'll check."

Marshall gave them his mom's cell phone number, too, and said he'd call back. He tried again to calm his hysterical mother. He gave up and called the police again. This time, he was told, "Okay. He authorized us to give his cell phone number, so here it is."

Marshall disconnected and dialed the number he'd been given. McGuire answered in the whiny, nasal voice that garnered a lot of good-natured teasing at the station house. "Hey, meet me out here at the Grape Creek Cemetery."

"I got your message and I'm on the way."

McGuire was close enough to the cemetery by then that Marshall was able to look up and spot him approaching on the highway. Sergeant Dave Jones, a special crimes investigator with the Texas Department of Public Safety rode with him. Officer Bill Mabe, who was on nearby Sutton Road securing the gate to Terrell Sheen's 7777 Ranch, headed toward the cemetery, too.

Marshall called Sheen and warned him to stay away from the ranch. McGuire exited Route 87 at March Road, heading for the graveyard in the fading sunshine of a dying late winter day. He was the first member of law enforcement to arrive on the scene. Although only in his forties, McGuire's silver and blonde hair was already thinning in spots, and he carried a few extra pounds on his frame. His ruddy complexion gave him the look of excitability in contrast to his unflappable nature.

McGuire spotted Marshall standing in the lane behind the super cab truck. Inside, McGuire saw Lloyd in the driver's seat and Judy in the front passenger seat with her infant grandson Shane on her lap. Wendi was in the back with her other son, 3-year-old Tristan.

McGuire and Jones stepped out of the car and approached Marshall. McGuire asked, "What do you need?"

"Have you searched the pond on Mr. Sheen's ranch?" Marshall said.

"No, we have not," McGuire admitted.

"You need to," Marshall said as Mabe's vehicle pulled into the cemetery. Now in his fifties, Mabe had the rough looks of a dignified manual laborer who'd spent many years working hard, getting things done. He combed his dark hair straight back, drawing attention to his high forehead. As he listened, his bright blue eyes settled on Marshall explaining the situation: "Michael Severance's body is in the pond. My sister said she didn't kill him, but she moved his body to the pond."

"Are you talking about the pond on Terrell Sheen's ranch?" Mabe asked.

"Yes," Marshall said, and walked up to the rear passenger door of the pick-up truck and opened it.

McGuire followed him, standing back a couple of feet listening to the conversation and observing the distress emanating from the truck cab.

In a raised emotional voice, Wendi said, "I didn't kill him, but somebody did. I thought that one of you did it," she said, referring to her family, "so I moved the body to protect you."

Lloyd sat in stunned silence. Judy babbled incoherently, near hysteria, denying that she'd killed anyone. Wendi repeated, "I did it to protect you. I did it for you."

Marshall interrupted them. "The police are here and they need to take Wendi into custody. Wendi, you need to get out of the pick-up truck now."

"No. No, don't do it, Wendi," Judy shouted. "Marshall, we'll take her. They don't have to take her."

"They need to take her," Marshall insisted.

"No, you're not going to take her," Judy said to her son.

Marshall ignored her. "Wendi," he said, "you just need to go."

Wendi paused, considering her mother's objections, then

stepped out into the grass and stood close to her brother. Marshall turned to the officers and said, "You need to arrest her. She found Michael Severance dead, and disposed of his body in the stock tank at Terrell Sheen's Four Sevens Ranch."

"What are you?" Wendi asked. "A cop or my brother?"

"I'm both," Marshall said. He clenched his jaw tight. He knew he was doing the right thing. But he also knew he was disappointing his sister.

Mabe took a step toward Wendi and said, "You need to come with us, Ms. Davidson. You are not in custody, but we need to ask you a few questions."

As Wendi turned to go with him, Marshall put a hand on her forearm. "Keep your mouth shut until you've been able to talk to an attorney."

As Mabe deposited Wendi in the back seat of McGuire's car, McGuire asked Marshall if he could come into town to the police station on Beauregard Avenue. Marshall agreed to come in, but said, "I will not investigate my own sister. That is your job. I don't want her talking to anybody until we get her a lawyer."

Marshall watched as the police vehicle pulled out of the cemetery toward the setting sun. He kept his eyes on the silhouette of his only sibling sitting in the back seat of a patrol car, on her way to an interrogation room to be questioned about her involvement in the murder of her own husband.

Marshall's heart sunk. His loyalties were divided. Now that the deed was done, sharp pangs of regret criss-crossed his heart.

TWO

Officer Mabe followed Wendi's car as Marshall drove it over to the Davidsons' spread. Marshall climbed into the police car and rode back to the cemetery to retrieve his vehicle before going to the police station.

Texas Ranger Shawn Palmer pulled his pick-up truck into the parking lot at the San Angelo Police Department on Beauregard Avenue at 7:30. He lengthened his stature with the traditional Texas Rangers cowboy hat. His boots gave a longer stride and a cocky staccato to his walk. With his brush-cut reddish-blonde hair, ruddy complexion and strong jaw, he could have been typecast in the role of a lawman in a western movie.

He went to an interview room and joined Detectives Dennis McGuire and Brian Elkins. They weren't getting any answers from Wendi. Elkins left when Palmer entered the room.

When Palmer asked the first question, Wendi smirked and said, "I want an attorney." McGuire and Palmer left her alone in that interview room and went two doors down the hall to speak with her brother.

Marshall Davidson reiterated the sequence of events that evening, telling the investigators that his sister had discovered her husband's dead body in the veterinary clinic on Saturday, January 15, 2005. He said that Wendi insisted that she was not the murderer, but since she knew many of her family members hated Mike, she believed one of them had killed him.

When directly asked if he believed that Wendi had murdered Mike, Marshall said, "It looks real bad when someone moves a body."

Palmer asked Marshall if he believed that Wendi could have transported Mike from the clinic and dumped him into the water without help. "She can pick me up, and he was my size. She didn't have to move him very far to get him in there. Yeah, it's possible she could do it."

At the end of the interview, Marshall asked if he could speak to his sister. McGuire and Palmer exchanged a glance and nodded. "Just make sure you leave the door open a crack," McGuire instructed.

The two investigators empathized with their fellow law enforcement officer. No doubt about it, Marshall was in an awkward position. He had done his duty and reported the information about his sister to authorities. But here in the police station, he was balking at answering any other questions. His family loyalty now seemed to be stronger than his promise to uphold the law. Palmer and McGuire felt sorry for him then—but not for long.

In another room, Wendi waited. She yelled at Marshall when he entered. "How could you?"

Marshall held out his arms in the universal sign of entreaty. "Wendi," he said.

"How could you turn me in? I am your sister."

"What you did is what you did."

"How could you?"

"You need to settle down, Wendi," Marshall said.

Wendi continued to rant at him about family, loyalty and her innocent desire to protect her parents. Marshall brushed her off. "Here's what's going to happen. They're going to book you in, and, at some point, take you to the county jail. The kids will be taken care of, so you don't have to worry about them. What do you need us to do with the clinic and everything?"

Wendi ignored his questions and lit into another tirade. After ten minutes, Marshall gave up and left the room.

At the moment, McGuire and Palmer had no body and were not ready to make the legal assumption that the missing Air Force staff sergeant, Michael Severance, had died as the result of homicide. They did have all they needed, however, to charge her with a different felony. McGuire had heard her admit that she'd disposed of the body of a man who'd died under suspicious circumstances. Both of the investigators had heard the corroborating testimony from Marshall.

Palmer went to his office in the Texas Department of Public Safety building out on the Loop and prepared an affidavit for an arrest warrant on a tampering with evidence charge, a third-degree felony punishable by up to 10 years in prison and a $10,000 fine. The affidavit claimed that the deceased body was evidence or contained evidence. When Wendi Davidson transported and concealed the body, she'd prevented investigators from having access to it.

He presented the document to Judge Eddie Howard, Justice of the Peace, Precinct 4, and swore to its honesty and accuracy. Howard signed the warrant and set bond for $500,000. Sergeant Palmer arrested her at 11:31 P.M. and turned over her custody to San Angelo Police Department Officer David Kahn, who transferred her to the Tom Green County Jail.

Palmer called Terrell Sheen and told him about the recent developments in the missing persons investigation of Michael Severance. He informed the property owner that officers had secured the area of the pond on Sheen's 7777 Ranch on Sutton Road. Sheen agreed to meet with Palmer at the location the following morning to grant his permission for a search of the property.

Palmer went home to get a few hours of sleep before he had to relieve the officers securing the ranch overnight. At 5:30 the next morning, he went through the gate at 7777 Ranch, drove down the one-lane caliche road through fields where cattle roamed, and parked next to a barn.

He was joined at the pond by Investigator McGuire. Together, they awaited the arrival of the others. The scrubby land, filled with prickly pear cactus and stunted trees, came to life around them with the rising of the sun. Bird song filled the air and a breeze blew through leaves, churning up dust. Palmer videotaped the area.

At 9, people began to arrive at the gate. The first two were San Angelo Police Department evidence technician Rosalind Hinds, and ranch owner Terrell Sheen. Fifteen minutes later, they were joined by United States Air Force Office of Special Investigations Special Agents Greg McCormick and Arch Harner and their evidence tech Julie Lecea. Soon after, Terrell Sheen signed a consent-to-search form and Hinds videotaped and photographed the ranch entrance, the one-lane road and the pond.

Around 10, another influx of officers arrived: Sergeant David Jones with the special crimes division of the Texas Department of Public Safety, investigators from the Tom Green County Sheriff's Office and the San Angelo Police Department along with the state trooper dive team. In half an hour, the underwater crew was ready to explore the depths of the pond in their search for the missing Michael Severance.

THREE

As the sun beat down on the shade-starved ranch, the officers from four different law enforcement agencies gathered around the stock pond as the divers took turns exploring the murky water for the body and any other evidence. Palmer watched for a couple of hours before setting out to find ranch hand Jose Romero. Jose lived in a trailer house northeast of the pond. Palmer questioned him in Spanish. Jose readily admitted to seeing either Wendi or her distinctive red Camaro on the property on more than one occasion.

Just after 2 P.M., the dive team made a discovery: a body submerged in the water near the wire fence that transected the middle of the pond—it was on the far side of the fence away from the dock. Attempts to videotape the evidence with an underwater camera failed.

Palmer, McGuire, evidence tech Hinds and the dive team took a boat out to the spot where the body was located. Above its location, Hinds took the temperature of the water six inches deep. She dutifully recorded 52 degrees Fahrenheit.

The body was weighted down by a variety of objects. The divers detached a cinder block, tire rim, brake drum and boat anchor fastened to the body with baling wire and plastic ties. The body floated up toward the surface, back first. As it emerged, Palmer noted that it was definitely the remains of a white male wearing maroon boxer shorts with

injuries on the back consistent with stab wounds. It resem-
bled the photographs he'd seen of Michael Severance—the
cold water had preserved the body well.

Palmer and McGuire helped guide the body, still encum-
bered with other weights, over to the bank of the pond. Palmer
handed a new unwrapped white sheet to the dive team. The
divers slipped it under the body and used it to lift Michael
out of the water.

A rock was still attached to the neck with baling wire and
plastic ties. Another cinder block was tied to the left ankle
with a plastic tie and monofilament line. Palmer saw additional groups of injuries on the abdomen and chest that also
appeared to have been made by a sharp object. Before leaving the water, the divers secured all of the items they'd removed from the submerged body and then detached the
items still connected and secured them as evidence, placing
them inside a body bag.

The moment Terrell Sheen learned a body was found, he
called Lloyd Davidson. Lloyd called Judy, then tore away
from his job site without a word of explanation to anyone.

Judge Eddie Howard arrived on the scene and pronounced
the victim deceased just before 4 P.M. The body went into
another bag and, with the objects, was transported to the
Lubbock County Medical Examiner's Office.

Before leaving the area around the pond, Rosalind Hinds
secured other possible evidence—sections of rope, boat
oars, fishing line, a fillet knife, a brick with string attached
and pieces of rust from the aluminum boat. She then went
with Ranger Palmer to the nearby barn.

Pulling open the door, they were greeted by a noise that
sounded like old bones jostling in a pile of dried leaves. The
meaning of that distinctive grating was clear: rattlesnakes.
Palmer and Hinds stood still; awareness of peril tightened
their muscles and made their breathing shallow. They knew
the slightest movement could agitate a snake into striking.
They relaxed when they spotted the wooden enclosure over
to one side. They knew why the vipers were in the barn.
It was almost time for the Jaycee's 47th Rattlesnake

Round-Up in Sweetwater, Texas, just 70 miles due north of San Angelo.

The enclosure held dozens of captive snakes. Jose Romero was a snake hunter. From October to March, like folks all over West Texas, he smoked the rattlers out of their dens and gathered them up for the annual event. In days, he'd move his haul out of the barn and transport them up to the big event.

When he arrived with the 30,000 others who visited the town of 11,000 for the festival, he'd take his snakes to the Nolan County Coliseum, where they'd be weighed to determine the amount of money he'd get paid. The first 1,500 pounds to arrive earned top dollar—anywhere from $3 to $10 per pound, depending on the year. The rest of the squirming mass went for fifty cents a pound. A lot of the hunters got in town days before the event to get at the head of the line for the larger pay-out.

After the weigh-in, the vipers were pitched into an above-ground pit with thousands of others. Standing amongst them was a man protected by boots and chaps, and carrying tongs. He'd shuffle the live snakes aside and pluck out the occasional dead one.

From there, the snakes moved to the milking pit where a team extracted venom for use by scientists developing treatments for blood clots and tumors. Then they were decapitated, skinned, beer-battered and fried. Craftsmen used their heads, hides and rattles for hat bands, key chains and other souvenirs.

At the moment, though, they were just a live squirming, stinking mass of rippling flesh whose tails created an ominous crescendo as the grand finale for today's grisly work—the recovery of a body that had spent seven weeks underwater. Before leaving the outbuilding, Hinds took possession of an unopened package of plastic ties as well as a container of ties and a pair of fencing pliers. Sergeant Mabe took custody of the aluminum boat. Just before 7 that evening, the job was done and everyone headed out the gate and toward the highway.

They knew Wendi had disposed of her husband's body—but how did Michael Severance die? All options were open until the completion of the autopsy report in Lubbock. Suicide, accident or homicide—all had to be considered. If the medical examiner found signs of foul play, the investigators had no doubt that their prime suspect was 26-year-old veterinarian Wendi Mae Davidson.

FOUR

Judy Elliott was born on November 23, 1953, and grew up in
Mertzon, a town of 800, southwest of San Angelo in the adja-
cent county of Irion, graduating from Mertzon High School.
She was a real daddy's girl. Her older sister, Yvonne—
known in the family as Cissy—and her brother Darrell
always knew she was their father's favorite.

Lloyd Davidson was a few months older, born on March
14, 1953. Neither one of them has ever stepped outside of the
state. They've spent their lives in West Texas, a place filled
with cowboys, loners and folks seeking escape from the
mainstream. A land where brown is a more common color
than green. It has two saving graces. The first is that it is not
all flat. Around San Angelo, the rolling hills soften the
harshness of the environment and entice your exploration
beyond the next rise. The second is the sky. It is enormous.
In some parts of the country, it is confined to a vast empty
space right above your head. Out here, though, it fills the
field of vision, covering like a huge dome of blue, arching up
from the ground and curving overhead, encapsulating the
world.

San Angelo itself feels like an outpost in the middle of
nowhere. Driving northwest from Kerrville, the beauty of
the Texas Hill Country fades in the rear-view mirror as you
pass through miles and miles of nothing. That void encircles
the city like a moat, cutting it off from the rest of the world.

The closest city of comparable size is Abilene and it's

ninety miles away. And this is not the Abilene of song. That
one is in Kansas. Lots of people love living in Abilene, Texas,
but no one ever wrote lyrics calling it "the prettiest little town"
they'd "ever seen."

San Angelo does have some pleasant features in the midst
of its drabness. The Concho River runs through it, the waters giving the promise of life. The downtown area is charm-
ing with its western architecture and eclectic shops. And the
people are kind to strangers and more than willing to lend a
helping hand.

In this frontier environment, Judy and Lloyd met and
married in 1974. They moved out to their ranch north of San
Angelo where they have lived ever since. Lloyd didn't believe in credit cards or mortgages. He built their home with
his own hands, using the money they'd saved for that purpose. Their house sat an eighth of a mile from the road, just
over a little hump in the driveway.

Judy was 23 and Lloyd 24 when their first child, Wendi
Mae, was born on July 23, 1978. The next year, they wel-
comed their second child, Marshall Anthony, to the family
on September 10. Two new residents in a decade of growth
in San Angelo and the surrounding Tom Green County—the
population increased by nearly 20 percent between 1970
and 1980.

Before the children were born, Judy worked as a secretary at Angelo State University. In her earlier thirties, Judy
became a full-time homemaker after a diagnosis of lupus
took her out of the workplace and put her on Social Security
Disability.

While the kids grew up, Lloyd worked at the Levi Strauss
factory. The ranch where they raised Wendi and Marshall
was secluded and the family centered their life there. Neither Judy nor Lloyd was involved in a church or any social
organizations. They had few friends and pretty much kept to
themselves by choice.

There were frequent visits to Judy's parents' home when
Wendi and Marshall were little. Judy's sister Cissy had a
trailer there for a while, but then her father built a house for

her with Lloyd's help. Holidays were a cherished gathering time at the Elliot home. On Memorial Day, Fourth of July and Labor Day weekends, they all gathered to grill all day, swim in the pool and listen to music from the juke box on the back patio.

When Judy's father died in 1987, her mother Jessie Mae was devastated, and too distraught to do anything to hold the extended family together. For a while, family gatherings moved to Lloyd and Judy's house, but they weren't too keen on hosting these events. In time, the get-togethers ended, and contact diminished and nearly disappeared. At home, Judy focused on the children, and Lloyd on building an out-door aviary and creating an exotic bird business. He started with pigeons, parakeets and cockatiels, and expanded from there.

The Davidson place was always home to a menagerie of animals. Wendi got her first dog when she was 3 years old. She named him Licky Candlestick. Wendi's best friend at Grape Creek Elementary, Stacey McGinley, visited on occasion. But for the most part, the family maintained their unit of four against the world. The kids, as a result, spent a lot of time exploring their immediate environment. They performed acts of kindness for the wildlife they encountered, rescuing a bird with a broken wing or nursing a baby raccoon whose mother had been killed by a car or other mishap. Wendi was only 7 years old when she first expressed her desire to be a veterinarian when she grew up.

Neither she nor her brother Marshall had any serious childhood injuries or illnesses. Wendi's only trip to the hospital was for a routine tonsillectomy. The two children grew quite close. While both of them were still at Grape Creek Elementary School, Marshall came home one day with ripped clothing and scratches on his face and arms. He told Wendi that a classmate had beaten him with an old tree root. The next day in school, Wendi tracked down the boy in the cafeteria. She got in his face and screamed threats at him and warned him to leave her little brother alone.

Wendi's love of animals grew when she attended Water

Valley High School. She excelled in her animal science class as well as all of the rest of her agricultural studies. Charlie Fleming, her retired vocational Ag teacher said, "She was one of the best students I ever had. A smart, sweet kid." Charlie kept up with Wendi's progress long after her graduation from high school, taking great pride in his former student's accomplishments.

Both Lloyd and Judy were active in the school's agricultural program when their children were at Water Valley High. They helped out at the school, enthusiastically supported every fundraiser and volunteered to help students at shows. "Anything I asked them to do, they did," Charlie said.

Wendi showed goats at the Tom Green County, San Angelo and Odessa Stock Shows. It was a good way to raise scholarship money for college. She was very involved in Future Farmers of America, where she became the club's treasurer when she was a senior. That same year, her younger brother Marshall was also an officer in the group, serving as sentinel.

Wendi also took part in cheerleading, basketball and volleyball. In twelfth grade, she received All Star Honorable Mention for her role as a Police Officer in a one-act play, *The Tell Tale Heart*. The list of extracurricular activities on her college application was quite impressive.

Because of poor social skills—an inability to relate to others and to understand the impact her actions and words had on those around her—she had a difficult time with peer relationships, particularly with other girls. She was not popular at school. In fact, the other cheerleaders did not seem to like her at all. Her negative experiences with these girls soured her on people a bit.

Her best friend, Chris Collier, was a boy. She dated him for a while when she was 16, but they weren't interested in each other in that way and drifted back into a comfortable friendship. Wendi didn't have any serious high school romances. Chris remained a constant presence in her life throughout high school. They had a mutual love for animals and once worked together to untangle a deer that had gotten caught in a barbed wire fence. Beneath her yearbook picture, Wendi wrote that her lifelong career ambition was to be a veterinarian.

She worked hard and got good grades—a combination that stirred up jealousy in others. Wendi had no patience for those who lacked her drive to excel. In academics, Wendi kicked off her first year at the high school by earning Outstanding Achievement awards in Geometry, Ag Science and Honors American History, as well as induction into the National Honor Society. But she was not happy when graduation rolled around. Despite her efforts, she did not graduate as valedictorian. She came in second place as salutatorian.

Judy and Lloyd were proud just the same. They purchased an ad in the annual yearbook addressed to "Wendi, Our Baby Girl." It read:

> *You have built a very strong foundation and nothing can stop you. Just know and remember we love you very much and we could never be more proud of you than we are right now.*

From high school, Wendi went to college in town at Angelo State University in the fall of 1996. She continued to live at home. During the summers, she worked at North Concho Veterinary Clinic. She had a steady boyfriend, Shay Kelton, the grandson of San Angelo's venerable legend, western writer Elmer Kelton.

Her brother Marshall also had a summer job. He worked for a veterinarian, Dr. Terrell Sheen, but not at the animal clinic. In addition to his practice, Sheen had a highly successful business as one of the leading landlords in town. Marshall did maintenance jobs on his rental properties and ranch work—fencing, setting up deer feeders, gathering cows and goats—on Sheen's 7777 Ranch in Grape Creek and on his other property in Mertzon.

Marshall missed having his sister with him at Water Valley High School, but he made his own academic mark. He was one of the charter members of his high school's National

Forensic League, an educational honor society for students with law enforcement aspirations, founded by Bruno Jacob in 1925.

For all of Wendi's life, she'd lived in the same house with a father who worked at the same factory. The only change in her family structure was the addition of her brother when she was too young to remember being an only child. In 1998, all of that changed.

FIVE

At the beginning of 1998, Lloyd learned that he was about to lose his job. Levi Strauss, in a cost-cutting measure, was closing eleven of its plants in the United States—including the one in San Angelo—and moving the operations to the Caribbean and Mexico. After more than twenty years of being a company man, he was unemployed.

Marshall introduced his dad to Terrell Sheen. Following his advice, Lloyd went into business as a self-employed contractor. He worked almost exclusively for Sheen.

In May of 1998, Marshall graduated from Water Valley High. Beneath his yearbook photo, he wrote:

> *My fondest memory is being attacked at Primarily Primates by a Black Leopard.*

His parents purchased an ad in the yearbook to celebrate his graduation just as they had for Wendi two years earlier. It read:

> *Our bouncing baby boy. How the years have flown. As a tiny baby, you were always hard to hold back when you saw something you wanted. Look at you now, pointed in the right direction, a strong mind and body. You're unbeatable. Hold on to your dreams and you will succeed because you're a winner. Just know and remember we love you very much and could*

never be more proud of you than we are right now. No matter where you go or what you do, remember you'll always be in our hearts.
Love,
Dad, Mom & Wendi.

Marshall did not plan to move away from home in the fall—he had a full scholarship to Angelo State University. He would not, however, join Wendi there. His sister had accomplished something that not many were able to do: She completed all of her prerequisite courses and was accepted into the only College of Veterinary Medicine in the state, at Texas A&M, after just two years of undergraduate studies. Only 20 percent of veterinary students enter the school on that fast track. Wendi was moving to College Station, heading east to a different physical environment, a more challenging academic situation and a whole new world at Texas A&M.

At more than 30,000 students, the population of the university was larger than the surrounding town. It sat on a huge expanse of rolling acres—a trip from a class on the east side to another on the west side was so far to travel that students without cars resorted to bicycles to get across campus on time.

The social fabric was enriched by a wealth of tradition. Originally an all-male school, A&M had been co-ed for decades, but many of the Corps ideals remained an integral part of the experience. Football was king, and the legend of the twelfth man ruled every game—all the students stood throughout all four quarters, indicating their symbolic willingness to step on to the field and help the team.

The annual bonfire before the gridiron contest with the University of Texas was the stuff of legend. For weeks, students, wearing decorated hardhats called "pots," headed to the cut site to chop down trees that were hauled to the construction site. There, they stacked a pyramid of logs that reached to the sky with an outhouse in UT's burnt orange and white colors perched on top before the fire was lit.

Wendi was a student the year the tradition came to a tragic end. On November 18, 1999, a nearly completed stack collapsed, killing twelve students. A pall spread across the campus as universal grief consumed the entire student body.

Wendi plowed into her course work with the same enthusiastic determination she'd demonstrated in high school. The demands of the curriculum were high—some say veterinary school is more difficult than medical school because of the need to learn about multiple species.

First-year studies—forty hours over two semesters—included gross and microscopic anatomy, microbiology, physiology and clinic work. The veterinary school at Texas A&M was the only one in the country to offer hands-on training for the first-year student. At this level, it was all elementary animal care, working with the colony of teaching animals at the school, becoming comfortable handling their patients, checking vital signs and drawing blood.

All the while, Wendi was immersed in a field of study with a whole new vocabulary so extensive that it took most students two years to master it all. In the summers, she worked as an assistant at Terrell Sheen's veterinary clinic in San Angelo.

Wendi delved into parasitology, pathology, pharmacology, toxicology, surgery and anesthesia classes—another forty hours or more with the addition of electives—in her second year. The last year of classroom studies focused on small and large animal medicine and surgery. For the first time, Wendi got experience in the operating room.

The fourth year of veterinary medicine took Wendi out of the classroom and into thirty weeks of basic care rotations and twelve weeks of clinic rotations that allow students to determine and hone in on their career path whether with small or large animals, a mixed practice or non-clinical work. During this part of her studies, Wendi put in a lot of time at the campus veterinary hospital under the direct supervision of a faculty member.

She worked hard at her course of studies, but did take some time to socialize. She became pregnant and had an abortion. Then she began a sexual relationship with Jason Burdine, another student at A&M. Wendi soon moved on to a boy named Chase. Although they were intimate, she never learned his last name. After Chase, she started up with her next sexual partner, Ryan Reitz.

Ryan and Wendi lived in the same trailer park. When she'd received a piece of his mail in error, she called. The relationship started from that happenstance. When Ryan attempted to end it, Wendi played the pregnancy card again.

At first, Ryan did not believe her. He thought he was infertile. He accompanied Wendi to the doctor and received confirmation that she was with child. Judy and Lloyd met with Ryan's parents to discuss the repercussions of the situation and to make plans for the future.

The Reitz family was in agreement. Ryan would support the child, but he would not marry Wendi. Judy was furious. "If he's not going to do the right thing, then we want nothing to do with him," she snapped as she stormed out of the room.

Counting up the days, Wendi realized that Ryan wasn't the only paternal suspect. She had no idea of how to contact Chase, but she knew where to find Jason Burdine. She told him that he was the father.

Initially, Jason wanted nothing to do with Wendi or the child. He thought about it for a while, though, and had a change of attitude. "You'll never get to see the baby," he threatened Wendi. He vowed to take the infant away as soon as it was born.

In this hostile environment, Wendi carried her second pregnancy to term, while performing the required rotations to earn her veterinary degree. Her son, Tristan, was born on October 29, 2001. Judy moved to College Station to care for the infant while Wendi finished school.

DNA samples went to a lab. Ryan Reitz was eliminated as the possible father. Wendi called and let him know. For some bizarre reason, she jotted a note to him suggesting that he should come up and see the baby. Ryan passed up the invitation without comment.

The DNA evidence should have made the paternity clear.

Not everyone, however, seemed to receive the same results. Jason Burdine insisted that he'd read a DNA report that eliminated him as the possible father. Years later, Judy Davidson said, in sworn testimony, that Jason was the father. In the same series of depositions, Wendi swore that she did not know the paternity of Tristan.

Nonetheless, Jason visited Wendi soon after Tristan's birth and then again right before Wendi left College Station after her graduation from veterinary school on May 10, 2002. Jason did not maintain contact with Wendi after her move.

As Wendi's brother Marshall said, "She always seemed to find the wrong guy."

SIX

After graduation, Wendi and Tristan moved to Abilene. Although she was still ninety miles away from San Angelo, she was now close to home by West Texas standards. That same spring, Marshall graduated from Angelo State University with a major in Animal Science and a minor in Range and Wildlife Management. It was his turn to move far from home. He accepted a park ranger position at Lake Corpus Christi State Park and moved to Mathis, 320 miles away.

Wendi got a job as a veterinarian at Abilene Animal Hospital. In October of that year, Dr. Larry Ellis purchased the clinic and kept all of the existing employees. He owned extensive real estate holdings in the area and offered his veterinarians a place to live in one of his properties in addition to their salaries. Wendi accepted this perk and moved into an Ellis-owned house with her son.

About a week after she started working there, Ryan Goode, a clinic employee and the teenage son of another veterinarian who worked for Ellis, came by Wendi's apartment to drop off a pager. She invited him inside to watch a movie. Before the night was over, they were in bed. Within a week, Wendi was discussing a long-term relationship. "I just graduated from high school and I'm going to Texas Tech in the fall," he objected.

"I can move to Lubbock with you," Wendi offered.

At that point, Ryan was blunt, "I am not interested in a long-term relationship." Wendi was in tears. Ryan was stunned by the depth of her attachment to him. He realized he was in too deep. Two weeks after it started, the personal relationship was over.

She dated the brother of a co-worker for a few weeks. When she told him she was pregnant, he disappeared. She claimed later that she'd had a miscarriage.

Wendi transferred her affections to a sick schnauzer. He needed regular medication that the pet owner could not afford. Wendi was supposed to euthanize the animal. Instead, she spirited him out of the clinic and into her home.

Any time an animal was scheduled for euthanasia, Wendi ranted, raved and argued against the decision. One staff member described her behavior as a temper tantrum. She preached against the practice to all who would listen, claiming that the only unconditional love possible on this earth came from the animals in our lives. Children were the next best thing, she said, but they always grew up.

It was one of many issues she had with Dr. Ellis. Whenever he tried to tell her how to do a procedure or instruct her on correcting a mistake, she appeared to be paying attention—and then disregarded what he'd said. Although Ellis had thirty years of experience and Wendi was fresh from veterinary school, she gave the impression that she regarded herself as the expert.

Her next sexual relationship lasted longer than the last two. Jeremy Gonzales moved into her place. They were together for nine months and Wendi claimed they were in love. All was well until Jeremy lost his job. According to Wendi, that's when he started using drugs and fell into a deep depression. The final straw came when he beat on her dog. She tossed him out of the house. Some questioned her version of events, blaming the end of the relationship on pressure from her parents. They were very displeased that their daughter would get involved with a Hispanic male.

One night after work, she was watching television when there was a knock on her back door. She grabbed her gun and chambered a bullet. Now, the knocking was in the front of the house. Jeremy kicked that door open. He got in her face and yelled at her, but she could not bring herself to pull the trigger. He took the gun away.

Holding it to his head, he swore he was going to kill himself. She coaxed the gun out of his hand and he ran into the kitchen and grabbed a knife. He continued to threaten to kill himself while Wendi pleaded with him.

The disturbance was loud enough that it attracted the attention of an off-duty police officer who lived across the street. He talked Jeremy into leaving. After the officer went back across the street, taking the gun out of the house when he left, Jeremy returned, raging again. Wendi called 9-1-1 and a uniformed officer talked to him outside, warning him to leave and never return.

A co-worker introduced Wendi to Joel Bird, from Robert Lee, a small town in between San Angelo and Abilene. Wendi got pregnant again. Her parents met with Joel's mother to make wedding plans. Judy was half-hearted about the marriage. She didn't think Joel was good enough for her daughter. She said that Joel was lazy and didn't help out Wendi at all.

Soon, with Judy's encouragement, the wedding was off. Judy claimed that Wendi had broken up with Joel because he was using drugs.

Judy was picking up Tristan for a visit in San Angelo when Joel stopped by the house. According to Judy, he was very upset, crying and begging Wendi to resume the relationship.

According to Wendi's brother Marshall, though, his sister was the one who was distressed about the end of the romance. She could barely talk when she told him about the break-up because she was crying so hard.

"What's the matter, Wendi?" he asked.

"I think I loved him," Wendi sobbed.

Wendi terminated that pregnancy and found a Chihuahua to love. After his broken leg would not heal, Dr. Ellis ordered Wendi to euthanize the dog. She told Mandy Ellis, the business manager, that she'd put the dog to sleep; in reality, she'd taken it home.

She kept him in her bathtub because of the pus oozing from his leg. Wendi eventually conquered the dog's infection and gave him to Candy Branch. Candy made an appointment with Dr. Ellis and brought him into the clinic, where he amputated the leg. The Chihuahua went home with his new owner and thrived.

Then one night near Thanksgiving 2003, Wendi went out to a bar and picked up an Air Force staff sergeant at Dyess Air Force Base. Michael Severance was a long way from home. After joining the Air Force, he'd left the woods of Maine when he was stationed in dusty West Texas. Although he had fallen into the rural rhythm of the area with alacrity, after meeting Wendi, his life would never be the same.

SEVEN

Maine native Leslie Severance joined the United States Air Force in 1976 and was stationed at Loring Air Force Base in Limestone, Maine. Located in the far northern part of the state, Loring was the easternmost base in the continental United States.

As a mega base, Loring had the best geostrategic location of the three Strategic Air Command centers in the northeast, along with the largest capacity for weapon and fuel storage in all the command. Built in the 1950s when the military focused on cold war readiness, Loring was designed to accommodate one hundred B-36 bombers.

Leslie worked as a jet engine mechanic. He was on leave near Christmas in 1976, when he made a trip down south to his aunt's home in Danforth, Maine. His cousin introduced him to Valerie Smith. Valerie was a New Jersey native, but her parents had moved up to Maine five years earlier. Leslie and Valerie got married in 1978.

Valerie was pregnant with their first child when Leslie decided to leave the Air Force in 1980. They knew if they moved to a big city, Leslie's training and experience as a jet engine mechanic would guarantee a job with high pay. But Valerie and Leslie were not interested in urban life. They made a conscious decision to settle in a place where it would be good to raise kids. Their first home was in Winn, on the banks of the Penobscot River—population 400.

The nearest city of any size was Bangor, proud home of a thirty-one-foot-tall statue of Paul Bunyan. Winn was north of that city—about an hour away—in the middle of the Maine Highlands, an outdoorsman's paradise. Springtime through summer, the mountains filled with bicycle riders, the rivers and lakes with kayaks, and bibbed tourists scoffed down lobster everywhere. In the fall, crisp autumn air heralded a vibrant display of reds, golds and yellows through the woods and over the mountain passes. In winter, cross-country skis, snowmobiles and snowshoes were the normal mode of transport.

Leslie was in Winn on terminal leave—he'd spend the last days of his Air Force commitment at home—when his son Michael was born on July 20, 1980. Their second son, Frank, was born in December 1982.

His oldest son soon earned the nickname of Bicycle Mike. Mike, Leslie said, had been fascinated with speed from a very early age. No matter how cold it was, he had to be outside and he had to be moving. If it was too cold to ride, he'd hold on to his bike and walk it in circles in the driveway. He dreamed of turning 6 so he'd be old enough to compete in the bike race on Children's Day at the Springfield Fair, about eight miles away.

Mike was riding his bike without training wheels when he was 4 years old. He raced when he was 6 and came in in third place at the 136th annual Springfield Fair.

In other ways, he did not live up to the old adage "Boys will be boys." He was stubbornly resistant to being cajoled into mischief by his brother or his friends.

In 1987, the family bought a place two miles outside of the town of Lee—population 800—and settled down for good. Their nearest neighbor was a quarter of a mile away. It was an old-fashioned kind of place where everyone knows everyone's business. "We look out for one another—particularly the kids," Leslie said. "If you see anyone's kid acting up, you'd ask them, 'You think your mother and father would be proud of you for doing that?'"

Leslie got a job a dozen miles away in a town of 5,000 at the Lincoln Paper and Tissue Company. He still worked there in 2009 as lead shipper.

Valerie got a job as a school bus driver after Frank started school. It allowed her to earn the money needed to provide little extras for her boys and still be at home with them after school. The Severances never had a lot in the material sense, but Valerie was innovative, making the most of what they had. The family was rich in other ways—a wealth of friends and a home filled with love.

It was the positive environment at their house that drew others like a magnet. People were always dropping by to share their company. If it was dinner time and Valerie had planned a quiet dinner for four, when unexpected company arrived on the doorstep, somehow she could manage to stretch it all to satisfy the hunger of an army of relatives and neighbors.

Mike attended kindergarten through sixth grade at Winn Elementary, a school that has since has been abandoned and demolished. He then went to Mount Jefferson Junior High School, where he competed in skiing events and played soccer and baseball. Valerie often volunteered for extra bus runs for school sports events. Not only did she earn some additional pay, but it enabled her to stand on the sidelines and cheer on her oldest son.

Mike and his brother Frank were close as young boys in spite of—or possibly because of—their different personalities. Mike was quiet and reserved. Frank was gregarious and outgoing. Both were very close to their mother, a passionate, hard-working, strong-willed woman. "She was the fire of the family," said Shirley Harvey, Valerie's best friend and Leslie's cousin.

Valerie possessed a traditional attitude toward hearth and home. She viewed her job taking care of her husband and her boys as her mission in life, and she would let nothing stand in the way—not even illness. Diagnosed with lupus, she still did not slow down. She went to work every day and put a home-cooked meal on the table every night. She took medications that caused severe rashes, and the disease itself was the source of incredible pain and yet, she soldiered on with her responsibilities to her family.

In fact, she did, at times, take it a bit too far. She developed an abscess on the back of one leg, located in the exact spot that rubbed against the school bus driver's seat. She ignored it. When Shirley chastised her about it, she refused to go to the doctor; instead she cleansed it and bandaged it and kept pushing forward.

Finally, it reached a point where she was limping so badly she could barely walk. Shirley looked at it again—it was red, inflamed and hot to the touch. Shirley rushed Valerie to the hospital, where Valerie underwent emergency surgery that removed a fist-sized piece of her upper calf, but saved her leg. Valerie was back behind the wheel of the school bus two days later. Valerie was a rock. Les, Frank and Michael did not think they could survive without her—and knew they never wanted to try.

EIGHT

Mike was only 14 years old on a fateful morning in late February 1995. Les was getting ready to go to work at the mill. Valerie was preparing for her day of getting the boys up for class and doing her job as a school bus driver.

Les heard an odd noise coming from the bedroom. He went to investigate and found his wife on the floor, out cold. He tried to rouse her. When that failed, he hustled the boys out of bed. "Hurry, hurry! Something's wrong with your mother. We need to get her to the hospital."

Les rushed her to a hospital in Bangor. Valerie had experienced a brain aneurysm. At first, doctors were very optimistic. When she came in, she knew her name and address. Doctors told the family that was unusual and promising.

The family's hope soared. Then Valerie took a turn for the worse. Over the next few days, her condition wavered between highs and lows as she endured the surgery and other procedures the physician used to try to save her life. "She'd overcome so many things, we really expected her to pull out of this, too," Shirley Harvey said.

When the medical personnel used up all the options available at that facility, they transported her to a hospital in Boston for additional treatments that went beyond the resources in Maine. Shirley wanted to be by Valerie's side, but she had a more important task. Les took Valerie's mother and sister south to Massachusetts and Shirley stayed behind to care for Frank and Michael.

In Boston, doctors performed a procedure that they hoped would save Valerie's life—but instead, it turned her into nothing more than a physical shell, kept alive by a life-support system. After that, Valerie never gave any indication of knowing that Les or her mother or sister were there. She demonstrated no awareness of her surroundings. She responded to nothing. On March 8, Les made the most gut-wrenching decision of his life. He authorized the physician to pull the plug to the machines that artificially maintained Valerie's physical existence. Now, Les was a widower with two boys to raise on his own. The love of his life was no longer by his side to lighten his journey through the years. The family fire had burned out.

Les was totally unprepared for this responsibility. Valerie had been a stay-at-home mom who'd taken care of everything. She paid all of the bills—Les didn't even know where she'd kept the checkbook. He didn't know how to cook, clean or wash the laundry. The first month of dealing with his grief and rebuilding structure for his family was overwhelming.

Mike saw his father stagger under his burden and assumed the role of caretaker. He automatically made it his responsibility to look after his little brother and his dad.

Mike became keeper of the minute details of the family. When they went to the bank after his mother's death to straighten out the situation there, the banker filling out paperwork asked Leslie for Michael's Social Security number. Leslie said, "I'll have to get back to you with that."

Mike said, "I know it, Dad," and rattled off the digits. Then the banker asked for Leslie's Social Security number. Leslie didn't know that off the top of his head, either. Mike did. Everyone turned to Mike when Frank's number was needed and, sure enough, Mike knew that, too.

That summer, Les traveled with his sons to Pennsylvania and stayed at the home of Valerie's Aunt Lenore. He took the boys to their first experience at a major league baseball game to watch the Phillies play. The caps they got at the ballpark became prized possessions. When they left in the morning, Lenore was surprised and delighted to discover that her two young grand-nephews had made their beds without being asked.

Mike returned to his first year of high school at the Lee Academy—it was a unique educational environment, one of only twenty town academies in the country. It had opened a century-and-a-half earlier, in 1845, when there was no public school system in Maine. Several towns got together and started one on their own. Lee Academy grew into the major educational institution of the region east of Lincoln and as far as north as the Canadian border.

This private, independent school teaches ninth through twelfth grades as well as a thirteenth year for students who need additional preparation before going to the university. The student body consisted of about 200 day students from nineteen different towns—the students and their parents elect to attend this school, some riding the bus for an hour-and-a-half for the privilege of going there. Additionally, there were about eighty dormitory students each year from other states and several countries. The students were drawn to the academy because of its long, well-established reputation, the small, safe rural environment and the solid academic program with a low student-to-teacher ratio.

The dormitory students pay tuition. The day students' cost is covered by their local town government and the state. Maine sets the rate at roughly $8,000 per local child and reimbursed the school accordingly. Fifty percent of the academy's budget is public money. Mike thrived at the school.

In 1996, a convenience store clerk caught Leslie's eye. Brinda Leighton was working that job as a stopgap measure. It was a way for her to earn money until the beginning of tourist season. At that time, she planned to move with her girls down to Bar Harbor, where jobs were plentiful and paid well.

Brinda was not looking for romance. She'd been separated from her husband for a year-and-a-half. His infidelity still stung, and she didn't believe she was ready for a new relationship. Then along came Les. His stops at the store grew in frequency. He talked a lot about losing his wife and about how much he'd loved her. He told Brinda about his two boys.

Soon, he was asking leading questions. Did she like children? Did she like being a mother? Brinda said yes, telling Les about her two daughters.

Finally, Les made his next move. "You wanna go out for a cup of coffee?"

Brinda was hooked. How could she deny a man who applied no pressure? How could she pass up that innocent invitation? It was their first date of many. They found it easy to talk to one another, enjoyed each other's company and discovered that they had a lot in common.

The new relationship posed a number of challenges. Les still grieved for Valerie. Brinda was still reluctant to trust any man. They both worried about the impact on their children.

In July, though, they plunged in and merged their households. Brinda, with 10-year-old Brooke and 13-year-old Nicole, moved into the home of Les and his two sons, 15-year-old Mike and 12-year-old Frank.

The four children got along from the start, even though young Frank could not understand why his family needed any additional members. Brinda was cautious with the boys and respectful of their mother. She never tried to replace her, and pictures of Valerie remained scattered throughout the home.

The two boys still hurt from the sudden loss of their mom. Mike handled it a lot better. He didn't outwardly display his grief, but was able to cope by talking with Brinda and Nicole about his memories of his mother—the camping trips and family activities and the fun of having her for their school bus driver.

Mike was a lot more accepting of the reality of his new life than Frank. Being older, he had a better understanding of adult relationships and could see the importance of Brinda in his dad's life. Frank, however, seemed stuck in the anger phase of his grief. He didn't freely share his thoughts about his mother and tended to keep the three Leighton women at arm's length. He was never hostile to them, but he never invited the close relationships with them that they had with Mike.

For her part, Nicole was delighted to have the older brother she'd always wanted. Nicole and Brooke continued to attend school in Lincoln after the move. Mike helped Nicole transition to the new neighborhood, introducing her to friends and taking her to different activities and places.

Mike and Nicole were close in age and had an interest in athletics in common. Nicole played basketball and field hockey. Mike focused on track and skiing. Together they jogged to get into condition and keep in shape for their sports.

While a lot of kids go in for one type of skiing or another, Mike wanted to do it all—slalom, downhill, cross country. He excelled at all three, and competed in the Penobscot conference, winning fourth place in the multi-discipline Ski-meister competition. He also ran cross country. In his senior year, his school team was eliminated before the state finals, but Mike made it as an individual.

Frank was big into basketball. Even though it wasn't Mike's favorite ball game, he and his friends would play with Frank at the house where they had a basketball hoop. Because of this practice with the older kids, Frank soon excelled at the sport. In many ways, the boys' lives went on as they had before the Leightons joined the family.

NINE

Brinda and Les focused on caring for the children and building a new life together. Brinda understood and accepted Leslie's love for Valerie. She listened to him as he talked of his loss and hugged him as he continued to cry over his wife's death for the next four years.

They always put off the idea of marriage out of consideration for the boys, and in Valerie's memory. As the years went by, it didn't matter as much. They were comfortable together, acting married and thinking of their household as a blended stepfamily.

The new family celebrated Thanksgiving in a big way. Their home filled every year with friends, cousins and friends of their cousins. Brinda and Les worked side-by-side in the kitchen turning out a traditional feast complete with an enormous stuffed turkey and plenty of pumpkin pie.

Because Brinda's girls maintained a relationship with their dad after the divorce, Christmas logistics were a bit more complex. They settled into a routine that worked for everyone. Nicole and Brooke spent Christmas Eve with their dad and Christmas morning with their mom, Les and the boys. They exchanged gifts and enjoyed a festive holiday breakfast around the big dining table. The ease of slipping into this routine was facilitated by the relationship between Les and Brinda's ex-husband. The two men worked together at the mill and had always gotten along well.

Although introverted, Michael loved a good joke. He cut

school one day to go fishing. At the end of the day, he went
to the school, told Headmaster Barry McLaughlin what he
had done and gave him the fish, earning laughs instead of
punishment.

Mike pushed the limits at bit at home, too. He decided to
teach his stepsisters how to drive. He coached them in his
old '72 Dodge Dart as they drove the dirt road around their
home. During one lesson, the trio was surprised by the
earlier-than-expected return home of Brinda and Les.

"What are you doing, Michael?" Les asked. "Those girls
are under-age. They shouldn't be behind the wheel on any
public road. Give me your license." Mike turned it over to
his dad, who kept him grounded for a week—a monumental
hardship for any teenage boy.

Mike was too shy to ask girls out. When his senior prom
rolled around, Nicole asked, "Who's your date for the prom?"

"I didn't ask anyone," Mike admitted.

"That's not right. You will have a date," Nicole insisted
and immediately called her best friend, Erica Voisine. The
two girls decided to escort Michael to the prom. They
planned to stay for a short while and then head home, leaving Mike with friends.

Mike's prom dates were not traditional, and neither was
the transportation he used to get them there. He coaxed the
loan of a Peterbilt out of the owner down in Winn. He
loaded up the two girls and drove up onto the front lawn of
the headmaster's house on campus. As students arrived in
cars and limos, dressed up in their finest party duds, they
stopped to view the spectacle. Their first reaction was bewil-
derment, but soon they were cheering Mike for his stunt. The
headmaster came out of his house and said, "Okay, Mike.
You've had your fifteen minutes of fame. Now get your truck
off my lawn."

Mike backed the big rig cab off of the grass, the crowd
dissipated and all went inside for the big dance. Mike was the
topic of conversation all night. Nicole and Erica had so much
fun with Mike and his friends that they didn't leave until the
night was over.

Despite his impish nature, Mike was a serious student, graduating with honors. His best friend throughout school was Luke House. Frank's best friend was Blair Emery. After high school, Luke's brother Joel and Blair both joined the Army. Mike went into the Air Force. Every one of them would make it to the conflict in the Middle East. All three of those new servicemen made the small town of Lee proud. They were all fine, polite young men who didn't swear in front of women. Not one of those three young men returned home alive.

TEN

Mike wanted to earn a living driving semis. He got his class-one license right out of high school and hoped to get a job running short-haul routes. His father had no objection to his choice of career, but thought it was too early for him to settle down in Maine. "Mike, you need to see the world first. You need to know what's out there before you can really know that here is where you want to be."

Leslie suggested that Mike join the armed forces. "I was in the Air Force, so I'm a little biased, but it beats the Army. In the Air Force, you don't have to go camping, sleep in a tent or carry a gun."

Mike agreed, signed up and began active duty on September 28, 1998. The Air Force stationed him at Dyess Air Force Base in Abilene, Texas. Nicole and Mike kept up their sibling-like connection, talking on the phone once or twice a week whenever his work permitted it. When he came home on two weeks' leave, Mike, Nicole, Frank and Brooke hung out together, driving around in Mike's old clunker.

Nicole noticed a big change in her stepbrother after joining the Air Force. He was still reserved, but the painful shyness had faded away, replaced with a core of self-confidence. It seemed to Nicole as if he had found himself and his place in the world.

Mike found his first steady girlfriend in Texas, Hillary Langley. The young woman had been wounded by a recent date rape. She did not trust easily, but Michael's gentleness broke through her defenses, helped her heal and captured her heart. They dated for months and Mike became a well-loved member of her family. He had a lot in common with her father Frank and brother Graham. They rode four-wheelers together, ate homemade ice cream and went on hunting trips. Hillary's mother, Janis, had an international Coke can collection. Every time that Mike was deployed, he brought back a can from a different country for her.

Mike, however, was only 20 years old and not ready to settle down. When the relationship grew serious, he backed off. He showed Hillary the respect of sitting down with her and explaining his feelings. He wanted to maintain a connection with her family, though, and did so with her blessing.

In 2000, Mike got a new roommate, Shane Zubaty. It was the beginning of a great friendship—so much so that Mike vowed to name his first son Shane. His military life was pretty peaceful until September 11, 2001, when hijacked planes took down the twin towers, slammed into the Pentagon and crashed in a field in Pennsylvania.

As a C-130 crew chief, Mike's services were needed in Operation Enduring Freedom. He landed in Uzbekistan at Karshi-Khanabad Air Base—known as K-2 to the servicemen. When the United States took over the old Soviet-era base, it was cluttered with equipment from the 1970s, left behind when the Russians abandoned the facility. The conditions there were harsh—the land a flat-to-rolling sandy desert.

K-2 was a small facility, one square mile in size. It became home to Camp Stronghold Freedom, an army logistics operation. Air-conditioned tents were laid out in a grid along streets with names borrowed from New York—Fifth Avenue, Wall Street, the Long Island Expressway.

Mike called home to talk to his father. "Dad, remember what you told me about the Air Force? Well, I've got an M-16 on my back and I'm sleeping in a tent. Do you think I'm camping?"

C-130 crews, like Mike's, ferried people and supplies into Afghanistan for the conflict. Mike was one of the first to touch down on Afghani soil.

On one three-hour stopover in that country, the crew retired to a tent for a few beers. They were all exhausted, but Mike was the first to drift off to sleep. While he dozed, a prankster shaved off half of Mike's eyebrows. Mike was ticked off when he saw the damage in the mirror, but that just made his buddies laugh even harder.

Always on the look-out for the enemy, Mike sometimes spent ten to twelve hours at a stretch patrolling the air. The night vision goggles provided to the crew did not have straps. That meant Mike had to press his face against the porthole to hold them on for hours at a time. But Mike wasn't a slacker. His commander had to speak to him about his enthusiasm for the job. "Don't volunteer so much—let the others go on some of these dangerous missions."

He was deployed to the Middle East five times. Because of the secrecy of his missions, his family back in Maine often had no idea of his location. One time when he flew out of Kuwait, kids threw rocks at his plane. Mike shook his head in dismay. "They sure forgot fast," he told his dad.

Mike took his re-enlistment oath in Kuwait balanced on the wing of a C-130. Mike got a kick out of the odd ceremony, telling his dad that the flag painted on the plane was the only one in the area and there had to be a flag to make it official.

In between deployments, he performed regular duties with the 317th Aircraft Maintenance Squadron at Dyess Air Force Base. In his spare time, he took up the two-step, a popular Texas dance seldom seen in his home state. He also loved racing all-terrain vehicles. He was good enough that he was hired to run an exhibition race at a Big Truck Event. He won the race and popped a wheelie the whole length of the course. In a coincidence that reflected the similar personalities of Mike and Nicole, while she was racing four-wheelers in Texas, Nicole was doing the same in Maine.

His experience with these vehicles led him to seek a new challenge. In the summer of 2003, he dropped in to Mary and Danny Hogue's racing garage in Abilene eager to try his hand at West Texas dirt track racing. He didn't want to go through the normal levels of competition in the sport, starting with the Bombers class and working through Junior Minis, Hobby Stocks, Mini-Modifieds, I Stocks and Limited Late Models and Modifieds. He wanted to go straight to the top and start with Modified Stock Racing.

The Hogues thought he was nuts. Mike had no car, no tools, no racing suit and not much money for anything. Soon, though, they realized he had the spirit of a competitor and the determination of a warrior. Since he had no cash to invest in a car, Danny agreed to trade a car for Mike's Raptor 4-wheel all-terrain vehicle. They made the deal on a handshake.

Mike always loved speed, and now he embraced the swirling red Texas dust and the extreme noise of the track. As a racer, Mike was fearless but never cocky. He spun out, survived crashes and kept coming back for more. He saved all the money he could for parts and repairs. He even went so far as to eat nothing but ramen noodles for a two-week stretch to get the money to feed his hobby.

Mike was not one for empty boasting. He didn't mention the purchase to family or his Air Force buddies until he was sure he was up to the challenge. He was a strong believer in the old maxim "Actions speak louder than words." After four races, he was confident enough to share his new interest and invite them out to a race.

He went with his new racing friends on a rafting trip on the Guadalupe River in New Braunfels. Nestled in the beauty of the Texas Hill Country, the pretty town was a world away from dry, dusty West Texas. Beer flowed and food was abundant. Mike kept a tight rein on his consumption, though, in order to focus on everyone's safety. Whenever anyone fell off their raft, he jumped in and helped them out of the water whether he knew them or not.

Still true to his quiet nature, he spent time around others in racing on the sidelines absorbing knowledge. One of his friends, Russ Fletcher, built custom engine motors for stock cars. Many a time, he'd be out working on a car and get a feeling that someone was watching. "Mike, is that you?"

"Yep," Mike answered.

"How long you been here?"

"Oh, 'bout fifteen, twenty minutes."

His new racing acquaintances found it hard not to like Mike. He just always seemed to do the right thing by instinct. One day at a race, someone knocked over a guy's cooler, dumping out the ice and beer. When the owner returned, the ice was a puddle and the brew was warm. The ranting began at high volume.

Mike looked over, assessed the situation, got in his car and drove away without saying a word. The man with the violated cooler was still complaining when Mike returned with a fresh supply of cold beer and ice.

Frank moved down to Abilene to live with Mike in 2002. Mike was in Afghanistan when his brother Frank was involved in a nasty motor vehicle accident. When Mike was back in Texas, he took his brother for a ride. It was all fun until Mike whipped the vehicle around and headed straight for a ditch like the one that had caused Frank's injuries.

Frank freaked. "Do you realize I was already involved in one accident?"

"Well, Frank, you've got to face your fears sooner or later," Mike said with a grin.

One night in December 2003, 23-year-old Staff Sergeant Michael Severance went out to a bar with his buddies to have a few beers. That evening, instead of returning to the apartment he shared with Frank, he picked up 25-year-old Wendi Davidson and spent the night in her bed.

ELEVEN

Wendi's carelessness in her personal life carried over to her veterinary career. She'd already taken risks violating her employer's wishes by bringing two dogs home from the Abilene veterinary clinic. She would do it again—but this time, the consequences were far more serious.

A client brought in a litter of sick kittens. Dr. Ellis examined them and determined that they were all riddled with ringworm, a highly contagious fungal infection. In a one-cat home, feline ringworm is a serious problem because of its ability to transmit to dogs and humans, particularly young children. In a clinic or shelter, it is a disaster. The spores can remain alive and dormant in bedding, on grooming equipment, on any unsanitized surface for as long as thirteen months.

Dr. Ellis isolated the kittens from other animals while he confirmed his diagnosis. When he was certain, he instructed Wendi to euthanize them. Wendi got out the drugs and loaded a syringe, but when she looked at the little creatures with their cute faces and tiny little paws, she looked away. When they mewed at her, she was done. She simply could not do it. She decided, again, that she knew best. She smuggled the kittens out of the clinic and took them home to nurse back to health. She took this action despite the fact that she was putting her own son, Tristan, at risk.

When she believed the little creatures were free of infestation, she returned them one at a time. Unfortunately, she was wrong. The little cats were still contagious. As she and others tended to them and then took care of other animals, all the felines at the clinic were exposed. The animals there for treatment of an illness were at greatest risk because their immune systems were already compromised. Before the disease ran its course, twenty-eight cats had to be euthanized.

Melissa Casey bore the emotional burden for Wendi's behavior. She was the one who had to hold each pet while Dr. Ellis administered a life-ending injection. Then Melissa carried the small corpses to the freezer and gently placed them inside. It broke her heart.

Mandy Ellis delivered the news to Wendi that she was responsible for the deaths of more than two dozen cats. Wendi was horrified—and out of a job. To a co-worker, she claimed that she was not fired, she'd quit. She said, "I'm not going to put up with his motherfucking lack of ethics." In her mind, she was not at fault—Ellis was.

She moved to Lubbock, where she got a job with Dr. Gary Schwede. She convinced him that she was the wronged party in Abilene and that ethical differences between herself and Dr. Ellis forced her to leave. She said that he and his wife Mandy were "immoral people. They lied to people for services they didn't do. They were very rude to every employee they had. They were just awful people." Wendi had no problem shredding Larry and Mandy Ellis to bits to preserve her own reputation—truth was irrelevant.

Right after she moved to Lubbock, she discovered another complication in her life. She was pregnant.

Meanwhile, Michael Severance had no idea that Wendi was making plans to alter his future. Up in Abilene, he lived the normal life of a young single man in the service. He did his job, went out with his brother and his Air Force buddies and got more involved in the stock car racing world, developing new friendships outside his military circle. He wanted to learn enough to be able to build a racing engine on his own.

Then Wendi called with the news of his impending fatherhood. He was stunned and confused. He talked to Frank about his options. Still undecided, he called his father. "Hey, Dad. I'm going to be a daddy."

"What? How long have you known this girl?"

"It was a one-night stand, and I don't know what I should do."

"What do you want to do?"

"I don't know, but family is important. I don't want my child to grow up with just one parent," Mike said.

"Worst case scenario is, you get married, it doesn't work, you get divorced and you have to pay child support," Les said. "But if you don't get married, you'll still have to pay child support."

Mike had a lot to think about. He was only 23 years old. He wasn't really ready to settle down yet. He barely knew Wendi. But there was a strong internal pull toward doing the right thing.

He called his now–married and pregnant stepsister, Nicole. A little ways into the conversation, he said, "Oh, by the way, there's going to be a second baby in the family."

"What?! You're having a kid?"

He told her about Wendi and shared his excitement about becoming a father.

He thought about it for a couple of months before asking Wendi to marry him. When she agreed, he called his dad right away and gave him the news.

"Have you told her parents about the baby yet?" Les asked.

"No. We're not sure how they're going to react."

"You gotta tell them. They need to know. If it was my daughter, I would want to know."

Judy and Lloyd had no idea that Wendi had a boyfriend until she showed up at their ranch in April of 2004 with a gangly, quiet young man named Michael Severance in tow. It was the first encounter between Mike and the Davidsons. Judy took an instant dislike to Mike even before she learned that he'd knocked up her only daughter.

When Wendi informed her parents that she was pregnant again, Judy's feelings became even more hostile. She was not mollified with the news that Wendi and Michael planned to get married as soon as the baby was born. Like other prospective grooms in Wendi's life, Judy found Mike unworthy.

It was an awkward introduction. Mike was more reserved than usual. He didn't engage in lengthy conversation, but he did answer most questions posed to him with a simple "Yes" or "No." "I found out that his brother had a car wreck. I found out that his mother had passed away. And other than that, nothing," Judy said.

After that first encounter, Judy made her animosity toward Mike clear to Wendi. She said he was "rude, disrespectful and lazy." She'd said those same words about previous boyfriends, and now made it clear that she did not approve of the marriage. In fact, she rarely let a day pass without telling her daughter how much she hated Mike.

After the visit Wendi returned to work in Lubbock and Mike went back to the base in Abilene. Marshall visited his sister in Lubbock one weekend and together, they drove to Abilene for the two men to meet. Mike was quiet but sociable. The three played Putt-Putt and then went to a bar for a few drinks.

Mike seldom made the drive to visit Wendi in Lubbock. By late spring, Wendi feared that he was slipping away. She complained bitterly to her brother Marshall. He was appalled at the situation—his sister was pregnant out of wedlock again. Nonetheless, he mustered up the patience to listen as she expressed her anguish.

"I don't think he wants anything to do with the baby," she sobbed. "He doesn't even want to see me anymore. I call and call and call, and he doesn't answer the phone. I wanted him to come down this weekend, but he had a car race and didn't want to talk to me about it."

"Wendi, you know, the best thing if he doesn't want to have anything to do with the child is just . . . You've managed on your own so far. You'll pull through on this one, too."

Michael, however, had made a commitment to his unborn child and was determined to see it through. With his bachelor life coming to a close, his 22-year-old brother Frank moved back to Maine.

When the wedding date was set, Wendi called Marshall. "We're going to get married. The date is set for September thirteen."

"Mom doesn't want this marriage, Wendi. She doesn't like him."

Wendi said, "I love him."

"Just make sure you know what you're getting into," her brother said.

Despite her pleasure at the upcoming nuptials, Wendi had little faith in any man's promises, and Mike was no exception. No matter what happened, Wendi knew that she needed now, more than ever, to return to San Angelo to be close to her family. She wanted to set up a large animal practice there. She also knew her days were numbered at the clinic in Lubbock—she was about to be fired again. Her first plans were to open a clinic out in Grape Creek near her parents' home.

Lloyd and Judy urged her to care for small animals. There's more money in it, they told her, and the start-up costs were lower. Wendi suggested a compromise: she would care for all animals. The Davidsons were opposed to that idea as well. They enlisted Marshall's help. He sided with his parents, but still Wendi held firm. She preferred working with large animals.

The Davidsons asked for the counsel of Lloyd's employer, retired veterinarian Terrell Sheen. The three of them sat down with Wendi. "You need to stick with small animals," Judy said.

Terrell nodded his head. "Your parents are right. That's where the money is—I know from experience. A large animal practice costs too much to set up. It's just not worth it."

Still Wendi did not budge. A reality check was planned for the young vet. Terrell arranged for Wendi to assist in a necropsy of a horse. A chain saw was not normally used in that procedure because it was too messy, but this was a designed object lesson. When the chain saw came out to cut off the animal's head, Wendi had seen enough. She set aside her preferences and meekly agreed to her parents' plan.

Wendi was very young to set up her own veterinary business. Large animals or small, it was an expensive proposition. But she had the support of her family and, more important, the financial assistance of Terrell Sheen. When Dr. Freddy Miller retired, his clinic building on Sherwood Way, one of the major thoroughfares in town, sat vacant. Terrell purchased that property for Wendi's use.

Lloyd and Judy dumped $40,000 into building renovations and equipment. Marshall pitched in by purchasing supplies. Terrell rented the facility to Wendi for a low $1,500 a month. In addition to clinic space, the building housed a small living area.

Through the last few months of their pregnancies, Wendi and Mike's stepsister Nicole chatted on the phone often. Since both were expecting, they had more in common with each other than they did with Mike at that time. It would be the second child for Wendi, but a new experience for Nicole. She turned to Wendi for information and advice. They both relied on each other for support.

On August 10, Nicole gave birth to Kaiden. That month, Wendi left Lubbock and moved into her parents' house as the construction on the new clinic continued. Although Mike maintained his place in Abilene, near the end of the month he moved into the Davidsons' house, too, commuting the ninety miles to Abilene to work at Dyess Air Force Base. Judy's hatred of Mike grew even more. She resented the slightest glimpse of him in his boxer shorts during his early morning preparation for work.

The elder Davidsons weren't exactly respectful of the young couple's privacy. One day, Wendi and Mike checked Tristan's baby monitor on the kitchen counter to make sure it was turned off. Then they went into the bedroom to spend some time alone. When they emerged, Mike realized that someone had turned the monitor back on, enabling them to listen to everything that was said and done in the bedroom.

Ten days after he'd moved in with his in-laws, Mike's son

Shane was born on September 1, 2004. Judy wasn't exactly a proud grandmother. She told her stepfather, "I'd like to send that little bastard to where he came from."

Wendi, Mike, Tristan and Shane moved into the one-bedroom residence inside the clinic building. Leslie Severance traveled from Maine to meet Wendi and her family and his new grandson. He planned to spend a couple of weeks with his son and be present for the wedding. The date set for the service was September 13, 2004. Leslie had no idea that his predictions for a worst case scenario were far too optimistic. He would learn the hard way how bad things could really get.

TWELVE

Shortly before the wedding, Les Severance flew into Abilene. He stayed at Mike's place with his son, Wendi and new grandson Shane. Mike took him up to Dyess Air Force Base and out to meet his racing friends. Les liked Wendi right away, but he loved Shane on sight. He held him and fed him as often as possible, beaming with pride. He often took care of both the boys, allowing the couple time on their own.

The night before the wedding, they all went out to a carnival. Tristan, of course, wanted to get on the rides. On one of them, though, he got scared and started crying. The operator immediately shut down the equipment and helped Tristan get off.

Tristan ran past Wendi's outstretched arms and went straight to Mike, hollering, "I want my daddy. I want my Mikey. I want my daddy. I want my Mikey."

Mike bent down, picked him up and comforted him until he calmed down. Les was amazed that in such a short time, Mike had formed so intense a bond with the little boy.

They all drove down to San Angelo early on the day of the wedding and went by the clinic to check on the remodeling in progress under Lloyd Davidson's supervision. Wendi was breastfeeding in the car while Leslie wandered through the clinic alone. The place was crawling with workers. Around the corner, Les spotted a person he described as a "little cowboy," wearing the big hat, boots, large belt buckle and jeans. The man walked up to Les and said, "So you must be the dad?"

Les held out his hand and said, "Yeah, I'm Michael's father."

The man didn't shake his hand at first. Instead he took a step backwards and looked Les up and down as if we were appraising a horse. Then he stepped forward and, stuck his hand out, and the two men shook. The man didn't say a word. He simply spun around on his heels and left. Les guessed that he'd just met Lloyd Davidson, but he didn't know for sure.

He continued his self-guided tour until he met a woman. She said, "So you must be the dad?"

"Yeah I'm Michael's dad," Les said.

"I'm Wendi's mom," Judy said and then turned around and left without saying another word.

Les walked into the room where a group of men were busy working. They all appeared to be Mexican—an ethnicity not seen often in the wilds of Maine. He was fascinated by watching them work and listening to them talk in Spanish. He was curious if their construction methods were the same as the ones he was used to seeing in his home state.

The foreman noticed him and asked him in English, "Are you the father of the guy marrying this veterinarian?"

"Yes," he said, sticking out his hand. "I'm Les Severance."

The foreman cocked his head at Les's unusual accent. "Where you from?" he asked with a smile.

"I'm from Maine."

"Wow. That's a long way off."

"Yeah, it is," Les said.

"Do you have any Mexicans in Maine?"

"We had some once. They came up to pick our potatoes."

"Those weren't Mexicans," the foreman joked.

"They weren't?"

"No, it's too cold in Maine for Mexicans. They must have been Eskimos."

Les and the foreman were laughing together when Lloyd and Judy walked past the men without speaking. Les shook his head.

"They're mad at your son for marrying their daughter, no?"

"You think so?" Les asked.

"*Mucho*," he replied.

The wedding was a simple affair. Judy ordered flowers for Wendi and brought a wedding cake. They all gathered downtown in the small room next to the Precinct 4 Justice of the Peace office on September 13, 2004, just after 4 o'clock in the afternoon. Judge Eddie Howard presided.

The party was small, just Wendi and Mike, 3-year-old Tristan and 12-day-old Shane, Lloyd and Judy and Les, along with Deputy Linda Moore as the official witness. Before the ceremony started, Judy spoke to Tristan in a loud voice, obviously wanting others to hear. "Did you get scared on that ride?"

Tristan nodded his head.

"Tristan, you need to kick that bad man. He scared you. You should have kicked that man."

The service was short—over nearly as soon as it started. It was punctuated by Judy stomping out of the room in tears, slamming the door immediately after Wendi said "I do."

Both sides of the family were supposed to meet at Zentner's Daughter Steak House on Knickerbocker Road for an after-wedding celebration. Lloyd and a sobbing Judy drove off with Tristan. Wendi, Mike, Les and Shane left in Wendi's car and arrived at the restaurant first.

They waited for the Davidsons and Tristan to arrive. They were beginning to get worried when Wendi got a call on her cell phone. It was her mom saying that they couldn't make it. She either didn't give Wendi a reason or Wendi chose not to share it. Les could only assume it was because Judy and Lloyd didn't like Mike.

When Les returned to Maine, he told family friend Shirley Harvey that Wendi seemed "to be a nice young lady, but her parents are something else. I've never met anyone like that. They're ignorant and cold."

Shirley asked, "How does Michael put up with that?"

"He just lets it roll off his back."

Les was glad he'd gone to Texas to meet his son's wife and baby, and happy he'd been there to see the young couple exchange vows. He sure couldn't say that he'd enjoyed meeting Wendi's parents. He worried about how much impact Judy's negativity would have on Mike's relationship with his new wife. He was concerned that Judy would make a lot of trouble for his son and possibly destroy his marriage. He didn't know that he'd witnessed the planting of the seeds of his son's destruction.

THIRTEEN

Life for the newlyweds was anything but routine. Instead of having time to get to know one another, they had the responsibilities and stresses of a striving young couple married for years.

Caring for a newborn puts demands on any relationship. In addition to little Shane, active 4-year-old Tristan needed a lot of attention, too. Mike worked on bonding with his stepson—just the two of them going to McDonald's or playing together. By all accounts, that was going well. Tristan usually called his stepfather "Mikey," but as time went by, he called him "Daddy" more and more.

Mike was a loving and affectionate father to Shane. He was always willing to hold him and care for him when they were home together. Often, though, he was away. His commute to work chewed up a lot of his day, and his hours were erratic, with night duty assignments and training schedules on top of his regular work.

Adding to the stress were the cramped quarters they called home. The tiny one-bedroom apartment was too small for comfort with four occupants. A door from the clinic waiting room led into the apartment. There was no real kitchen—just a sink, a toaster oven, a couple of hotplates and a microwave. In order to reach the bathroom, they had to go out the back door and in another door to the kennel area. It was a full bath with a commode, sink, shower and tub that, in addition to being used by the family, was where dogs were bathed.

Fortunately, Tristan often stayed with his grandparents, where he had his own bedroom. That eased the space issue to some degree, but it was still a difficult situation.

The biggest threat to the family's peace and tranquility, however, was the rush to get the clinic opened for business. A newlywed 26-year-old woman with a newborn rarely embarked on an undertaking as ambitious as this one. With all the details running through Wendi's head every minute of every day, she was excited and excitable, stressed and peevish. It led to a lot of bickering between her and her husband. Her mother's daily negative comments about Mike inflamed the situation.

Wendi complained to her brother Marshall about the incessant spats. He didn't want to get in the middle of it and said, "Y'all are married. That's your business."

When Wendi didn't take the hint that Marshall didn't want to talk about her marital problems, he borrowed words from his mother's mouth, saying, "He's lazy. He won't get out there and work. He just grabs the baby up as an excuse."

"Well, I know, but I love him."

Marshall sighed. "As I said, that's your business."

Finally in October the doors to Advanced Animal Care opened for business. Terrell Sheen, with an obvious expression of pride toward his protégée, stood by Wendi's side in the photograph in the newspaper ad that announced the new veterinary clinic.

The white one-story box of a building stood alone in a potholed parking lot with patchy, uneven paving. Towering above it, a billboard proclaimed the grand opening of the practice. A small slab of cement sat before the front door. It was just large enough for the chair that sat to the right of the entrance.

Inside, a small but comfortable waiting area with a receptionist counter greeted the new clients. One wall was lined with shelves containing pet care products. An array of leashes for sale hung beside them. Another wall had two doors. One led to the examination rooms and a public bathroom, another to the apartment.

The arrival of patients made the clinic complete. Word-of-mouth, advertising and the convenient, visible location all helped bring them in to Wendi for treatment. One of the first was Charlie Fleming, Wendi's high school Ag teacher. Charlie wanted to pay when Wendi took care of his cat, but she refused his money. She owed him a debt of gratitude for his encouragement and instruction, and she wanted to honor the special place he held in her life.

Diane Slater was another new patient. Her cat Hansel had a urinary tract infection. She was very happy with the way Wendi cared for Hansel. She told the San Angelo *Standard-Times*: "I just got good vibes from her. She talks to you. She doesn't rush you out of there." Diane left smiling with medication, special food and an instant fondness for the new veterinarian in town.

With the business open, Judy Davidson spent her days at the clinic. She volunteered her services as a receptionist and secretary. Since she was receiving Social Security disability payments each month because of her lupus, she could not get a paycheck for the job she did. She placed supply orders and made it clear to vendors that she could see through their sales games and was not going to purchase anything that was not a necessity.

She expected her son-in-law to assist Wendi in the business. It was irrelevant to her that he had a job of his own with a long road trip to go with it. She didn't like it when he slept late—it didn't matter to her that he might have worked all through the night. In her mind, he was supposed to be up and at it each morning when the doors opened. She never bothered to learn anything about his schedule or make accommodations for it.

She magnified every empty beer bottle into a serious drinking problem and credited Mike with every one of them—never Wendi. She resented his stock car racing and hated it when Wendi went with him to a race. She thought it was a dangerous hobby that no responsible husband and father would have. And every day, Judy told her daughter about how much she loathed Mike, couldn't stand him, hated him. It was unrelenting.

Marshall was visiting his parents one weekend when his normally non-confrontational brother-in-law got into an argument with Judy. After Judy stormed off, Mike said, "She's not going to tell me what to do. It's my marriage and I'll do whatever I want."

"Y'all just need to get along," Marshall urged.

"That's fine, but she wants me to do stuff, and it's my marriage and I'm going to run it the way I want to run it."

"You're right," Marshall agreed.

The living quarters at the clinic were too small for the family of four. Judy offered her home—said that Wendi, Mike and the boys could live out there. But Judy's hostility toward her son-in-law made that an untenable solution.

Hillary Langley, Mike's old girlfriend, was disappointed when she learned of Mike's marriage. She'd still hoped that they would get back together someday. Mike drove the 75 miles to Tuscola to visit her family in October.

Frank was a home builder and Mike sought his advice on buying or building a home for his new family. While he was in Tuscola, Mike took a spin in Frank's new Corvette. Frank and Janis were a bit concerned after the visit. Mike did talk about Shane, and flashed around baby pictures, but, although a newlywed, he barely mentioned his wife. They worried that things were not going well for him. It was the last time they ever saw him.

Mike and Wendi went out with real estate agent Joe Stephens in search of a place out in the country with enough land to raise horses and other large animals. Joe showed them a five-acre tract with a manufactured home in Grape Creek. After Mike and Wendi saw it, Judy and Lloyd contacted Joe, and went out to view it, too. They definitely wanted Wendi to buy a home near theirs, and were pleased with the location. But to Joe, it seemed that that was all they found pleasing. In minutes, he picked up on their negative attitude toward their son-in-law.

Mike and Wendi, though, weren't convinced that it was the right place for them. Joe took them out to another spread twenty miles north of town. It was larger and more rugged—definitely rattlesnake country. The house on the land was site-built, but it was one hundred years old and its clumsy, amateurish construction was not up to contemporary standards. The young couple liked it just the same.

Joe thought the two were happy together. Mike often commented on how much he liked the San Angelo area and the people who lived there. Joe figured he must love it—and Wendi—a lot, since he was willing to commute all the way to Abilene to be here with her.

Even though they were drawn to that property, Mike and Wendi decided the timing wasn't right. If they bought now, Wendi would be stuck with handling the move with two young children on her own. Mike was scheduled for another deployment on January 24. They told Joe they'd get back with him when Mike returned from overseas.

For now, the living and working situation continued. When Mike wasn't in Abilene, he'd make lunch for Wendi. Many times he offered to fix something for his mother-in-law, too, but she always turned him down. She didn't want "to eat anything that man prepared."

In a phone call to Maine family friend Shirley Harvey that November, Mike said, "I think my mother-in-law is trying to kill me." Shirley did not take his comment literally.

Tristan was around the clinic all day, every day, too. He watched movies and played with toys in the apartment, sat in his grandmother's lap at the reception desk and played games with her in between clients. When Jamie Crouch started working part-time on weekdays, she pitched in with the kids, too.

Some days, Lloyd and Judy cared for both of their grandchildren overnight to give the couple time for an evening out. Other times, Tristan went with his grandparents and Jamie kept Shane.

Despite Judy's complaints about Mike's drinking, others didn't see it. Wendi and Mike often visited Jessie Mae and Emmett Eggemeyer, Judy's mother and stepfather. Emmett said that on the many occasions they visited, he'd seen Mike drink only a beer or two, and never saw him intoxicated. Around Christmas of 2004, Wendi laughed and said, "If I ever learned that Mike was unfaithful, I'd have him on the table at the clinic." Emmett thought she was only joking about euthanizing her husband. Soon, it wouldn't be funny at all.

While in the Air Force, Mike participated in Operation Enduring Freedom and Operation Iraqi Freedom. He landed in Afghanistan, Iraq, Saudi Arabia, Kuwait and Uzbekistan. He took part in 515 sorties and was part of 232 peacekeeping missions, achieving a 99 percent departure reliability rating and accumulating 922 flying hours as a crew chief. He survived the perils of war. But he would not survive five months of marriage to Wendi Davidson.

FOURTEEN

In a Christmas phone call home, Mike told his dad, "I have two sons. I don't need any more. Wendi's getting her tubes tied." He shared his plans to drive down to Boston during the January trip to visit Shirley Harvey, who was in a hospital with leukemia.

At the end of his conversation, Wendi got on the phone and talked to her father-in-law about how excited she was to be coming to Maine. She said she was really looking forward to meeting all of Mike's family and friends.

Mike got a break from his congested and chaotic home life after Christmas. On December 29, he and Derrick Fesmire traveled to Wichita Falls near the Red River, the natural barrier that divides Texas and Oklahoma. They participated in a two-week Air Force leadership training course.

While Mike was gone, Wendi was in charge of getting everything ready for a trip to Maine. Before Mike left, she'd blocked out the dates on the office calendar—no appointments, no boarders while they were gone.

The airline tickets were purchased. Mike coordinated their arrival with his dad. Everyone was expecting them. Mike thought Wendi was excited about the upcoming trip—her first outside of Texas in her whole life. Yet she did no packing and made no personal preparations.

They were scheduled to fly to Bangor in the early morning hours of January 16. Living in Texas all of their lives, neither Wendi nor her children had adequate clothing in their wardrobe for a mid-winter excursion that far north. But while Mike was away, Wendi didn't do any shopping. She bought no cold-weather gear—not for herself, not for either one of the kids. Was she really planning on making the trip?

On January 5, other trouble was brewing in the Davidson family. Judy paid a visit to her stepfather, Emmett Egge-meyer. Emmett had married Judy's mother, Jessie Mae El-liott, nineteen years earlier after the death of Judy's father. Now, Jessie Mae was bedridden and dying of cancer.

Judy told him how much she hated Mike and how she wished he were dead. Then, she tried to bully Emmett into giving her control over her mother and her mother's finances, both before and after her death. Emmett did not oblige.

On January 11, Judy visited her ailing mother and, ac-cording to Emmett, tricked the frail woman into signing papers giving Lloyd and Judy power of attorney and making them co-executors of Jessie Mae's estate. When Emmett learned what she had done, he was furious at Judy's manipu-lation of his helpless wife.

Mike returned from training on January 12, excited about the trip back home. He was looking forward to seeing his family, but what he talked about the most was Tristan. It would be the young boy's first chance to see snow when he traveled to Maine. Mike called home frequently to check on the weather. He couldn't wait to share this experience with his stepson. He planned to take him sledding and teach him how to make snowballs and build a snow fort.

The only cloud hanging over the anticipated trip was Wendi. Since his return from Wichita Falls, Mike was puz-zled at how distant she seemed—not willing to talk or warm up to him at all. She didn't seem pleased that he'd returned home. He called his dad, chatted about the weather in Maine and the travel plans. Then, he shared his concern about Wendi giving him the cold shoulder.

He didn't know that during his absence, his mother-in-law had worked overtime to poison Wendi's mind against him, his family and the trip back East. Judy and Lloyd were adamant in their opposition to the planned visit to Mike's home state. Judy tried to discourage Wendi from going through with the trip. "It's not going to be good for business. You're just opening and now you're closing down for a week. It's bad business."

"Hey, it's just one week," Wendi said. "Things can wait. I'll be back."

When that argument didn't work, Judy tried emotional warfare. She planted the suspicion in Wendi's mind that a conspiracy was afoot. Judy warned Wendi that the Severance family might not let her come back to Texas, or wouldn't let her bring Shane home. Although Judy had no proof to reinforce her theory, she'd always been a destructive influence on Wendi's thinking.

On the morning of January 13, Mike helped Wendi out at the clinic. He carried a puppy back for an x-ray. He set the animal, attached to an IV, on an examination table and walked out of the room. He returned immediately and was chastised by Wendi. "Are you just going to leave the puppy on the table by itself?" She lit into him, calling him stupid. Her outburst distressed Shane, who fussed and cried in response.

Without saying a word, Mike picked up the little dog and placed him in a crate. He then got Shane and drove off to visit friends in Abilene without telling Wendi where he was going.

A little while later, Wendi went into the apartment looking for him. He wasn't there and neither was the baby. She went outside and saw that Mike's pick-up truck was gone. She called Mike's cell phone, but he didn't answer. She instantly became distraught and burst into tears. "Maybe they've been in a wreck. Maybe they're on the side of the road somewhere," she moaned to her mother. "Why would he take off with the baby?"

Judy had nothing worthwhile to offer—no comfort, just another venomous remark about her son-in-law. Wendi called Mike again. This time he answered. "Where are you?"

"I'm in Abilene visiting some friends. We'll be back soon."

By 4:30, he was home, and the two children headed out

the door with Judy. Lately, Wendi's parents had kept the boys overnight three or four times a week. Mike was not pleased with the frequency, but what Judy wanted, Judy got. He knew better than to engage in a battle he could not win with his mother-in-law.

Friday morning, Judy returned to the clinic with her grand-children in tow. Wendi kept busy all day, examining her furry patients, handing out medications to their owners, per-forming surgery and continuing Jamie's training as a veteri-nary assistant.

Mike made arrangements for repairs to his truck. Some-one had rammed into the side of the bed and left an unsightly dent. Mike thought the best time to get the work done was while they were away. He made an appointment to drop the pick-up off at a body shop on Saturday morning. He also contacted the insurance company, setting up the free re-placement car rental for use in Maine rather than Texas.

Since Wendi and Mike knew they had to stay home Sat-urday night because of their early flight Sunday morning, they wanted to go out for dinner and dancing Friday eve-ning. Wendi asked Jamie if she could baby-sit the boys.

"Why are you asking Jamie?" Judy wanted to know.

"You had them last night, Mom. It's too hard on you to have them two nights in a row."

"Well, let me take Tristan. Jamie's young and inexperi-enced. The two of them are too much for her."

When the clinic closed, Judy left with her older grandson and Jamie took the baby. Mike called Derrick and Julie Fes-mire, asking them if they wanted to come down for a night of dancing. The Abilene couple couldn't get a sitter on the short notice. Within days, regret for not making it down to San Angelo that night piled up high on Derrick's shoulders.

Wendi and Mike went across the street and had dinner at Buffalo Wild Wings, leaving the restaurant at 7:40. After dinner, Wendi and Mike went to Graham Central Station, where they danced and had a few drinks. They crossed the street to the clinic. Between the beer and his excitement about the upcoming trip, Mike was exuberant and full of wild energy. He jumped in his pick-up and drove in crazy circles around the parking lot.

Wendi went inside. The truth of what happened in the next twenty-four hours remains unclear, but based on the evidence later compiled and examined, the state of Texas was able to reconstruct what they suspect happened.

Inside the apartment, Wendi poured a beer for her husband. Then she dropped five veterinary phenobarbital pills into his drink. The drug was highly soluble and the strong flavor of the beer easily overrode the medicinal taste. It was not a fatal dose, but it was enough to ensure eight to twelve hours of deep sleep.

A grinning Mike came through the door and downed his beer. He undressed and collapsed on the bed. Wendi waited until she was certain that he was unconscious. Then she slammed a syringe full of Beuthanasia-D, a common veterinary euthanizing solution, into her husband's chest. The liquid contained a lethal dose of pentobarbital diluted with phenytoin, a substance added to drop the active agent from a schedule two down to a schedule three narcotic (a restriction affecting wholesale purchasing). It would be only a matter of time before the drugs shut down his respiratory function and his heart.

There was only one more thing Wendi needed to do—dispose of the body of the man she'd promised to love and cherish "till death do us part."

FIFTEEN

Wendi got in Mike's pick-up and backed it up to the rear door of the clinic. She chose an angle that took advantage of the slight depression in the ground in front of the entrance leading inside. She lowered the tailgate and eyeballed its height. On flat ground, the distance was just under three feet. Her strategic parking got it closer to a height of two feet.

She dragged the body across the lintel and hoisted the top part of his frame onto the lowered gate panel. She crawled into the truck bed and, sticking her hands under his arms, jerked him all the way up. She pulled the burden completely into the back of the pick-up. Then she jumped down and slammed the tailgate shut.

She threw a covering over his body and went into the outbuilding behind the clinic and returned with an old brake drum and a concrete block. She hoisted them into the truck bed, weighing down a couple of corners to keep her cargo concealed from view. Then she tossed a spool of baling wire and a reel of fishing line into the cab.

She left town, heading north on Route 87 toward the community of Grape Creek where her parents lived. She angled off the highway onto March Road. When it forked, she left the paved surface, going straight on Sutton Road.

The surface of this byway was caliche, a light-colored layer of dirt that split into shingles like sheets of mica. In other parts of the country, people refer to this soil as "hard-pan." Nothing can grow from it but clouds of dust. The ride over it was rough, but Wendi had been raised in this part of Texas. She was used to bouncing a pick-up truck over rugged back roads.

She followed the fence line of the 7777 Ranch until she reached the main gate. A lot of spreads out here had tall arches spanning the gate with metal artwork on top proclaiming the name of the property. Here, though, was just a simple metal entryway locked shut to keep out intruders. Wendi had the key. She opened it up and pushed it all the way back. She climbed in the truck and pulled through across the cattle guard. On the other side, she stopped, put on the emergency brake and got out. She pushed the gate shut, but didn't lock it.

The narrow, one-lane caliche drive went up and down hills, past weed-like mesquite and cedar trees and sparse brush for a mile before reaching the stock tank. Out of sight of the road, it was surrounded by acres of rolling hills devoid of homes and prying eyes.

In Texas, a stock tank refers to a large pond. There was a boat dock on one end, and it was stocked with fish every year for laid-back summertime recreation.

Wendi pulled up to the dock head first, pointing her headlights in the direction of the stock tank. She rolled Michael's body out of the bed and grabbed his feet, dragging him face down across the ground and onto the covered wooden platform built over the edge of the pond. Then, she returned to the truck and retrieved the supplies needed to weigh down the body.

She looped one end of the baling wire around his neck and twisted it tight—but not too tight, so as not to sever the neck. On the other end, she attached the brake drum. She tied fishing line around the cinder block and secured it to his left leg.

What was she thinking as she went about her gruesome task? How could she do this? Lying before her in nothing but red boxer shorts, his winter-white skin glowing in the gleam of her headlights, was the man who'd shared her bed—a man she'd claimed to love. Mike was only 24 years old. He'd served his country, he'd cared for his baby, he'd loved life. Wendi had gone with him to look at homes where they could build a future together. Now, she stood by his corpse, in the middle of nowhere, in the dark of night, treating him like useless trash.

She pushed his body to the edge and rolled him off into the water. When the sound of the splash disrupted the eerie quiet of the wilderness, did it make her jump? She needed to stay until the last of his body passed under the black surface of the water and the ripples smoothed to glass.

She stalked back to Mike's pick-up truck, backed it up, put it in gear and headed out of the ranch and back to her apartment in the clinic. She climbed into her empty bed—a place she'd tried so hard and so often to fill with a man. She sought just a few hours of sleep before her mother arrived to open the clinic.

She believed she'd committed the perfect murder.

SIXTEEN

Judy arrived at the clinic between 7:15 and 7:30 that morning. As soon as she got there, Wendi left to pick up Shane from Jamie. Since no surgeries were ever scheduled on Saturdays, it was Jamie's day off. Wendi returned in time for the clinic to open at 8 A.M.

She laid Shane down in the designated area of the office that housed his bed with its colorful mobile, a swing and baby's toys. She left the door open in order to hear him if he cried.

The door to the bedroom remained closed. Judy thought she heard sounds of movement from the apartment. She asked Wendi if Mike was coming out to help with patients that morning.

"Nah. He's too hung over from last night," Wendi said.

Despite Mike's condition, Judy noticed that her daughter appeared to be in a very good mood. A couple hours after the clinic opened, Lloyd pulled into the back parking lot. He saw Mike's pick-up parked there—the truck that was supposed to be in the body shop that morning.

Lloyd sent Tristan inside and then he got to work on some outdoor chores. The clinic stayed open until 3 in the afternoon on Saturdays, but Judy was tired and Tristan was hungry. She left with her grandson a little after noon to feed the boy and get some rest. When Lloyd finished up in the back, he joined his wife at the house.

Wendi closed up the clinic at the regular time. She strapped

Shane into his car seat, hopped into Mike's pick-up truck and drove out to the Davidsons' place, arriving just after 4. They all had dinner together. While they ate, Judy continued to argue about the trip to Maine. Mike and Wendi had spent $1,500 for flight tickets for the four of them to travel back East, but still Judy persisted. "You shouldn't go, Wendi. It's bad business and a bad idea. Mike's been acting strange. What if he doesn't let you come back?"

After supper, Wendi loaded up the boys and drove over to her grandmother's house. She dropped off some shrimp for Jessie Mae and chatted with her by her bedside. "We're leaving for Maine in the morning," she said.

"I'm afraid I might die while you're gone. I might never see you again," Jessie Mae cried.

"You'll be okay," Wendi reassured her. "I'll be back and I'll come by and see you just as soon as I can."

Wendi talked with her step grandfather Emmett out in the yard. He glanced in the bed of the truck and noticed gravel and cement block chips.

Wendi returned with her two boys to her little apartment in the clinic. She later claimed that she'd discovered Mike's body then. She said she'd found him in bed. Then she said she'd found him on the floor of the clinic. In all likelihood, both stories were nothing but self-serving lies. She did not see his body. Little Tristan did not experience that trauma. Mike was now lying on the bottom of a cold stock tank in the middle of a desolate ranch.

SEVENTEEN

At some point after disposing of her husband's body, Wendi called the airline, cancelling the family's four tickets for the flight to Maine. Around 5 A.M. on Sunday, she picked up the phone and called the Severance home in Maine.

Leslie had already left for work. Brinda answered the phone. "Where is Michael? Have you seen Michael?" Wendi asked.

" 'Where is Michael?' What are you talking about? You are supposed to be getting on an airplane to fly here. You're not at the airport?" Brinda said.

"No. I can't find Michael. I don't know where he is. He didn't come home last night."

"He wouldn't miss a trip back home. Are you ready to leave when he shows up?"

"I haven't even started packing yet. But we'll fly out just as soon as I find him."

Brinda could not believe what she was hearing. The flight was just a couple hours away and Wendi hadn't packed? Where was Mike? He was on leave—but had something happened? Had he been called in to work because of a national emergency? She sat stunned for a few minutes and then called her daughter Nicole.

Together, they wondered if, for some unknown reason, Mike was on his way there alone. Brinda called the airport. She learned that the tickets for the flight had been cancelled that morning. Dread uncoiled, releasing an overload of acid into her stomach. She called the bus lines and the trains, but could not find any passenger named Michael Severance. She spent hours on the telephone, talking to everyone she knew, trying to find Mike. She walked past the snowsuit, boots and sled she'd bought for Tristan, and burst into tears. She was desperate to locate Mike before Les returned home from his twelve-hour shift.

Nicole called Wendi several times that day for updates, but there never were any new developments. Nicole got more frantic with every passing hour. She was baffled by Wendi's attitude. Mike's wife acted as if it was no big deal at all.

In Texas, Marshall Davidson called his parents to remind them that he'd be coming to San Angelo on Monday and to ask about his grandmother's health.

"Mike's gone missing," Judy said.

"Missing?"

"He's not here. He was supposed to go on that trip to Maine, and we don't know where he is," Judy said.

Lloyd got on the other phone and joined the conversation. "He's been wanting out of the military. Maybe he made the trip to Maine early and went off to Canada."

Judy said, "I can't believe it, but he ran off on Wendi, and left the baby and everything."

"I'll be there tomorrow," Marshall assured his parents.

Les got home from work that evening at 6. One look at Brinda's face and he sensed something was wrong. "You don't look ready to go. We've got to drive down to Bangor, the plane will be in soon."

"Mike isn't coming, Les," Brinda told him.

"What do you mean, Mike's not coming?"

"Mike is missing, Les. Wendi called this morning. She wanted to know if he was here. I've been on the phone all day trying to find him."

"Something's wrong," Les said. "He wouldn't miss coming home." He called Wendi and questioned her.

"We left Mike at home and I took his truck and the kids

over to my parents' house and I haven't seen him since," she said.

"Mike's truck was supposed to be in the shop. He had an appointment to take it in Saturday morning. What were you doing with it?" Les asked.

"Oh, we forgot to take it in," Wendi said.

Leslie knew how much his son cared about that truck. He knew he wouldn't forget to take it in. Leslie was devastated. They'd rented a hall and planned a reception for Michael and his new bride. They were so excited about the arrival of his son and family. Now, all that anticipation turned to cinders—replaced by a churning anxiety. Leslie Severance knew something bad had to have happened to his son, but he knew nothing more.

Soon after talking to Les, Wendi and her father went to the San Angelo Police Department to file a missing persons report. She provided the necessary details to Officer Lucien Thomas and was told that an investigator would come to see her on Monday morning. Wendi then called the Air Force and reported that Staff Sergeant Michael Severance was missing from his home.

On Monday morning, although Advanced Animal Care was scheduled to be closed, Wendi opened it for business. Judy reported to work, picked up her grandsons and took them to day care. When Detective Dennis McGuire of the San Angelo Police Department arrived at Advanced Animal Care, Marshall Davidson was there with his sister. McGuire asked questions and looked around the facility and the apartment.

Wendi insisted she did not know the location of Michael Severance. "He's been acting strangely over the last couple of weeks. He's been drinking heavy and spending lot of time at Buffalo Wild Wings and Graham Station."

"And that's unusual for him?"

"It is out of character. And he's been disappearing for hours at a time without telling me where he's going. I got home Saturday night about eight, and he wasn't here. And I haven't heard from him since then," Wendi added.

When McGuire asked about Michael's job, she told him that he was in the Air Force and on leave until Monday, January 24. "We were supposed to fly to Maine to visit his parents yesterday morning, but we didn't go, because he was gone. I called the airline and they checked and said he didn't fly out by himself. I don't know where he is."

"What did he take with him?" McGuire asked.

"There's two hundred-twenty-one dollars missing from the cash register. Mike knew the money was kept there, and he could get into the till. I think he took it," Wendi accused. She didn't bother to explain that it was only in small bills, making it a huge wad of cash to stuff in a pocket.

McGuire walked through the clinic noticing a knife with a blue handle, and mentally noting the computer and the types of drugs on hand. He did not confiscate anything. As he went through the couple's apartment, McGuire noticed that all Michael's clothing still appeared to be there, and none of the luggage was missing. Behind the building, Michael's 2004 blue Dodge pick-up sat in the lot, as did Wendi's 2001 red Chevrolet Camaro. Inside the cab of the truck, McGuire found Michael's cell phone.

McGuire brought the phone inside and continued to look around the clinic. In Maine, Frank Severance dialed the cell number of his missing brother just before 3:30 that afternoon. McGuire told Marshall to answer. As Frank heard the click of someone connecting the phone, his heart soared. He believed for a brief moment that he'd hear Mike's voice and all would be well. He'd have a story the two of them would laugh about for years to come. Instead, there was another voice on the line—someone he did not recognize. "Who is this?" Frank demanded.

Marshall explained that he was Wendi's brother and that Mike's phone was found in his pick-up. Frank was rattled by hearing a strange voice and even more unsettled by learning that wherever Mike was, he didn't take his cell.

Les called the San Angelo Police Department and received another shock. He couldn't believe the callousness of the unidentified man who spoke to him. "We'll probably find him shacked up somewhere with a whore."

This description did not fit the son Les knew he'd raised. Next, he called Mike's commanding officer, Captain Bill Walker at Dyess Air Force Base. Les repeated his concerns, explained the plans to fly to Maine and held his breath.

"Let me look into this and get back to you," Walker said.

Les was bewildered. The way the day was going, he didn't think he'd hear back from the Air Force any time soon. He felt so helpless. When the phone rang fifteen minutes later, he could barely believe Walker was on the other end of the line. "You are absolutely right," the captain said. "This is not characteristic of Michael. Something is wrong. I can't do anything official until he's AWOL. He's on leave and doesn't have to report for duty until January twenty-fourth. But I'll look into it. It doesn't sound right."

Relief washed over Les. His son was still missing, but at least now someone obviously cared—someone believed in Michael. The insensitive comment made to Les by someone at the police department had left a sour taste in his mouth and it would permanently skew the family's view of the investigation into the disappearance of Michael Severance.

EIGHTEEN

Frank Langley got the word that Michael Severance was missing from the local news. He heard that Wendi was postulating that Mike had committed suicide. He called the OSI office at Dyess Air Force Base. "Michael Severance didn't commit suicide. Search the highways for an accident and look at his wife. Something's wrong here."

When investigators suggested that Mike had gone AWOL, Frank batted down that possibility, too. "Mike thought a lot of the service. He's a stand-up guy. No way he'd walk off without a word."

On Tuesday, January 18, two days after she'd reported her husband missing, Wendi took her mother's advice and paid a visit to attorney Tim Edwards. Right after she left for her appointment at the lawyer's office, Les called the clinic. Judy told him that Wendi was putting down a dog. Les didn't understand the significance of that phrase until much later.

Wendi filed a petition for divorce, stating:

The marriage has become insupportable because of discord or conflict of personalities between Petitioner and Respondent that destroys the legitimate ends of the marriage relationship and prevents any reasonable expectation of reconciliation.

Wendi requested that health insurance be provided for their child, Shane Michael Severance, through her estranged husband's place of employment, that Mike make child support payments and Wendi be awarded the ultimate determination of where Shane would live. She requested that the court divide the community property and acknowledge that she had separate property that should be excluded from that settlement.

She didn't stop there, though. Wendi also obtained a restraining order forbidding Michael from contacting her in person or by telephone, and from writing to her in "vulgar, profane, obscene or indecent language or in a coarse or offensive manner." Michael was forbidden to threaten, take unlawful action against Wendi, or to cause bodily harm to her or one of the children. And the list of what he could and could not do went on and on.

Wendi knew he was not capable of doing any of these things. She knew he was dead, and she knew where his body rested. That was the greatest obscenity of all.

NINETEEN

The same day that Wendi filed for divorce, the 7th Security Forces Squadron at Dyess Air Force Base referred Mike's disappearance to the Office of Special Investigations. On Wednesday, January 19, Special Agents Arch Harner and Greg McCormick drove down to San Angelo to the residence of the missing airman.

They verified that Mike was not at his home, that he had not taken any military clothing or any other equipment necessary for his position and hadn't left in any personal vehicle. In response to their questions, Wendi said, "Mike talked about not wanting to go on his next deployment and how easy it would be to disappear into Canada."

The agents were surprised at how unemotional and apathetic Wendi appeared. When they ran through the list of possibilities, including everything from the question of suicide to the likelihood of another woman, Wendi's demeanor did not change. Most wives of missing men show something—worry, fear, anger—but Wendi was devoid of any expected human response in the initial volley of the queries.

Then, almost as if a cartoon light bulb had formed over her head, Wendi seemed to understand that the agents wanted her to be upset. She teared up once she picked up on the unspoken cue, but the reaction appeared mechanical and artificially induced. The sorrow did not show itself in her eyes.

* * *

By January 24, San Angelo Police Department investigator Dennis McGuire was beginning to feel uneasy about the Michael Severance case. There was a world of possibilities. Michael could have gone AWOL and be hiding out in the countryside or he could have fled to Canada. Perhaps, as suggested by Wendi's family, Michael had committed suicide. And then there was the possibility of homicide. McGuire had seen no definite signs of foul play, but that might only mean the killer had been careful. McGuire needed answers, and to get them quickly, he needed help.

The San Angelo Police Department had a heavy case load investigating incidents that they knew were criminal. They had every crime you'd find in Dallas, but with lower numbers. They had a big city to police, with minimum staff and a small-town mentality. They'd even had to launch a major education effort to teach citizens to lock their cars and houses.

In this case, all they had was a missing person and the knowledge that adults had the right to abandon family and friends without warning. It was a far more serious matter for the military. They had few desertion cases. Most of the time when an airman went AWOL, he was found within a couple of days, usually at his mother's house. This case was unusual.

McGuire referred the case to the San Angelo Major Crimes Task Force, calling a meeting of representatives of the law enforcement agencies impacted by any of the scenarios. At 2 P.M., the task force members, Lieutenant Randy Swick from the sheriff's office, Texas Department of Public Safety Special Crimes Sergeant David Jones and Texas Ranger Shawn Palmer gathered at the San Angelo Police Department. Because of this case's connection to the Air Force, Agent Greg McCormick of the Air Force Office of Special Investigations was also asked to attend. Detective McGuire briefed them all.

McCormick noted that Michael had not reported to duty that morning and was now AWOL, which, for the Air Force, meant that a serious violation had been committed. For their investigators, on that day, the case had turned criminal.

Palmer noticed an uncomfortable undercurrent at the conference table. There seemed to be an unspoken animosity between McCormick and McGuire. Being in a position of minimal responsibility, he did not pursue the problem. But what he noted was a clear conflict of agency objectives.

In correspondence a few months later, the Air Force acknowledged the friction and blamed it on Special Agent McCormick's belief that the San Angelo Police Department was uncooperative and lacked enthusiasm for the investigation. The agents, the letter read,

> became somewhat frustrated. Their perception was there did not seem to be a sense of urgency by others to help locate an active duty Air Force member who was missing under suspicious circumstances.

Palmer left the meeting with three responsibilities and started to work right away. He contacted Budget Rent A Car at the San Angelo Regional Airport terminal. They reviewed their records, as well as the records of the other rental car agencies operating out of that facility. No one had rented a car to Michael Severance.

He then contacted Crime Analyst Melanie Schramm to request a search for any computer queries made in reference to Mike, or to either his truck or Wendi's car. After that, Palmer put in a request for the cell phone records for the number listed in Mike's name. An administrative subpoena was served on Sprint communication company on January 25.

That same day, the OSI agents interviewed Judy Davidson who said, "Mike hated the military and talked about going to Canada." Lloyd repeated the comments made by his daughter and his wife. He mentioned that his employer, Terrell Sheen, owned more than a thousand acres that the family, including his son-in-law, could access at any time. "Maybe Mike is hiding out there," he added.

Wendi faced additional concerns that Tuesday. She was served with papers from the court relating to her divorce petition. She was required—along with Mike—to attend and complete a Children's Interest Seminar provided by For Kids' Sake, a non-profit agency, within sixty days of her original filing.

Wendi and Lloyd both underwent a polygraph examination administered by Detective James Johnson, at the San Angelo Police Department, at the request of the Air Force. The results were inconclusive. One of Wendi's attorneys leaked the information that she'd passed a lie detector test. It is uncertain if he was referring to the same polygraph examination. But there is a reason why the results of these exams are not admissible in many courtrooms. Although a nice addition to the arsenal of law enforcement's collection of investigative tools, it is not perfect.

The instrument records three levels of autonomic arousal—heart rate/blood pressure, respiration and skin conductivity. But the idea that these psycho-physiology changes are constants and can accurately predict a person's veracity is closer to myth than reality.

Whether the subject possesses guilty knowledge or not, results can reach a dead end with no conclusions possible. Innocent but anxious people are found deceptive. Sociopaths lie and are found to be truthful. In fact, the most trustworthy results often are created by the placebo effect—a person who believes in the infallibility of the testing is most likely to exhibit the types of changes in their readings that the examiner uses to gauge levels of deception.

The fallibility rate is believed by some to be only slightly more than chance. Even proponents of the device admit that many who administer the polygraph are inadequately or incompletely trained, skewing the results they obtain. Estimated accuracy rates range from 52 to 76 percent—not exactly conclusive indicators of honesty. It might sound like a scam, but some people advertising surefire methods for beating a lie detector test actually can help an interview subject do just that.

Wendi logged on to her computer and researched lie detector tests, looking for that kind of information. On January 26, she entered a search for details about the decomposition of dead bodies in water.

Wendi Davidson was an intelligent woman. But she had to doubt her own smarts when she found the information that pointed to her big mistake. The body she'd tossed in the stock tank would surely rise to the surface and reveal her secret.

She had to return to where she'd dumped the remains of her husband and cover up her error. She had no other choice.

TWENTY

Wendi read and learned. A corpse in water usually sinks because the specific gravity of a human body is very close to that of water. When she'd submerged the body, tissue decomposition from bacteria had begun, forming a gas by-product. That accumulation of a lighter substance decreased the specific gravity of the body, creating sufficient buoyancy to allow it to rise to the surface and float. Weights attached to the body may delay, but will not usually prevent, the body rising. In warm water, the body will drift to the surface in eight to ten days; in colder water, it would float in two to three weeks.

Wendi wasn't sure of how the water temperatures were defined or of the current reading at the stock tank. It was January, making her think she had the longer period of time. But, then again, she was in Texas and ponds just didn't get as cold there as they did up North—that made her lean toward the shorter period of time.

Either way, odds were that, at the very least, Mike's body was beginning to rise. The brake drum attached to his neck with baling wire, and the cinder block tied to his left leg were not enough. She needed more weight. She needed the body to stay underwater until decomposition of the tissue was complete.

She logged off the computer in her veterinary clinic and went out the back door. She scrounged through the barn, gathering up used auto parts and anything else of substantial weight to attach to the body.

When she finished scavenging in there, she still needed more. She planned to stop by the dump out at the 7777 Ranch to get additional items. She set the blue-handled boning knife she'd used in veterinary school on the seat of the pick-up truck when she climbed into the cab.

She exited the highway, out in the countryside. Near the fence line, a short distance before the gate, was a large pile of discarded material. The ranch owner, Terrell Sheen, liked to call it a brush pile, but it looked just like a dump to everybody else. Wendi unearthed a few more hefty items to weigh down the body and tossed them in the back of the truck.

She pulled into the ranch and locked the gate behind her and drove the mile out to the stock tank. Standing on the dock, her eyes scanned across the surface. Nothing stuck above the water. Just below the surface, though, she saw a shape. As she'd suspected, the body was rising.

She didn't know that at about the same time she spotted the body, someone spotted her car. Fortunately for Wendi—unfortunately for everyone who cared about Michael Severance—when hired hand Jose Romero saw her vehicle, he'd thought little of it at the time. He didn't interrupt her or try to find out what she was doing. He'd seen her out at the ranch many times before.

She got into the little boat and rowed out to the body. She reached down for it, but with the brake drum and cinder block attached, it was too heavy for her to lift. With the oar she pushed on it, guiding the corpse over to the bank, resting it half in the mud, half in the water.

She tied the boat up to the dock, disembarked and got down in the mud by the body of her husband. She had two tasks to perform. First, she wanted to make it easier for the gas to escape from his body. So she stabbed him with the blue-handled knife—through his chest into the lungs, the diaphragm and downward into the abdomen. She thrust the knife into the lower abdomen, ripping it open. She drove the knife into clusters of wounds in his right flank and into his right arm. She rolled him over and slammed the blade into his back again and again.

Homicide investigators have often said that a preponderance of wounds were evidence of overkill, and indicated anger toward the victim. But she'd killed Mike weeks earlier. Was Wendi now furious with her husband for foiling her plans to conceal her crime? Or was she driven by desperation to hide the secret of her ugly actions? Was it possible that her mind was elsewhere—that she stabbed at someone or something else? Was it a vain attempt to eliminate malevolent demons residing in her psyche?

Whatever made her exhibit this level of fury, it wasn't possible, in the midst of her rampage, that she spared one kind thought for the individual loved by his family and friends—for the man who was the only daddy either of her sons had ever known. After forty-one thrusts of the knife, she stopped desecrating his body.

Her second chore was to weigh the body down with more objects to delay its rise to the surface. It took several trips from the truck to the dock, but she soon had all she needed by her side. She lost a couple of items in the muck at the side of the pond trying to tie them to the partially submerged body. She switched to plan B.

She dragged him up on the dock and slid the body into the boat. Then, she loaded up cinder blocks, an anchor and a tire wheel rim, along with yellow braided rope and plastic zip ties. She climbed inside, and when she was certain the load was well balanced, she moved the boat out to the center of the water, where a submerged fence separated the pond into two sections.

She methodically fastened the contents of the boat to both ankles, both wrists and the left elbow with plastic zip ties, attaching 145 pounds of weight to Mike's 155-pound body. Then she eased the body and objects out of the boat, guided it past the fence and into the water on the smaller side of the pond away from the boat dock. She sat and watched until his body sunk to the bottom and disappeared from sight. It was hard work, but she'd accomplished what she'd set out to do. She undoubtedly felt pride in a job well done.

She returned to the dock, tied up the boat and got in her truck. She drove back down the caliche lane to the road. She got in and out of the truck to open and then close the gate. Before she left, she locked it tight. She then drove off convinced no one would ever find the body—certain that her husband would remain a missing person forever.

TWENTY-ONE

Up in Maine, hope was fading fast. The day Michael should have reported for duty had come and gone. Family members called OSI nearly every day urging immediate action. They were fearful that if Mike were not found soon, there was no possibility that they would ever see him alive again.

Major Bill Walker called Les every couple of days. Some days, he had an update to report. Other times, he called to see how the family was coping.

Les now knew that Mike had left more than his cell phone and truck behind. His wallet had been left at home and he was reported to have last been seen wearing a tight pair of jeans and a tee shirt—no hat and no jacket. Where would Mike stuff more than $200 in small bills? And how could he handle the January nights with lows at 44 degrees?

Investigators from the police department kept asking: "Do you think Mike ran off to Canada?"

Les knew in his heart that his son would not go AWOL, but he based his response on logic. "Why would he leave Texas and go to Canada when he could come home and slip across the border with ease?" Although the sense of what he said was clear to Les, he felt that it went right over the investigators' heads.

On January 28, the Air Force sent a team to San Angelo to conduct a search of the two square miles around Michael's home. They found no evidence pointing to the whereabouts

of their missing staff sergeant. OSI Special Agent Greg Mc-
Cormick and San Angelo Police Department Detective Bill
McGuire paid another visit to the clinic during that search
to talk to Wendi Davidson. They didn't learn any new information from the interview, but he did get something else of
interest. She gave McCormick permission to conduct a forensic investigation of her laptop. He made a mirror image
copy of the hard drive and took it with him for later analysis.

Marshall dropped into the San Angelo Regional Office of
Texas Parks and Wildlife to ask Major Steve Whiteaker
about the game warden job opening in Tom Green County.
He was interested in a transfer to another game warden position in his hometown. "I won't have two years as game warden until the end of June." Two years was the minimum
amount of time the agency required before a standard transfer request could be issued.

"You'll probably miss the opportunity then, because the
current academy class would have their assignments long
before that. Most likely, a rookie will fill the position."

Marshall explained the situation with his missing
brother-in-law and complained about the police "harassing
his parents." Whiteaker thought it odd that Marshall considered it harassment for law enforcement to ask his parents
questions about Mike's disappearance and to look around
their property.

On February 15 at 10 A.M., the Major Crimes Task Force
gathered again to update one another and plan their next
moves. Although no concrete evidence existed, the suspicions regarding foul play were now high. Those concerns
thrust Texas Ranger Palmer into a more active role in the
investigation.

He followed up on two phone calls made to Mike's cell
phone on January 20—one at 12:58 A.M., the second at 1:30.
Both were less than one minute in duration and originated
from the telephone of Lauren Hahn. She did recall placing
late-night calls, but could not remember the date or even the

reason for them. She knew Mike, she said, because she used to date Jeff Holden, who was either a cousin of or close friend to Mike.

Palmer and McGuire traveled to Hamlin, Texas, a small town with a shrinking population of approximately 2,000, a two-and-a-half-hour drive from San Angelo. They met Jeff Holden at the local police department. With Jeff's consent, they searched his residence to make sure Mike was not hiding there.

Jeff told them he'd known Mike for four or five years and they went out together to nightclubs. Mike drank beer, he said, but did not smoke and did not use drugs. Jeff hadn't known about Mike's marriage until after it happened, but didn't think it was going well. "Two or three months ago, Mike told me the relationship was on the rocks and he was thinking about calling it quits." Jeff denied that Mike hated the military and insisted that his friend was looking forward to his next deployment.

OSI Agent McCormick and his immediate supervisor Arch Harner suspected that Wendi or her family knew something about Mike's whereabouts. They decided that they needed tracking devices on all of their vehicles. Harner contacted regional headquarters to inquire about the process. His first step, they told him: Check to see if any devices were available.

Harner found out that there were three trackers they could use. Next, he notified the OSI staff judge advocate in the OSI legal office. They approved of the scope and intentions of the investigation. Harner applied to the regional commander for authorization. He received approval to install a tracker on Wendi's car and on the two trucks belonging to Judy and Lloyd Davidson. Unfortunately, when he obtained the three promised devices, one of them was unsuitable for their purposes.

McCormick called Palmer and apprised him of their plans. Palmer was uneasy about their decision. He knew OSI followed appropriate military protocol for a deserter investigation, but he worried because their process was not in line with the proper procedure for a civilian criminal investigation. In that kind of case, Palmer needed a search warrant approved by a sitting judge. He was concerned that the Air Force actions could jeopardize a future prosecution in the event that foul play and a perpetrator were identified.

At McCormick's request, Palmer went to Advanced Animal Care to perform surveillance in advance of the placement of the tracker. While there, he spoke to Lloyd, who once again repeated his statement that his son-in-law had fled to avoid deployment overseas.

Despite Palmer's reservations, he met Harner and McCormick in the veterinary clinic parking lot at 12:40 A.M. on January 26. The Air Force had already installed a tracker on Judy's pick-up, now they placed the equipment on the undercarriage of Wendi's red Camaro. The device they installed was not a real-time tracker. In other words, they could not determine exactly where Wendi was at any given time. However, it kept a log of everywhere she went. They simply had to pull up in the vicinity of her car and download the geographical coordinates from the global positioning system.

They may not know Wendi's location every moment, but they'd know every place she'd traveled. With any luck, that information would be all they needed to determine what had happened to Michael Severance.

TWENTY-TWO

It was business as usual at Advanced Animal Care. Wendi still had a loyal base of customers. Folks wondered about the mystery of her missing husband, but Mike wasn't from around those parts and Wendi was. Few wanted to believe that the local girl–turned–professional woman had anything to do with the disappearance of her husband.

Wendi still had her mind on making sure Mike's death remained unknown. She wanted to eliminate the record of her online searches into lie detector tests and body decomposition. She asked if Jamie, her veterinary assistant, knew anything about searching Internet history. "I think Mike was looking at porn on this computer," she lied. Jamie told her what little she knew, and promised to ask her fiancé Tim Schwarz if he knew more. Tim came into the clinic and talked to them both. He explained that while you can delete the cache of files relating to browsing activity, the data still remained on the hard drive, where a forensic computer specialist could find it. Wendi processed the reality that she couldn't conceal her tracks and put her mind to creating a reasonable and innocent-sounding purpose for her searches.

Wendi didn't know it yet, but that wasn't the only data that was a potential problem for her. On February 28, Special Agent McCormick downloaded the information on the tracker attached to Wendi's car. He discovered that on February 27 at 12:30 P.M., her vehicle had traveled to a remote location near

Sutton Road in Tom Green County. It had stopped briefly and then left.

McCormick and Harner contacted Palmer the next day and told him they were pursuing details about the location. The trail to the coordinates took them to gated private property, but not to the exact spot. A little digging and they knew the land was owned by Terrell Sheen. They went to his office and asked for permission to search it.

Sheen was willing to allow them on to the property, but he wanted to go with them. The three agreed to meet at the property on the morning of March 3. Sheen arrived as promised and gave McCormick and Harner a tour of the entire ranch. He allowed the investigators access to all the outbuildings and pointed out the different ponds. They identified the spot where Wendi had parked her car on February 27—it was right beside the largest stock tank of them all.

Her visit to the pond, combined with the Internet search about body decomposition, tended to lead them to the conclusion that Wendi had murdered her husband and disposed of his body on the 7777 Ranch. They hesitated, though. There were other interpretations of the facts. Terrell Sheen had close ties to the Davidson family. Wendi could have had a legitimate reason to be on his property. She knew that the Air Force had searched the swampy area near her home— maybe she was just fearful about what they might find. It all looked suspicious, but not conclusive. As long as there was any room for doubt—any possibility that Mike was alive— the Air Force deserter investigation still progressed.

On March 4, McCormick and Harner drove into town and up the Loop to the Texas Department of Public Safety building where Ranger Shawn Palmer had his office. The military investigators revealed all they had learned about the property and the forensic analysis of Wendi's computer. Palmer contacted additional officers to form a round-the-clock surveillance of their suspect. By 5 P.M., Palmer and three others staked out Advanced Animal Care.

When Wendi pulled away from her clinic and headed

home early that evening, two law enforcement vehicles were
on her tail. She drove out to Grape Creek Cemetery and then
over to her parents' home on nearby Rollin Acres Road. She
brought along a pistol, telling her brother, "The detectives
took this to test-fire and get the ballistics off of it. They said
it was misfiring, and I talked to someone else and they said
it should be cleaned."

That day, Shane Zubaty, Mike's former roommate in
Abilene, who now lived in Florida, opened a letter from
Wendi Davidson:

> *I really wish I knew where Mike was so everyone
> would be at peace, but I don't know and I realize that
> I may never know what happened. I have come to the
> logical conclusion that Mike left everything to start a
> new life. The other possibility is that the military may
> have something to do with his disappearance . . . I
> have two small children to raise and a business to
> run. Wherever he may be I love him, but I am trying
> to move on with my life."

She wrote that she realized after her husband's disappearance that she didn't really know any of his friends and co-
workers "other than he hated work and did not want to
deploy." She invited Shane to visit whenever he came to
Texas, because she would like to meet her son's namesake.

Shane said that the letter was chilling. He had heard no
indication that Wendi was responsible for Michael's death,
but now he wondered. He thought about traveling to Texas,
meeting her and drawing his own conclusions.

At 11 P.M., the watchers were relieved by a new surveillance
team led by Detective McGuire. They followed Wendi when
she drove back to her place in town, arriving at 8:18 the next
morning. Nearly two hours later the men on stake-out
watched as a Ford Excursion entered the parking lot and
pulled away hauling Mike's racing car.

The task force convened on the hill by the car wash overlooking the clinic at 2 P.M. In the pouring rain, the overnight team briefed them and left for home. If developments continued to progress as anticipated, a homicide investigation would soon be in full swing, making Texas Ranger Sergeant Shawn Palmer the lead investigator.

At 2:30, Palmer approached the clinic with DPS Special Crimes Sergeant David Jones. Wendi had agreed to discuss the disappearance of her husband. Initially, she appeared calm and emotionless as she answered their questions. She reiterated her story with nonchalance, telling the men about her trip to her parents' home on January 15 and her return to an empty apartment that night.

She didn't flinch when Palmer questioned her about searching the Internet for information about the decomposition of a body in water. It seemed apparent that she'd given it some thought beforehand. "When they searched the creek back there, I wanted to know if they would be able to see a body if someone dumped Mike there. I wanted to be prepared for what they might find," she said. She talked about not wanting to lose it when she saw the condition of his remains after being in water for so long.

"Why did you look up information about polygraph results?" Palmer asked.

"The police just gave me a lie detector test. I was curious," she shrugged. She rattled on a bit about her scientific nature and proclivity for questioning everything in her quest for knowledge.

When Palmer's questions turned to Terrell Sheen's ranch, her demeanor changed. Her eyes shifted, her posture became rigid, her brazenness evaporated. The rambling chat was over. Her answers turned short and curt. "My parents and I have access to that property," she said.

"When were you last out there?" Palmer pressed.

"A week or two ago."

"Why were you out there then?"

"I went with my dad to cut wood," she answered.

"Did you go to the stock tank?"

"The stock tank?" she stalled.

"Yes, the stock tank."

"There's three tanks out there."

"How many have a dock?" Palmer asked.

"Well, uh, well," she stammered, looking at the floor. She raised her head. "Just one."

A telephone call interrupted the interview. Wendi said, "I've got to get that," and explained that it was her rotation as the after-hours veterinarian on call for a group of San Angelo animal doctors.

Jason Geron was on the other end of the line. Wendi was not his veterinarian, but this was an emergency. His Bengal cat, Enoch, had been on top of the garage door when Jason had opened it. Enoch was caught between the door and the ceiling. He was in obvious pain and his leg didn't look right. Wendi gave him directions to her clinic and then explained the situation to the investigators.

Palmer and Jones left before Jason arrived. They returned to the car wash on the hill joining the rest of the team. The injury sounded serious, making them believe they had a lot of time. They took cover from the pounding rain in a position where they did not have a total view of the clinic. They immediately decided that the ranch needed to be watched round the clock. Air Force Special Agents Harner and McCormick volunteered for the first shift.

They didn't realize how desperate Wendi was in the aftermath of the interview. Jason entered the clinic with his daughter and his beautiful marbled dark and light brown cat. The veterinarian hurried through the examination and rushed Enoch into the back for a quick x-ray. She came back, told them the leg was not broken, gave them medication and hustled them out the door. The abruptness of the visit left Jason feeling a bit unnerved. He hoped he'd never have to rely on her services again.

Not one of the officers noticed when Wendi slipped out of the parking lot in record time. But when Harner and McCormick pulled out on the road, they spotted the red Camaro ahead of them and tailed her. While Harner drove, McCormick called Palmer and asked for instructions. Palmer told them there was no need to follow her. They needed to focus on securing the ranch. No one thought that she would be careless enough to go straight to the ranch immediately after being questioned about it. Harner and McCormick both suspected foul play now, but doubt still existed. The desertion investigation continued.

"We'll be out there all night. We better stop for some vittles," McCormick said. Harner pulled into a gas station/convenience store and the men stocked up.

Back in San Angelo, Palmer's conviction that Mike's death was homicide overrode all of his doubts. Nothing beat redundancy for making sure all the bases were covered. He sent Bill Mabe of the San Angelo Police Department out to the ranch.

Prepared for the long haul, Harner and McCormick turned off the highway and followed March Road. When they veered right, they noticed that the day's downpours had taken a toll on the unpaved caliche surface of Sutton Road. Deep swerving tracks left evidence that someone else had traveled that way—most likely in a two-wheel-drive vehicle. When they passed the final dog-leg in the road before reaching their destination, they spotted the red Camaro. Then they saw Wendi in her blue scrubs standing in front of the gate, fiddling with the lock.

She made no attempt to avoid them. By the time Harner brought the Expedition to a stop, Wendi was standing on the driver's side of their vehicle. Harner rolled down the window. "What are you all doing out here?" she demanded.

"What are *you* doing here?" he asked.

"I came out to check on a horse," she said with a defiant ring in her voice.

"You can't do that," Harner said. "No one can have access to this ranch at this time."

Wendi walked away, opened the gate and pulled her car through. Harner and McCormick hesitated. They did not normally have the authority to stop a civilian on private property who refused to obey their instructions.

Before they could take any action, Officer Mabe pulled

up. Wendi's hands were on the gate preparing to pull it shut behind her. Mabe stopped her. "You cannot close that gate. You have to leave the property now."

"Why? What are you doing out here?" she asked.

"Why are *you* out here?" he echoed.

"I have some horses on the property and I need to take care of them," she snapped back, taking out her anger toward the San Angelo Police Department on its representative.

Mabe stood his ground. "Where are your horses?"

Wendi pointed in a southwesterly direction. "Back there. They're in a pasture near the road."

"How do you think you're going to get back there in that car after all this rain?"

"There's a four-wheeler at the barn. I'll park the car there and take it to the pasture." They stared at each other for a moment and Wendi broke the silence. "Okay. I told you why I'm here, so why don't you tell me why you're here?"

"We're in the process of getting consent to search from Terrell Sheen or a search warrant from the judge. I'm here to secure the property until we can do a detailed search."

Wendi's cool façade slipped. Mabe saw no actual tears in her eyes, but her face contorted as if she were crying, and her voice wavered. Then Mabe heard a strange sound.

Wendi turned toward her car. "Oh, that's my baby." She walked over to the Camaro and opened the door.

Mabe saw an infant strapped in a car seat in the back. He didn't see any rain gear in the car, and neither Wendi nor the baby wore adequate clothing for the day's weather. He wondered what she'd planned to do with her child when she hopped on to the ATV that was exposed to the elements.

She turned back to Mabe and peppered him with questions about his presence at the ranch.

Mabe patiently explained, repeating, "We are attempting to get authorization to search the ranch."

"Why?" she demanded. "Why do you need to search the ranch? Only Terrell Sheen and my father have access to it."

"You need to leave, Doctor Davidson."

Wendi did not budge.

Mabe continued. "You are welcome to sit here outside of the gate, but you cannot enter the property."

Without a word, Wendi got into her car and backed it up to the road. Mabe closed the gate and followed her to the intersection of March and Sutton Roads to make sure she didn't try to access the ranch by the secondary entrance.

Mabe returned to the gate where the Air Force agents waited. Wendi's appearance at the ranch on that afternoon made it clear: the case was now a criminal investigation of a civilian. The military mission was done. Harner and Mc-Cormick stood down, turning the responsibility over to law enforcement. It was time for the civilians to gather the evidence needed to make Wendi Davidson pay for the death of airman Michael Severance.

TWENTY-THREE

Wendi struggled down Sutton Road, her gut clenching every time the rear end of her car fishtailed first one way and then the other in the mud. She had to be approaching panic. She lost her escort when she hit March Road and drove to the cemetery where her grandfather was buried. She didn't want to face her family, but knew she had to do so—they were now her only hope. Reluctantly, she called them to Grape Creek Cemetery.

Marshall knew something was wrong the moment he saw her. It took a while to get the information from her. Finally she explained that she'd come home, found Michael dead and disposed of his body. She insisted that she'd gotten rid of it because she was certain one of them had killed him and she didn't want any one of them to get caught.

Marshall Davidson's first response was to do what any law enforcement official should. He called the police department and eventually arranged for the bizarre meeting at Grape Creek Cemetery.

Meanwhile, Wendi still wanted to cover her tracks. She called her attorney Tim Edwards and told him to terminate the divorce proceedings. Authorities didn't know what she'd told her lawyer, but whatever it was, it was sufficient to impress him with the sense of urgency. He filed a notice of non-suit in the district court clerk's office at 8 P.M. that night.

If Judy, Lloyd and Marshall were not involved in Mike's death or the disposal of his body—as the evidence and their reaction at the cemetery indicated—it had to have been a through-the-looking-glass night for them. Their daughter was pointing a finger of guilt in their faces. At some point, they had to have suspected that Wendi had killed her husband. They might not want to believe it, but the thought had to have crossed their minds.

Judy and Lloyd did not publicly rebuke their son at the graveside that night at the cemetery as Wendi did. They returned to their home to care for their two grandsons and await the arrival of their children. Marshall, however, came back to the house alone, delivering the news of his sister's incarceration on a charge of tampering with evidence.

"How is she?" Judy asked.

"She's pretty tore up," Marshall answered. "She's crying and hysterical."

Their shock of that night's revelations dissipated, leaving in its wake their firm conviction that family always came first. They would do all they could to keep Wendi out of prison. After all, they'd never liked Mike. If they could bring their daughter back home, their despised son-in-law's death was insignificant.

Throughout Monday, Marshall called Palmer and McGuire to ask about the progress of the search of the ranch, but never talked to either one of them. Palmer wasn't interested in talking to anyone from the Davidson family until he completed the job at hand. Palmer believed that the diving team would find Mike's body—but believing was far from knowing. The disparity between the two gnawed at him from the moment he arrived at the ranch at 5:30 A.M.

The morning hours crawled by—each minute stretched longer by doubt and anticipation. Palmer assisted with the arrival and orientation of the diving team and the experts. After the divers hit the water at 10 A.M., Palmer remained close by for a couple of hours, as if with his presence, he could will Michael's body to reveal itself.

At noon, Palmer went across the ranch to interview hired hand Jose Romero. Eight-and-a-half hours after his arrival on the scene, Palmer got word that the troopers had discovered a body underwater. *Was it Michael? It had to be.* A tenuous thread of doubt remained as the divers descended with a video camera to provide evidence of identity. But the taping failed.

Palmer climbed into a boat with other members of the search team and headed to the center of the pond. Divers went back down into the water, removing weights and allowing their discovery to rise. The Texas Ranger watched as the back of the body broke the surface of the water. He was shocked to see how well the cold water had preserved the remains, and by how much the face looked like the photographs of Michael Severance.

When the gathering of evidence was completed at 7 P.M., Palmer, Jones and McGuire left the 7777 Ranch and drove over to Lloyd and Judy's home and delivered the news of the discovery in the stock tank.

The moment the Davidsons learned that a body had been found on Terrell Sheen's property, they knew that everything now looked worse for Wendi. Palmer informed Marshall that Wendi's car needed to be secured pending a search of the vehicle. Marshall agreed to drive the Camaro to the Texas Department of Public Safety offices. From there, Sergeant Jones gave him a ride to the San Angelo Police Department.

Just after 8 o'clock that night, Marshall sat down with Palmer and Jones. He insisted that Wendi had not given him any additional details concerning the disposal of Mike's body. He also explained the parentage of Wendi's two sons, adding that when his sister had first been pregnant with Shane, Mike doubted that he was the father. Then, suddenly, he said, they got married.

The fragile peace at the Severance home in Maine began to fracture at 9 P.M. Les was at work. Brinda answered the phone. The caller identified himself as a member of the Air Force and asked to speak to Leslie Severance.

Brinda said that he was not at home and asked to take a

message. "We'll call back. We need to speak to Mr. Severance."

"Is it about his son?"

"We are only authorized to speak to Leslie Severance."

Brinda was rattled. She tried to calm her thoughts. It
could be nothing more than a bureaucratic detail, and someone else wanting to ask the same questions about Michael's
whereabouts. She tried to convince herself that the call was
insignificant. She didn't have much success.

At 11 P.M., there was a knock at the door. Standing outside
were three men in Air Force uniforms. She flashed back to a
conversation she'd had with Mike just before his first overseas deployment. "If something bad happens to me, you'll
know when they come to the house," he warned. "If there are
three men, prepare yourself for the worst before you open the
door."

Brinda saw them and did not want to open the door. A
small piece of her heart insisted that if she refused to open
the door, it would not be true. She swallowed hard and faced
them. Again, they asked for Leslie Severance. "Did you find
Michael?"

"Are you his mother?"

"No," she admitted with regret.

"Then we can only speak to Leslie Severance. Where can
we find him?"

"He's at work. But you can't tell him there. Come in and
I'll call him. I'll tell him to come home."

The men stepped inside, but stood right by the door. Brinda
picked up the phone and called. "Les, you need to come
home."

"Why, Brinda? What's wrong?"

"You just need to come home. Now."

Brinda then called both of her daughters and Mike's
brother, Frank.

Nicole was the first to arrive, then Brooke walked through
the door. Both were full of questions, but none of the Air
Force officials would provide any answers. Les opened the

door, but before he could cross the threshold, one of the men blurted out, "We found your son in a pond."

Nicole raced to the bathroom and threw up. As she came back to the living room, Frank arrived and received the news. He said nothing. He turned around and left the house. He returned a half hour later with two of his cousins.

Les looked lost. He couldn't sit down. He couldn't stand still. He roamed around getting up and down, pacing from one room to the other. Brinda stayed close to him, feeling helpless, knowing there was nothing she could do to ease the pain of this horrible moment.

Nicole got on the telephone and called family members. She didn't want anyone to learn of Mike's fate from the newspaper or on the television.

The family stayed up all night, each lost in personal grief. Every one of them wanted to deny the reality of Mike's death. They had all anticipated this moment, but now that it was here, they didn't want to believe it. They took some comfort from one another's presence, but the newness of their pain left them numb—the plunge into the depths of suffering would come when they learned the full horror of Michael's fate.

TWENTY-FOUR

As soon as Michael's body arrived at the medical examiner's office in Lubbock, Dr. Sridhar Natarajan began the autopsy. He performed an exterior examination, first running a complete set of x-rays to search for any evidence of a retained foreign body—like a bullet. Finding none, he moved on to meticulously detailing the outward appearance, enumerating the evidence of decompositional change and the effects of weeks of submersion in water, including the bleaching, wrinkling and sloughing of skin.

He described the items found attached to the body and the ligatures still connected to it. The location of each of the forty-one stab wounds was noted. Then he proceeded through each biological system, remarking on its condition. He preserved samples from the body, preparing some for toxicological tests. It would be more than a month before he got back those test results, and more than three before he issued his final report.

Sergeant Jones and Lieutenant Frank Carter of the San Angelo Police Department waited just inside the door of the clinic early Tuesday morning, March 8, 2005. They watched Marshall as he made a series of telephone calls. Texas Ranger Palmer joined them there a few minutes after 7.

When Judy and Lloyd arrived nearly an hour later, Palmer told them, "We will be seeking a search warrant for the clinic. Officers will remain here to ensure that no evidence is disturbed."

"I need to get the babies' things," Judy said.

Palmer allowed her and Marshall to gather clothing, toys and any other items needed for the children, but asked them not to disturb anything else. Judy pulled a push pin from a calendar in the apartment and removed three rings. "Marshall, please remind your mother not to remove any articles that she does not need for the immediate care of the children," Palmer said.

Marshall whispered to her immediately. Judy placed a woman's two-ring wedding set and a man's gold wedding band on the desk in the crowded apartment.

When Detective McGuire arrived at the clinic, Palmer returned to the Texas Rangers' office to write up the details of the investigation in an affidavit to request authorization for a search warrant for 4240 Sherwood Way and for the 2001 Chevrolet Camaro.

After leaving the clinic, Judy took Tristan to the Children's Academy child-care center, where Jenny Pittman regarded him as a well-adjusted child. She began to doubt that assessment when Judy and Tristan arrived in tears. When Judy left, her grandson stopped crying, but he later demonstrated the beginnings of compulsive hand-washing. When it was time to line up to wash hands before a snack, Tristan was so over-eager, he cut in front of the other students.

At 3:40 that afternoon, Judge Tom Gossett signed a warrant to search the clinic. Palmer returned to Advanced Animal Care with the document in hand at 4 P.M. They knew Wendi had disposed of Mike's body; now they needed to find the evidence that confirmed that she was responsible for his death.

Palmer briefed an officer and a detective from the San Angelo Police Department at 4 P.M. He watched crime-scene technicians as they videotaped and photographed the area around the clinic. He noted a section of white rope hanging on a fence behind the building. It appeared to be consistent with one of the ropes found attached to Mike's body. He made sure it was digitally recorded.

At 5:35, with a uniformed patrol officer posted by the front door of the clinic, the search of the outside area began. Behind the barn were two vehicles, neither one appearing to be in working order. Inside one of them, Palmer spotted a pile of auto parts. In the other, military clothing and gear sat on the seats.

On the ground between the two vehicles, Palmer spotted a tire tool and confiscated it as possible evidence. A crime-scene technician did the same with a cotton apron found a short distance away.

Inside the barn, they took custody of two brake drums, a sleeping bag, bolt cutters, wire and a pair of pliers. The length of white rope was removed from the fence and bagged as evidence.

Detective McGuire inserted a key in the front door of the clinic and the team entered. The crime-scene techs went first, videotaping and photographing every inch of the interior. They recovered a lot of paperwork including documents from on top of the counter, invoice pads and an appointment book.

In the surgery area, Palmer noted several containers of medication, including a bottle of Beuthanasia-D Special. He recovered two pairs of scissors, six controlled substance logs and a set of bolt cutters. Palmer moved into the pre-operating room where he confiscated a few more pairs of scissors as well as two rolls of monofilament line and a wood-handled knife he found in a drawer.

He bent down and crawled under the sink, where he disconnected and removed the PVC trap from the water line. When he got off the floor, he headed into the examination room, seizing pliers and bandage scissors.

In the residential area, they approached an area with a desk and several shelves. Inside a briefcase found there, they confiscated a plastic knife holster, a sexual history list in Wendi's handwriting and a number of notes about

Jason Burdine, a number of used pregnancy tests and a
sexual device shaped like a male organ. They took custody
of the three rings left on the desk earlier that day by Judy
Davidson.

On one shelf there was a lockbox. Detective McGuire
opened it and said, "The last time I was in here, a pistol and
a blue-handled boning knife were in this box. They're not
here now." Those two items were not found anywhere in the
building. From the shelves, they confiscated bank statements, photographs, videotapes and a folding knife.

The techs swabbed several suspicious-looking stains and
sprayed luminol in the dog kennel area, but found no evidence of blood. They took possession of a stack of patient
file folders resting in a laundry basket.

While they searched, Judge Gossett signed two new
warrants—one authorizing an investigation of the contents
of the computer observed at the clinic, the other for the
search of the Chevrolet Camaro belonging to Wendi Davidson. Before leaving the clinic, Palmer took custody of the
Compaq laptop computer with its power cord and mouse, an
iomega Zip drive and disk and a high speed port hub.

Within fifteen minutes after leaving the premises,
Palmer, McGuire and Jones were following a tow truck as it
transported Wendi's car from the Texas DPS office to a sally
port at the Tom Green County Jail. Inside the car, officers
took possession of a blue spiral notebook, containing con-
version tables for medications, and a pair of pliers. A forensic tech processed the exterior for latent prints and vacuumed
the trunk to collect any trace evidence. He also removed a
stained section of carpet from that area.

While the car underwent its examination, Sergeant Jones
and Detective McGuire traveled out to the Davidsons' place
and spoke to Lloyd, who admitted seeing the blue-handled
knife and the pistol at Wendi's apartment. He believed that
Marshall had the pistol, and possibly the knife as well. This
news alarmed McGuire and Jones. Marshall was not playing
a role in the investigation of his sister, but he was a law en-

forcement officer and, as such, had certain responsibilities that went beyond family loyalty. If he had these items and was concealing them from the detectives, it was a serious obstruction—one that could cost him his job.

TWENTY-FIVE

At a quarter till 4 on March 8, Wendi picked up the telephone in Tom Greene County Jail totally unaware that her car was in the same facility that she was and, at that very moment, members of law enforcement were digging through it looking for evidence to incriminate her. She placed a collect call to her parents' home.

Marshall answered the line, telling the operator that he would accept the charges.

"Hey, Marshall, how are— How is everybody?" Wendi asked.

"Just peachy," Marshall said.

Wendi continued on, seemingly oblivious to her brother's sarcasm. She had a mission to accomplish with this call. There were things that needed to be done, and she wanted both her brother and her mother to make a list of the tasks she assigned to each of them. As soon as Marshall secured paper and a pen, she started. "All right. Shane might be covered by military insurance, 'cause I think he still has benefits even after his father's deceased. So I think he'll still have military insurance."

"I know, we've already talked about that."

"Okay. So write it down."

"I got it," Marshall said.

"All right. The life insurance policy as well. Check on that," Wendi ordered.

"Hunh?"

"Check on the life insurance policy, too," Wendi repeated.

"We are. We've talked about that, too."

"All right. I don't really want, you know, I don't want the money. I just think that, you know, even if we can't even use it for any of this," she said, referring to her legal expenses, "I still want Shane to have it."

"I know, and we're—we've been talking about that."

"Okay. And Mike's dad— Is he coming down here or something?"

"Maybe eventually, yeah."

"And he wants some of Mike's stuff?" he asked.

"Yeah."

"Okay. Well, he can have anything out in the barn. I have everything that I wanted to keep at y'all's house. There's not much there, but a few pictures, stuff like that, for Shane." Wendi's voice cracked.

"Are you okay, Wendi?"

She drew in a sharp sniffle. "I am, Marshall. I just miss y'all, and I'm very upset about Mike, you know."

"I know it's hard, Wendi. I know."

"'Cause before, I was just doing what I had to do, but now I'm very emotional, you know, 'cause now I can tell everybody what happened and it's— You know, it hurts to know that somebody you love— Marshall, I loved him so much, I really did, and I wish that I'd been thinking with my right mind, but . . ."

"Well . . ." Marshall said, at a loss for words.

"Obviously I wasn't, and I need to just suck it up."

"Well . . ."

"Okay. So . . . and I don't know about the Mustangs, if y'all want to go ahead and sell them or . . ."

"We're talking about that, too," her brother reassured her.

"Okay. Because I don't really think it matters at this point in time. I mean, I— You know— They're just as much mine as anybody's . . . Don't they still have the car and the clinic sealed off?"

"No. The clinic is ours now, and the car is going to be, probably tomorrow."

"Okay. Now, y'all need to check in my console. There was eight hundred and fifty dollars cash in there, because I had just taken it out of mine and Mike's bank account, and was going to— I had it in the safe like my safe at work, but I put it back in the console . . . But I have that money, because that's the only cash I had, and I just grabbed it and I was going to put it back in my bank account. But check, because that's a big chunk of change. I want to make sure no dirty cop took it."

"Okay. I wrote it down," Marshall said.

"Eight hundred and fifty bucks in the console," she emphasized.

"I wrote it down," he repeated.

"All right," she said.

"Oh, let me ask you a question. Did you get your saline and stuff?" he asked, referring to the supplies she needed for her contact lenses.

"That was another thing I had. I do, it's here, but they're still not letting me have it because I'm on suicide watch. I don't know what the hell I can do with saline, but they won't let me have it. So, I'm still . . ."

Marshall interrupted, "I thought they told you that you could have it as long as it was new."

"They said . . ." Wendi exhaled her frustration. "They brought it to me and said, 'Here, take your contacts out and we can take them.' I said, 'No, that's not the point.' I said, 'I cannot see without my contacts.' 'Well, we can't give you the stuff, and we can't be running them back and forth. So either take them out or leave them in.'

"And so I talked to the nurse, and they're all assholes. And I was, like, 'If the guard okays it and lets me put it in this lock-up box'—that, you know, they have keys for—I said, 'and she will let me take them out at night and put them back in, in the morning, will that be okay?' She said, 'I don't know, you'll have to talk to her.'

"So I still don't— I mean, that's still not resolved, but it will be okay."

"Well, do what you can on that end to get it," Marshall said. "We got it to you."

"I know. Thank you very much." The conversation turned to documents that Marshall needed to pick up from the clinic and get to her accountant. Then Wendi said, "I talked to the lawyer today and he still sounded really positive. He gave me my arrest warrant thing that they have for me."

"Uh-huh."

Wendi continued. "And, basically . . . they have all the facts in there and I . . . found out how they found all this out, because the computer thing, and then they put a tracker deal on my car in . . . February. So when I went to the ranch . . ."

Marshall cut her off. "Don't tell us all that."

"Well, it's public knowledge. It's in this public record thing. So it's in there and that's how they figured it out. But, I mean, I don't care. I mean, whatever. They can get me for whatever I did and just leave me the hell alone about the rest . . . But, anyway, he said that they were going to be working on trying to get me a psychologist to try to get me out of here," Wendi said, referring to their efforts to find a doctor who could attest that she did not need to be on suicide watch.

"Right," Marshall acknowledged.

"And going to try to get my bond reduced. Now, the jailers and the nurses keep telling me MHMR [Mental Health/Mental Retardation, a Texas state agency] is coming, and I better cooperate with them or I'm never getting out of there. I told them I was not speaking to MHMR, because my attorney advised me not to speak to them at all. He was getting me a private psychologist. They're giving me a real hard time about that. They told me, 'Well, if you don't talk to MHMR, you're never getting out of here.'"

Wendi told Marshall that although she was in jail on just one charge, tampering with evidence, the lawyer had warned that a homicide indictment was nearly guaranteed. "He told me we'll just have to wait and see," Wendi said. "He said on the autopsy, they don't have nothing, which— I don't know if that's a good thing or a bad thing . . ."

"I don't think they have done the autopsy yet," Marshall contradicted.

"He said it's already been done in Lubbock. They couldn't find anything. They sent samples off to some federal lab to see about toxicology . . . He said he doesn't know if there's anything in his system or not. I mean, if there is, they still can't prove that it was me or you or anybody else."

"I know," Marshall said. "Don't talk about the case."

"I know," Wendi sighed.

"You know they're listening."

"I know. I mean, I'm just talking about public knowledge, basically."

"Well, that's fine. Wait until it's public."

"All right. So he told me that somebody would be here pretty shortly to give me a paper to release his body to the military so they could bury him, cremate him, whatever they wanted to do . . . He told me to go ahead and sign that. Have y'all talked to his dad at all?"

"No, we have not."

". . . God, this is horrible. All right. Let me talk to Mama real quick."

When Judy came to the phone, she asked how her daughter was doing, prompting Wendi to give full vent to a round of whining and complaining. "I'll be much brighter when I get out of this little cell, because, I mean, it's about to drive me insane, because there's no TV, you know. I'm stuck here. The only girl that was normal—all the other ones are, like, really suicidal and crazy. But the other girl that was here, she was just handicapped, and she was actually a paralegal, so she told me, kind of— I didn't talk to her about my case at all."

"Well, I hope not, because you know they can plant people in there," Judy cautioned.

"I know. I didn't say nothing. All I did was talk to her about how the system works and everything. But anyway, she's gone; she got bonded today, so there's nobody normal in here. I mean, they're all in their cells. I can't see them or talk to them, just the fire watcher girl [slang for the staff member responsible for keeping a close eye on potentially suicidal prisoners] and they have fits and it's kind of scary. Like multiple personality and stuff like that. And there's no TV and there's nobody to talk to.

"I'm sitting in . . . my stupid little vest and my blanket and the stuff the attorney has give me . . . I try to sleep, but I can't hardly sleep. They only have lights off for five hours at night, and the rest of the time they're bright lights. And they're not off, they're just dim. But I'm able to eat better. You know, I'm still not eating a lot, but I'm eating better." Then Wendi asked, "Do you have a pencil and a paper?" and got down to business.

They talked about family matters, Tristan's day care and Shane's health insurance. Wendi perked up when Judy spoke of a possible source of regular income for Shane. "He should get Social Security benefits."

"Which is what?" Wendi asked.

"It's like I have," Judy said, referring to her disability checks.

"He'll get money each month?"

"Yeah . . . until he turns eighteen."

Wendi sounded pleased at this news and turned her questions to Shane's ear infection. The recording on the telephone line interrupted. "You have one minute left."

"All right," Wendi said. "I got a couple of other things, and if it goes dead, then I'll just ask you tomorrow. You know the name of that guy, the dog that bled in the front waiting room?"

"Yeah. I don't remember her name."

"But you can look it up, because it was January fifteenth, around that time," Wendi pushed.

"Okay. All right. What about it?"

"We need that name, and I need to get it to the lawyer as soon as possible, 'cause they're going to need him as a witness."

"All right," Judy said, sounding confused.

". . . You can tell they're very unstable. Who knows where they will be living when—a year or two years, so we need to get that to the lawyer so they can get some kind of statement."

"All right."

"Because I don't want two years from now somebody saying, 'There was blood on the front waiting room,' you know, 'where did that come from?' "

"All right."

"So I definitely need that name. It was around January fifteenth," Wendi insisted.

"All right."

"And we need the phone number, all that."

"All right."

Wendi then gave Judy a list of names of people who needed to be contacted about heartworm treatments. When the recording stepped in again to terminate the call, Wendi said, "Love you," and the conversation was over.

Wendi's agenda was clear: take care of finances and take care of me. Marshall and Judy seemed to be nothing more than tools to that end.

TWENTY-SIX

Immediately after getting off of the phone with his sister, Marshall called Major Steve Whiteaker at the San Angelo Regional Office of Texas Parks and Wildlife. "Have you heard the news about my sister, Wendi Davidson?" he asked.

"Yes. I heard she'd been arrested in connection with the disappearance of her husband."

"I tipped the police off about where they might find the body. I can be at your office in ten minutes. Do you have some time to talk?"

Whiteaker agreed to meet with him. As soon as Marshall arrived, he laid out his case for a hardship transfer to San Angelo. "My sister, Wendi, is in a lot of trouble and I'm going to try to gain custody of her two children. Zapata is not a good place to be raising kids, and here in San Angelo, I would have help from my family. In addition to the children's needs, my mother has lupus and my grandmother has cancer. I need to be here to help my dad take care of them."

"Hardship transfers are not easy to come by, Davidson. You are going to have to spell out the necessity for one very clearly to Colonel Pete Flores."

Marshall continued his argument. "Things have really gone bad lately due to my sister's problems. I was here in San Angelo visiting my parents the day that Wendi broke the news to them that she found her late husband dead, and assumed that one of her family members had killed him. So she took the body and put it in the pond on Terrell Sheen's ranch in an effort to protect the family."

"Who's Terrell Sheen?"

"He's a family friend and former veterinarian that I used to work for. Wendi and my dad have also worked for him, and Wendi keeps a horse out there on the ranch. The whole family pretty much has free roaming of the ranch at any time."

Marshall then explained the events of March 5 and the one charge filed against his sister. "They set a high bond in order to break the case. My parents pooled their money to hire Wendi an attorney, but they're already financially strapped because they put a lot of money into Wendi's vet clinic. After Wendi was arrested, I told her not to talk to anyone but her attorney. When I talk to Wendi by phone from the jail, the first thing I always tell her is to not tell me anything I might have to testify about later."

Then Marshall related a strange story about his father's friends that he said happened while his father was out in the field working on a tractor. "One of them lay down behind a dirt berm and stuck his hand up just barely above it. Another friend stood back with a camera and took a picture of my dad coming toward them. The picture makes it look like Dad was burying someone and the picture is floating around out there somewhere."

On March 9, Palmer and McGuire gathered up all the forensic exhibits that needed laboratory analysis, and drove to Austin. On the way out of town, Palmer called Detective Ron Sanders at the Tom Green County Sheriff's Office. "Marshall Davidson will be coming in to take possession of Wendi Davidson's vehicle today. You can release it to him. Could you give him a call and ask him to bring the blue-handled boning knife in with him that was removed from Advanced Animal Care? It's evidence in the homicide investigation and I'd like you to take custody of it."

Sanders called Marshall and he said that he'd bring the knife in and turn it over. When Marshall came into the office, however, his attitude had changed. Sanders walked out to greet him and noticed that Marshall appeared to be embarrassed, turning arrogant and dismissive when Sanders asked about the knife.

"I want to hang on to it until I talk to my sister's attorney about releasing it," he said in an irritated tone of voice.

"What about the clothing Wendi gave you?" Sanders asked.

"My dad told me you wanted that, and that you wanted the pistol, too. But I need to speak to the attorney first."

Sanders stared at him, surprised that a fellow law enforcement officer would withhold evidence and act so self-righteous about it. Marshall didn't flinch under his glare. Sanders turned and escorted him back to claim his sister's car.

In Austin, Palmer and McGuire completed the paperwork to maintain a record of a chain of custody and turned over their exhibits to the forensic investigators at headquarters. They still needed to recover the missing knife and pistol, but mostly, now, they had to wait for results from the state lab and from the toxicology tests performed on the samples taken during Mike's autopsy. They had their suspicions about what had happened to Michael Severance, but they knew it was possible that one of the labs would prove them wrong.

TWENTY-SEVEN

Up in Maine, the Severance family tried to hold it together. Nicole closed down the day-care facility she operated in her home for a month in order to help her mother with anything that was needed.

They desperately wanted to bring Michael home. Once the autopsy was completed, they thought it would be a simple matter to facilitate the transportation. They were appalled to discover that they had to wait for Wendi to sign a release form. It was a galling situation that only served to make their pain worse.

The other matter that ate away at their hearts was the fate of Shane. He was in the custody of the family responsible for the death of his father. They felt helpless to make any impact on events unrolling in faraway Texas.

While he was on the road, Marshall called Palmer's office and left a message in his voice mail. He wanted to get one of the records seized during the March 7 search, claiming that one of Wendi's patients needed their pet's veterinary records for a trip out of the country. It sounded plausible, but Palmer would soon learn that Marshall had really wanted the record to provide information to Wendi's attorney.

Early that evening, Wendi called and talked to Marshall once more. "I'm sorry to be calling again, but I just was thinking, this article in the paper, they said that you stated that he was dead in the bed."

"The article wasn't right, Wendi."

"I never said that, Marshall. He was dead . . ."

"Wendi . . ." he tried to interrupt.

". . . before in the back."

"Wendi. What did I say about the case? If you talk to me about the case, I'm hanging up."

"Okay. I'm just saying . . ."

"I didn't say that. You need to not worry about what you see in there," Marshall insisted.

"All right. Well, just listen."

"Okay."

"I think it's important that they have the facts."

"Wendi, listen to me. Your lawyer is handling it. I am not—if you say one more word about the case, I'm hanging up, I promise you."

"Well, I need to speak to my lawyer. Can you get him to come up here tomorrow?"

"I'm going to talk to him, but you have to understand, what the paper says is not the facts. That's not what's going to court."

"Okay."

"I've already told your lawyer that."

"Okay."

"He said— Well, that's why he doesn't want to talk to the paper is, they always skew it and, you know, do it however they benefit themselves."

Wendi sighed. "I know. I just— I mean— I'm not talking about any specifics. I'm just going to tell you that . . ."

Marshall raised his voice. "Wendi, you just told me a specific. Don't ever do it again."

"I'm not talking any specifics. I just want to make sure all the facts are straight."

"Well, that's what you need to tell your lawyer."

"Okay. I'm sorry. I just worry about this."

"Well, I can't believe that you just said that," Marshall responded.

"I'm repeating what was said in the newspaper."

"And then you repeated what you said."

"Well, it's the truth. I don't know."

"Huh?"

"It's the truth," Wendi repeated.

"Well, it may be. I don't want to know what room he was in. I don't care."

"All right. Whatever."

"But, yes, I know you never said the bed."

"I know. I just don't know why they always— A lot of that is lies."

"Well, I know, Wendi, but you need to think before you speak," Marshall urged her.

"All right. I'm just worried about in here and I'm worried about out there."

"Well, you don't need to worry about out here. We're taking care of it."

"But I do worry, because if I get bonded out, then I want to be able to run my business for a little while, forever—and how am I going to do that if they've taken half the freaking clinic?"

"If they've taken it?" Marshall asked.

"Did they take any of my equipment or supplies or anything?"

Marshall said, "No," then seemed to contradict himself by adding, "But all that will eventually come back."

"I hope soon, because . . ."

Marshall interrupted her again. "Well, you need to worry about what's going on in there. We'll worry about what we need to do out here."

"I know."

"You know, there's nothing you can do to help the situation . . . I'm telling you, we're taking care of our end. You need to keep your mouth shut about the case except to your lawyer."

"I know."

"Well, you keep forgetting."

"Is Tristan doing okay?"

"He's doing all right."

"Does he ask about me?"

"Every once in a while he'll mention something, and we just say that you've got a new job."

Wendi badgered him for specifics of Tristan's conversations about her, which Marshall couldn't recall. Then she asked, "Does he still sleep with Mom and Dad?"

"Yes, he's sleeping with Mom and Dad."

"Where does Shane sleep?"

"In his bed."

"Does he wake at night?" she asked.

"Every once in a while."

"Do you get up with him?"

"What?"

"Do you get up with him?" Wendi asked again.

"Yes, I get up with him and, yes, Mom gets up with him. I mean, you're acting like we're not taking care of them and . . ."

"I know you are, Marshall. It's just that I miss them."

"Well, I know you do, Wendi."

"I mean, I'm used to not being around you, and I'm used to not being around Mom and Dad, thank God. I'm not used to being around—not being around my kids."

"I know, Wendi . . . We're all working to try to get you back with them . . . Don't say anything you shouldn't, or anything else."

"I know. It's hard, because I'm in here by myself and all I have to do is sit and worry."

"I know, and we've already talked about that. We said that we know that's all you've got to do. And there's probably reason for concern."

"I'm trying to be strong, I am, but God, it's hard," Wendi moaned.

"Well, I know, Wendi, and I know how you are, that you can't, you know, be by yourself, and that's why it's so hard for you in there."

"It is."

"But, at the same time, if they put you in general population, you get stuck in a— with people you don't like, how is that going to be, too?"

"I don't know, Marshall. I don't know. But I just know this is horrible . . . I usually can't brush my teeth. I mean, I've been able to brush them twice since I've been here. I don't have any deodorant or shampoo or . . ."

"Have you done anything with your contacts?"

"No. They still haven't done anything. I'm just going to have to wait till I get out of here. There's nothing I can do about it. So . . ."

"Are you sleeping?" Marshall asked.

"Yeah, okay. I'm sleeping."

"They got you a bed, or do you sleep on the floor or what?"

"No, it's a metal rack and it has the little plastic net thing. It's all right. I mean, my physical needs are being met. I mean, the food sucks. Yesterday I had to eat a meal off the floor because it fell on the floor, and I either had to eat it or do without. So . . ."

"They wouldn't bring you another one?"

"No. That's all right. I don't care."

"Well, who threw it on the floor?"

"I dropped it trying to get it through the bars. That's all right. It's my fault, I guess. That's all right. You know what? I thank God every day that this is me and not any of y'all, and especially Mama, because Mama wouldn't make it, because you can't smoke, you can't drink coffee."

"I know."

"You know, you can't move around. God, Dad couldn't live— I mean, Dad would not be able to sit here. I don't think you would be able to do it. I don't think you would be able to sit here like this. I mean, if anybody is a good candidate, I guarantee you, I'm the best. I mean, it's horrible, but . . ."

"Well, we're trying to get you out, Wendi, but you— I mean, you've got to be prepared for the worst and hope for the best."

"I know. I tell myself that every day. Every day I tell myself that. And, you know, I know I shouldn't worry, but God, I worry about what everybody that knows me thinks. You know, what is Terrell thinking; what is Mr. Fleming thinking?" she asked.

"They're all just— They're all supporting you, Wendi . . . Everybody is in full support of you, just whatever, you know, they need to do to help." Wendi expressed a long list of worries and fears about losing friendships. Then she said, "I just wish I could change the whole past."

"Well, I know. We all wish it wouldn't have happened— anything wouldn't have happened. We wish you weren't in jail. But whatever happened happened, and you're in jail."

Wendi fretted about loose ends and finances, and then turned her words to her deceased husband. "I know this sounds maybe silly, but, you know, I just want Mike to be buried here, because he's my husband and the kids' daddy and . . ."

Marshall interrupted. "Wendi, you need to let that go. I mean, the last two times you've called, all you've talked about is him, and you need to worry about you, now. Okay?"

"But I don't want them to, like, ship him off to Maine."

"Well, that's where he was born and raised."

"But I'm his wife."

"What?"

"I'm his wife, Marshall."

"Yeah, but he's got family up there, too."

"I don't know what they want to do, but . . ."

Marshall cut her off. "I don't know what's going to happen yet. Like I said, you need to talk to your lawyer. But you need to think about his dad, you know, probably do what his dad wants to do. You know . . ."

It was Wendi's turn to interrupt. "It doesn't matter what I want to do?"

"Y'all have been married for a few months— Well, sure it matters, but y'all have been married for a few months. He's been his dad's forever."

"And what about Shane and Tristan?"

"What about them?" Marshall asked.

"That was their daddy."

"They're not going to be able to see him, Wendi. I don't understand what you're saying there. You know that as well as I do."

"Well, would you want Papa shipped off somewhere, you know?"

"Papa was born and raised here. You need to think, Wendi. You are— I don't know what to tell you. You're losing it. You need to pull yourself together and think about it, because you're thinking Shane—Well, Shane doesn't have a clue who he is."

"I know."

"Shane doesn't know who he is and–and Tristan knew him for a short time in the scheme of things. So . . ."

"I know."

"I mean, you're the only big one it's affecting, and it seems like it's getting worse and worse, and you need to think about other things than, you know, where he's going to be buried."

"I don't know. It just seems important to me . . ." Wendi insisted.

". . . It's like your lawyer said, he ought to just be cremated and spread over wherever, you know, his dad wants to spread him."

"Is that what they want to do?"

"That's what the lawyer said. I don't know what they want to do. I haven't talked to his dad or anything." Then, Marshall told his sister that he would not be able to visit her on Monday because he needed to go to a regional meeting and hoped at that time to have the opportunity to talk with the head of his department about getting transferred to San Angelo.

When the warning of the impending end of the call echoed in both receivers, Marshall was ready to terminate it. Wendi desperately wanted to keep him on the line until the last possible second. Marshall gave her that additional minute—it was no big deal. But soon, his devotion to his sister would cost him far more than a little time.

TWENTY-EIGHT

On March 10, Detective McGuire and Texas Ranger Palmer drove out to the Davidsons' place to speak with Marshall. "We understand that you removed some of Michael's clothing from the Advanced Animal Care clinic," Palmer said.

Marshall was argumentative, stopping just short of denying that the clothes were in his possession. When asked to describe exactly what he had, Marshall wasn't free with any details. He said, "Yeah. I have a couple of things—some shirts and stuff."

While Palmer secured the knife, Marshall spoke to McGuire. "Do not expect any assistance from me just because I am in law enforcement. Wendi Davidson is still my sister, and I am not going to help with the investigation."

That same day, the Davidsons' child custody attorney drafted a "Power of Attorney for Child Care" document for Wendi's signature. It named her brother Marshall as her "agent and attorney-in-fact" in order that he could ". . . provide for the care and control of" Shane; ". . . obtain any and all medical attention, aid, surgery or treatment reasonable and necessary for" him; and enroll him "in a public or private school . . ."

That afternoon, Wendi called Terrell Sheen. "Maybe several veterinarians could alternate working there, like Jody up the road and Janis Cortez and Doctor Russell, so we can pay some bills and not lose it."

Terrell did not seem very receptive to the idea. In fact, he suggested it might be time to sell her practice.

At 6:30 that evening, Wendi called home. Marshall said, "We talked to the other attorney about the kids, and what we'll probably do is give Mom and Dad custody of Shane, and they'll also have— Well, all three of us will be power of attorney over Tristan, and then I'll have power of attorney over you."

"Why is Shane going to Mom and Dad?" Wendi demanded.

"Huh?"

"Why is Shane going to Mom and Dad?" she repeated through clenched teeth.

"Because I don't have any what they call 'standing,' which means— Grandparents do, but I don't. And if we don't give it to Mom and Dad, and they do it wrong, do it with me, then that would give his family some grounds to come down and get him, because, basically, they've got the same grounds to come pick up the kid right now as anybody."

"No, not really, because don't I have say?"

"Huh?"

"I don't have any say anymore?" Wendi bristled.

"Not right now. You don't have physical control of him."

Wendi said, "He's not going to be going to Maine, I don't think."

"Well, right now, there's nothing that really could stop him other than we have physical custody of him right now. So we're going to get a temporary power of attorney. I'm going to get power of attorney over him for right now. That way, at least somebody will have some say so over them and then Mom and Dad will get temporary custody."

The conversation turned to Wendi's mental health evaluation. "Was there a psychiatrist coming or am I supposed to talk to MHMR?"

"No, the psychiatrist, he'll have him come up here pretty quick."

"MHMR is coming tomorrow."

"Well, you need to tell them that you— He basically said, No, I'm not crazy and I can't talk to you about the case."

Wendi objected to keeping silent, because she wanted to be moved out of the suicide watch unit.

Marshall insisted that she not talk to them unless her lawyer was there with her. "Look, they're probably going to try to beat it out of you to talk to them and everything else. Just say, 'No, not without my attorney. He's got somebody else supposed to come up here and talk to me.'"

Next, they discussed Marshall's encounter with Palmer and McGuire earlier that day. "Don't say anything back to me after I tell you, but basically, they want all the clothes that . . . you gave me, and they got that blue-handled knife that you left out there at the house. I don't want to know anything about it, but . . ."

"Well, I don't care. Whatever . . . Nobody has been here asking about Mike, what—what we're going to do with Mike?"

"No. I asked him about that, too," Marshall said, referring to the criminal attorney. "And he said somebody . . . from the military will probably come up there and have you sign off on something releasing it to the military so they can take care of . . ."

"And nobody has. So they're just going to let him rot?"

"Well, they will. No. I mean, I'm sure he's still up in wherever they sent him. But they— Somebody will come by . . . You don't talk to them or anything. You just sign whatever they give you so that they can handle the burial or however they're going to do it."

Wendi complained about not knowing what would happen to Mike's body and about not being able to talk freely to her brother.

Marshall said, "Well, if it's not about the case, it's fine."

Wendi babbled as she sought the right words to use. "Let me put it in some little metaphor. I just, you know, I know what all happened, and I guess in my mind, I just, you know— Why can't you just let dead dogs lie, you know?

And I don't know. I was kind of at peace knowing things, and now I don't know. You get what I'm saying?"

"Well," Marshall said again, "I don't want to know any more."

"But you do know what I'm saying?"

"I guess. I don't know. I don't want to know about the case."

Wendi expressed annoyance that her family wasn't making an all-out effort to get her out of the jail.

"The D.A. said charges are imminent. I mean, they're coming," Marshall said.

Everyone else seemed to take that as a matter of course, but Wendi seemed shocked. "The D.A. said that?"

"Yeah," Marshall said. "The D.A. said that to the attorney."

"I just don't understand why. I just don't know how they can do that when they don't know anything."

"Well, they can do it just based on the evidence they have got. You know, it's all circumstantial stuff, but that's how they're going to do it. But, you know, that's what we're waiting on and everybody kind of figured that. It wasn't no big secret, you know, and, anyway, so we're waiting on that and then we'll try to get your bond reduced and try to get you out of there."

"So basically, there is no ifs, ands or buts.' I mean, it's going to be just a matter of time that this is going to trial," Wendi said. She turned the conversation to the disappointing phone call she'd had that afternoon. "Terrell didn't sound happy when I talked to him."

"Why? He was happy here today."

That news unsettled Wendi, causing her to stammer a bit, then she said, "He was just very to the point: 'What can I do for you; is that all you need?' I mean, he just, I don't know. He was kind of hateful."

". . . He wasn't earlier. We all sat there and talked to him . . . He's behind you, trust me," Marshall assured his sister.

"It didn't sound like it. I mean, I don't really want to call him again, 'cause, I don't know, he hurt my feelings, I guess."

When she complained about having to call everyone collect, Marshall reminded her that she didn't need to call all the veterinarians in town.

"No," Wendi snapped back. "But I need to write them, but I can't even do that right now. I can't even have a freaking pencil or a piece of paper."

"You don't need to write them either, because anything you write down is going to be thrown into court, good, bad or indifferent."

"I know. But God, Marshall, I just need to be doing something. Damn it."

"Well, if we can get you out of there, you'll be able to watch TV and read or whatever."

Wendi continued her complaint. "I feel like I need to be trying to figure out what they're up to, you know, 'cause I . . ."

"You can't. That's what your lawyer does. He's got access to all that stuff."

"I mean, I just— For the life of me, I can't understand why they took my records unless they're going to try to get people to say bad things about me, you know, calling clients and stuff."

"Well, they're not going to, you know, they've got to do what they got to do, and our side has got to do what we got to do. I mean, we're not trying to hide anything, we're not trying to cover anything up, but we're going to, you know, we're not going to sit there and tell them, 'Well, when she was three, she picked her nose,' and everything else. I mean, that's irrelevant. I mean, we told them what we know, and we're going to move on from that. And everybody else, you know, if they call somebody else, they can tell them what they know and move on from that. And your attorney is going to get to do the same thing and twist it on them. We're saying, 'Well, you said this, but, you know, the same person said this.' I mean, that's how the game is played no matter where you go . . . Nothing you can do. I mean, anything you do is just adding to the fire that, you know, stuff that your attorney has got to justify," Marshall said, and turned the phone over to his dad.

Wendi asked her father, "Everything going okay?"

"Yeah, well, as well as can be expected. I mean, it's a lot better on us than it is on you, obviously, but it's still hell out here, too."

"I know. Damn it, Daddy. I mean, my whole life, I mean, I just tried to do things that . . ."

"Well, I know."

". . . help, you know, I always want to— I'm always worried about what y'all think."

"Well, you know, from this point on, you know, everything is a done deal. You just have to move forward from this point on. So . . ."

"I don't know," Wendi objected. "Everybody is like, 'You have never been in jail before?' I was like, 'No.' And they're like, 'Oh, she's trying to make it to the big top.' I mean, everybody is just . . ."

"Well, you know, if any of the inmates or anything try to talk to you about anything about the case, don't say anything to them either."

"I know," Wendi sighed. "I'm just worried that I'm going to be in here forever and then they're going to charge me and then it's just going to be ridiculous. I mean, I need to hurry up and get out so I can— I mean, I want to see my kids, but I need to work at the clinic to try and get money saved up so we can have money to—so y'all can take care of the kids and so we can fight my way out of this."

"I know," her dad said. "But see, you're worrying about that. You're working too far in the future. I mean, you need to worry about today and tomorrow right now . . . and the next day. You know, not weeks, months."

As the call was disconnected, Wendi shouted, "Love you!" but no one was there. Wendi seemed incapable of understanding and accepting that the act she'd committed had changed the landscape of her universe, building a barrier between her and the rest of the civilized world. In her mind, it was still all about her—everyone should be focused on her—and there were no signs that that would ever change.

TWENTY-NINE

In Abilene, at Dyess Air Force Base, those who had known Michael Severance as a friend or fellow airman gathered at the base chapel at 1:30 P.M. on March 11. Memorial services were common on any Air Force installation during a time of military conflict. But Mike's death was different. Although he'd died while in service to his country, he did not lose his life in the line of duty.

It was hard to take this loss in stride. There would have been sorrow if he'd lost his life under fire during one of his deployments to the Middle East, but no one could frame this incident in noble rhetoric. His life had been stolen in a selfish and senseless act of homicide.

Down the road in San Angelo, Lloyd Davidson answered the phone just after 9:30 that night. Wendi apologized for being angry the day before, complained about the hardships of jail, asked about Marshall's possible professional transfer to the area and inquired about her mother's health. After a few minutes, Lloyd turned the phone over to his wife.

"How are you?" Judy asked.

"Oh, hanging in there, day by day. I think I'll be better whenever I get, you know, around the TV, because time will pass faster."

"Well, did you get out?"

"Well, off suicide watch, but they haven't moved me out of the cell yet, so I'm still stuck here. So I don't know."

"You don't know why?" her mother asked.

"No. I asked them. They just don't even answer nothing. They just turn and walk away. So that's how everything is. You say, 'Can I use the phone?' and they just turn around and walk out. Not a 'Yes,' not a 'No,' not a 'Kiss my ass,' nothing."

Little Tristan got on the phone next and exchanged *love you*'s and *miss you*'s with his incarcerated mother. Then he asked, "Where you at?"

"Where am I at? Oh, I'm at this new place. I'm working," she said with a sob.

"You crying now?"

"Yeah, baby, I'm crying, 'cause I miss you and Shane. Is Shane doing good? Is Shane happy?"

"Yeah."

"Are you being a big boy for Mommy?"

"I'm a good boy."

"You are?"

"I don't cry anymore."

"You don't cry anymore?"

"Unh-uh."

"Oh golly, you're big."

In the manner of 3-year-olds everywhere, Tristan talked for a short while and then, without explanation, was ready to go. "Bye, Mommy. I love you."

When Judy returned to the phone, Wendi asked, "Mama, can you, on Monday, go to the clinic and get Mike's dad's number and either y'all or have the attorney call and find out what's going on, 'cause, Mama, I need to be there you know?"

"Monday?"

"Mama, I need to. Wouldn't you want to be at Daddy's funeral if he died?"

"Well, that's— You know, Wendi, the circumstances— I don't know that you can."

"Well, I don't know that I can or I can't, but dang it, I need to find out. I don't even know where he is or what's happening, and at least I knew before. And, you know, I know that sounds fucked up, but God dang it, you know . . ."

Judy interrupted Wendi's tirade. "Well, Wendi, honey, you might as well just calm down. I mean, I'm not calling up there."

"Then just get the phone number. It's in the Rolodex under 'Mike,' and it says 'Mike's dad.' Give it to the attorney and tell him that I want to know what they plan on doing, and what kind of services or arrangements, 'cause I really want to go. I really do. I'll fly up there by myself and go if they're doing it in Maine. And I don't care what they say, or anything else. Mommy, I loved him so much. And maybe y'all didn't like every little thing about him or something, but this is hard."

". . . God, I know it's hard, but . . ." Judy sympathized.

Like a pouty child, Wendi snapped back, "You don't."

Judy bristled, "I'm glad you think not."

"I mean, I know it's hard on you, in your shoes and everything, but golly, you know, it's one of those things that I just don't think it's right for Dad and Marshall to go out and shoot jackrabbits . . . but they do . . . And then here I was, and I don't feel like I did anything wrong. I mean, that's how I feel, deep down, but I know that it must be, you know . . . I know that society would think it was bad, but . . ."

"Okay, Wendi. That's enough. Okay? Just think about something else, talk about something else."

When Wendi spoke about the possibility of losing her veterinary license, she choked with sobs. "I'm going to get everybody in the world to sign a petition for the state board and everything I can, 'cause, you know, otherwise, I just threw seven years of my life away going to school."

"Well, Wendi, did you not think about that at all?"

"No, Mama," Wendi shrieked. "If I was thinking logically, I wouldn't be in this freaking boat!"

Judy calmed Wendi down and their conversation ended with an exchange of "I love you."

The next day, Wendi was out of the suicide watch unit

and in a little building behind the jail called "the barracks." Here, twenty women lived in one big room filled with bunk beds.

They all shared one television set. Early in the day, it was tuned to a Spanish-speaking channel, but after 4 o'clock, it turned over to stations with English language programming. Wendi wished she had some control over the channel selection, but was grateful that there was something to watch just the same.

When she called her mother, she shared her good news and then resumed complaining again. "I worry about everybody and it's ridiculous. Y'all are having to do my business stuff, all my tax stuff. And, boy, you know what I'm going to do the minute we get out? I'm going to go to the *Standard-Times* and get that ad, that free ad, and put a big old ad, Advanced Animal Care Now Open, blah, blah, blah."

"I don't know," her mother cautioned. "You're going to have to take it a day at a time."

Wendi continued on as if Judy had never spoken. "And I'm going to get all my records back, and if they don't get my records, then I'm going to get the attorney to demand that they make copies and provide manila folders, because I need to start calling all the clients and I need to start— We need to make sure we're sending out reminders and blah, blah, blah, because, you know, they've done everything they can to destroy, you know, everything and . . ."

"Well, Wendi, this is a pretty serious thing."

"Well, maybe it is, but they're making it a mountain from a molehill . . . If you were in here, you would think what I did was not too bad. I mean, it's just— It's different. That's why it makes news, but as far as, you know, I didn't do nothing violent. I didn't do nothing, you know, I didn't— I don't know, but, you know, whatever. And the only reason I lied about anything was because I had to. You know?"

"All right, well you need to talk to your attorney and . . ."

"And I need to find out what in the heck is going on with, you know, I guess Monday morning if y'all can call over there with their phone number—Mike's dad's phone number—and find out . . ."

"And find out what, honey?"

"I want to know are they having a funeral, are they not having a funeral or is it here, is it in Maine, where the heck is it? Because I need—I need to try to go."

"I don't think that would be a real wise decision."

"Well, maybe it wouldn't, Mama, but it's a one-time thing, you know. It's like getting married. It's a one-time deal, you know? You get married. You know, hopefully that's it . . . Mike is not going to be buried more than one time . . . He's my husband. He's Shane's daddy, and as much as people did or didn't like him, I loved him . . . and that doesn't change anything that happened in the past . . . It's something I can do now . . . Now, if it's in Maine, I don't know if I'm going to be able to go. It depends if I'm out of here or not, and I'm sure I have to get permission from somebody, but I've got credit on plane tickets, you know. And I know Tristan doesn't need to go, but I probably would take Shane."

"Well, that would be kind of stupid," Judy said.

"Well, it's not my fault what happened. It's not Shane's fault what happened and . . ."

"But they're not going to look at it that way."

"Well, I don't care what they look at . . . What I should have done is not even released his stupid body . . . I should have been the one to make that decision. The only reason I didn't is because, one, I'm in jail and I can't afford it, and, two, is I can't even wipe my own ass in here. How am I going to plan a funeral? . . . It's just not fair . . ."

"Well, there's a lot of things in this life that ain't fair."

". . . Maybe I deserve what I'm getting, but I don't feel like it . . . I guess it will either make me stronger or crazy or meaner. I'm not sure which one yet."

"Well, you better decide it's going to make you a stronger, better person," Judy said.

"Well, I guess I'll learn not to take crap from people.

This is ridiculous . . . Maybe everybody was just doing their job, but I'll tell you, one person I'd like to kick in the balls and that's that stupid, freaking McCormick guy. God, he's such a liar and ass."

"Wendi, that's what he does. That's his job."

Wendi griped about the trackers and warned her mother she'd better get the devices off of the two trucks. "It might not be on Daddy's. They might have been able to take it off of his without him knowing, but, you know— Stupid fuckers . . . Maybe I did do something wrong. They're twisting it all around . . . They're low-bag piece-of-shits . . ."

"Watch what you're saying," Judy admonished.

Judy's warning was too late. Despite knowing that her phone calls were being monitored, Wendi's self-centered carelessness had already put negative consequences in motion.

THIRTY

In between the morning and late afternoon visitation times at the jail on Monday, March 14, 2005, Lloyd and Judy filed a petition for custody of their grandson, Shane Severance, in the Tom Green County courthouse. Two days later, Leslie's San Angelo attorney, Thomas Goff, filed similar documents on his behalf.

On March 17, the medical examiner's office in Lubbock, after a forensic analysis of Air Force dental records, confirmed the identity of the body pulled from the water at the 7777 Ranch as that of Staff Sergeant Michael Severance. The office released his remains to the Severance family. Leslie's wait was over at last—his son was coming home.

Down the road at the San Angelo Police Department, Marshall Davidson met with McGuire and Palmer. Marshall appeared agitated and resentful that he had to turn over the clothing given to him by his sister. He'd previously insisted that he had only a couple of items belonging to Michael; however, on this day, he relinquished two jackets, sixteen shirts and two pairs of pants.

Palmer knew that Lloyd Davidson had removed cash from the console of the Camaro before it was searched. He also knew that Marshall had knowledge of his father's actions. It was time to test the game warden's honesty. "Do you know of anything being removed from Wendi's car before it was taken into custody?"

Marshall stood before him and lied, denying any awareness of the facts. Palmer and McGuire now knew they could expect only the worst from their fellow peace officer.

That same day, Marshall submitted his official hardship transfer request. He began his statement with a synopsis of current family events. Then, in contradiction of what he'd told Wendi days before, and in opposition to the papers filed by his parents earlier that week, he wrote:

My family decided the best course of action would be to award custody of her two children to me along with Power of Attorney to take care of my sister's financial and other needs. At this time, the 6-month-old's grandparents from Maine are also fighting for custody of my sister's six month old baby which means that I will have to appear in hearings in San Angelo.

I do not have a very extended family, so help both physically and financially is limited. Wendi is my only sister, my parents and two grandmothers are the only family I have in Texas that could be considered to take care of Wendi's children. Unfortunately, my grandmother on my father's side has been in a nursing home for several years, and my mother's mother has been diagnosed with cancer that has spread throughout her body and she is not expected to live more than two months.

My parents had loaned my sister the majority of their savings to open her veterinary clinic and now that money is lost because the clinic had to be closed. Although I have paid several thousand dollars to help with lawyer fees, my parents were also forced to find even more money to help pay for a retainer fee with more up and coming fees and expenses.

My mother has a terminal disease called Lupus which limits her ability to stay active for an extended period of time, and causes her to stay ill a majority of the time. She is on disability because she is unable to work and gets tired very easily. My grandmother's sickness and now this terrible situation has devastated her and has caused her to almost completely stop eating or sleeping and I can only hope she begins to accept the facts and settle her nerves before she is hospitalized. Right now, she is helping me with the children and it is imperative that she does, since I cannot and will not be able to do it by myself.

At this time, my family and I are financially unable to afford day care on a regular basis. My father has been in poor health for the past few years with several herniated discs in his back, and skin cancer. He works contract labor with no benefits, overtime or retirement. He returned to work as of the 9th to try to make ends meet.

It seems as if I have become a father of two overnight and it would be impossible for me to move the children to my current station in Zapata because it is 450 miles from San Angelo. I cannot raise the kids without the help of my parents and they cannot raise them without me.

Zapata County is my first duty station and officially my two years will be up on June 18th before, in normal circumstances, I could apply for a transfer. I've had people tell me that it is my decision to involve myself in this situation with the children, but I feel that it is my duty to care for these kids because I love them very much and because of the loss of their father and the incarceration of their mother, they are now my children to raise.

I have been dedicated to the department working as hard as possible to make strong cases. I have led District III in the number of cases I have filed. I have handled everything from commercial fishing violations, to seizing thousands of pounds of marijuana, and recovering stolen jet skis.

He then expounded on his loyalty to the agency, his commitment to his career, and the distraction to his job performance that would result if the transfer was not granted. He continued on, laying out his plans for the future.

If I am stationed in San Angelo, I plan on moving in with my parents at least for a few months for several reasons.

Hopefully, it would help ease the financial strain my family is in because hundreds of dollars that I currently pay in rent and bills could be used to support the current crisis. At the same time, day care expenses would be low, because my mother would be able to watch the children while I return to work except for those days that she is too ill to do so.

I do not want to cause the department any problems or concerns but hope that the department understands the seriousness of my situation. If there is apprehension from the department that I may interfere with the ongoing investigation or impede the investigation in any way, let me assure that I have not and will not do so in any manner.

Marshall wrapped up his request with a final statement of his need and the impact of this request.

I have never been a person that likes to shortcut anything, but I have never been in a situation of this magnitude, nor have any of my peers, that that is why I am officially requesting a hardship transfer. I understand that on paper my situation may not seem as desperate as some other Wardens' problems, but without relief of a transfer, I feel that my family's health and the development of my sister's children will suffer. I have faith that a transfer in this case would help to ease the dilemma I am facing, would not cause the division any undue strain and would be in the best interests of both.

It was a compelling document, but there was a flaw: There was a line between truth and lies, and one between exaggeration and reality. Marshall didn't seem to recognize either one.

THIRTY-ONE

That evening, Wendi spoke with her father.

"What I want is, I want somebody to try to get the damn bond reduced. I'll do that stupid house arrest thing . . . I don't know why they can't do that . . . it may take a year or two for the police to get all their investigation done."

". . . I've never heard of anything like that."

"Well, that's the kind of impression that [the attorney] gave me, that I may be sitting here a year or two before we find out anything."

"Yeah, but how can they do that and then, say, you went to trial and they found you innocent and you've already served a year?" Lloyd asked.

"I know. I haven't been convicted of nothing right now and I'm sitting in jail."

Lloyd listened to Wendi's complaints for a couple of minutes and then said, "They went out to Terrell's ranch again today."

"For what?"

"Looking in the caliche pit."

"Okay. Hmmm? Oh, because we were out there chopping wood, I guess."

"No. I don't know. They said something about there was some carpet in there. They went and looked under the carpet and everything . . . they're still talking to people and still getting stuff together."

"And in the meantime," Wendi whined, "I'm the one that's in trouble . . . and they don't even know what's going on."

"Well, yeah, you're in trouble because you're the one that did something . . ." Lloyd reminded her.

"I'm ready to go to court, and I'll tell everybody, God, the whole freaking public of San Angelo, what I did, and I'll do whatever I need to do, but I'm tired of sitting in here wondering every day what they think I might have done, you know?"

"Well, you pretty much know that what they think you've done. They think you did something to Mike, and they know what you did at the tank . . . so they're just trying to prove everything that they think. I mean, you know that."

"No, not really."

"Okay. What do you think? That you ran a stop sign or something? . . . You've got to look at it from their perspective. You know you're the one that did something with him, so they're trying to figure out why."

"I already told everybody why."

"Okay. Well, that's true, but . . . they probably think there's a lot more to it and they're going to try to prove there's a lot more to it than that," Lloyd said.

". . . If they think I'm such an evil, bad person, why don't they have me out there making a living, taking care of my kids and not going anywhere and staying there at the clinic? And then I won't be eating up taxpayers' dollars."

"Well, one thing is, that's not how the system works either. Why would they even have jails if the system worked that way?"

"I don't know, but there's a lot of people on house arrest."

Lloyd attempted to get his daughter to accept the reality of her situation: "Yeah, but it's usually for little dinky things, not for serious stuff."

"I don't know . . . I'm trying not to be bitchy but . . . most of the reason I'm in here is because, one, Marshall called the police, all right, so he's the one that did it. Then . . ."

"No!" Lloyd interrupted. "You're the one that did it."

"All right. So part of this is my fault," Wendi grudgingly

conceded. "But thanks to my brother, I'm here because he told . . . them to keep a close eye on me, so they put me on suicide watch . . . and three . . ."

"You're not on suicide watch anymore."

"You're right. I finally got out of that, but forever I had to deal with that. And then, three, the attorney's secretary said that it may be possible the reason why my bond is so high . . . is because somebody might have said I was a flight risk." With dripping sarcasm, Wendi added, "I can't imagine who that somebody might be."

"I don't know of anybody ever saying that, other than you said something about it one time . . . nobody else ever repeated it."

"I think you might want to talk to your son and ask if he said anything, because I . . ."

Lloyd cut her off again. "Wendi, you're trying to blame everybody but yourself."

"No. I'm just saying, dang it, I'm ready to go to court and I'll take whatever punishment they deal out for me for what I did, but this is not fair, Daddy, not to know . . ."

"Life is not fair . . . Do you think all this that's going on is fair to any of us? . . . We've got to go down to the other attorney tomorrow because Mike's grandmother or something is going to try to get Shane . . . We're fighting battles left and right," Lloyd said in obvious confusion about Leslie Severance's custody filing.

"Daddy, they can't . . ."

"And you keep blaming us," Lloyd added.

"They can't take Shane, Daddy."

"Well, why do you keep trying to turn things around and blame everybody but yourself?"

"I'm not, Daddy."

"I mean, you act like . . . we're not doing anything out here, and there's not a day goes by that we don't do something, either go to the lawyers or make phone calls . . . and fight. We're fighting battles every day, and then . . ."

"I know. It's hard," Wendi interjected.

". . . And then, you try to always turn it around. And as

far as Marshall calling them out there, they was already on to you. You told on yourself. You went out to the ranch . . . and they was waiting for you . . . You already did it to yourself right there."

"I know, Dad. I know it. Okay. It's just very, very hard."

"So don't be blaming Marshall for something you did," Lloyd continued. "I know it's got to be miserable in there, but we're not the ones that did all this, and we're trying to get you out of there, if possible, and if we don't do anything, it's going to be a lot worse."

Wendi changed the subject. "How can they get Shane? Because, they can't, right?"

"I don't know . . . she filed for custody or temporary custody or something. We're supposed to go down there tomorrow."

"Oh, my God," Wendi exclaimed.

Lloyd was exasperated. "Well, you knew that they would try. I mean, you always act like everything is a surprise, but you knew they'd try to get the baby."

"No, I didn't."

"Well, you should have," Lloyd admonished.

Father and daughter talked a bit more about the custody situation and then Lloyd returned the conversation to his daughter's attitude. "Everything is serious and you keep acting like it's running a stop sign or something. But, you know, this is serious stuff, and you act like we're not doing anything for you, and we're doing continuously . . . You sit in there and you think that nobody else is doing a thing, and everybody is out here fighting like hell."

"I know, and if I could be out there, I could fight, too."

"Well that's the whole thing," Lloyd said. "The person that does something is the one that's in jail, and the people that didn't is the ones that's out."

Wendi returned the conversation to the issue of Shane's future, wanting to know exactly which grandmother had applied for custody.

"I don't know yet. Guess we'll find out tomorrow when we go down there."

"Idiots. Well, oh my gosh. I know I screwed up, but I had good intentions," Wendi said.

"Hunh?"

"I know I screwed up, but I had good intentions," she repeated.

"Well, you know, everybody knows you screwed up, too, and, you know, nobody can figure out why. But . . ."

"I tried to tell y'all why," Wendi objected.

". . . People just make different choices, and I guess that's the one you made."

"This sucks," Wendi complained.

When the phone call ended, nobody said "I love you." It was apparent that Lloyd was losing patience with his daughter for refusing to see the gravity of the situation and avoiding responsibility for her own actions. But still, Lloyd was in this fight for the long haul. She was his daughter, and he was not ready to give up yet.

THIRTY-TWO

After the tense conversation between Lloyd and Wendi, Judy reached out to her daughter in a letter. She shared updates about the two boys and then wrote:

> *I am so very sorry for this big mess you are in, honey—but we are all trying so hard—please believe that. I want you outta there so we can be a family again. No matter what (as Dad says) when it comes "Right Down To It" Family is all that really matters. So hold onto that thought.*

Preparations for Michael's funeral began in Maine. In a strange coincidence, the first fundraising event, planned to help finance Leslie's custody fight for Shane, was scheduled for the day after they'd learned Mike was finally coming home.

More than two hundred tickets had already been sold for the event on Friday, March 18. They sold even more at the door. Before the night was over, a crowd exceeding 250 people had filled the Knights of Columbus Hall in Lincoln that evening. A D.J. filled the room with the thumping rhythm of dance tunes. The centerpiece was a large photo collage put together by stepsister Nicole and friend Heather Whitney. The event was an amalgam of grief-filled remembrance and a rousing good time.

"It was a strange situation," Leslie said. "We had a funeral planned for the next Thursday, but I kept remembering how much Michael loved to dance. It was scary at first, but then I relaxed and enjoyed the celebration of Michael's life with his friends and the community. I've never been hugged so many times in my life. It was good for me to see the support that I have, and that Michael had. It was overwhelming."

Wendi's timing was off when she called home on Saturday afternoon. Shane was crying, a dog was barking and Tristan was still sniffling from a fall from his little wagon. The little boy was not in the mood to talk, and soon abandoned his mother to her brother. Marshall sounded testy when he came to the phone.

Wendi asked him about her dogs and then moved to questions about her brother's job. "When will you know if they transfer you or not?"

"Around April, but, you know, I'm not holding my breath. Somebody else put in for it, too, so . . ."

"Yeah, but isn't yours kind of an . . . emergency thing?"

"Well, theirs is a hardship, too, so . . ."

"You know what it's about?" Wendi asked.

"Some sort of medical thing for his wife . . ."

"Well, crap."

"So I don't know. Hopefully, it won't end up costing me the job, but, well, we do what we have to do," Marshall said.

"What do you mean? You're not going to quit."

"Well, no, but if I run out of leave and still have to come up here for all the hearings and trial, and all that, I guess I'll do what I have to do . . ."

Wendi bristled at the thought. "You just can't lose your job . . . That's what you wanted to do your entire life, and this is my fault. If I lose my job, that's one thing, but you're not going to lose your job over this."

"Well, trust me," Marshall said, "I'm trying to work it out."

Wendi told him to go back to Zapata the next day if he needed to be there. Then she said, "I don't know what's going to happen with the kids, but they're my kids. I mean, you don't have to deal with it."

"Yeah I do. They're not just your kids."

"Well, I know, but I don't want you to lose your entire life over . . . some petty mistake that I made." Marshall then turned the conversation to the impending custody hearing between the Davidsons and Leslie Severance.

Wendi said, with callow indifference toward her grieving father-in-law, "Well, all you have to do is, once he comes down for court, just ask for a continuance, and then that just means he has to go back to Maine and they have to reset a trial date. And then, when he comes back down, ask for a continuance." She moved to outlining her goal to get out of jail by April 1.

"If I were you," Marshall said, "I'd look at the worst—that it's murder—and then you're going to have to come up with a defense against it. And then, even if not, if they never go there, then it's tampering with evidence right now, and chances are you're still going to be convicted of a felony."

"Yeah, maybe so, but . . . my guess is, I'll probably get probation over it." She talked about her plans to keep the clinic open as its business manager if she temporarily lost her license. She demonstrated a firm conviction that she would get out of jail and, after overcoming a few minor obstacles, her life would continue on as if nothing had ever happened—as if the world would set aside Mike's death as irrelevant. Obviously, she had already done just that.

Wendi Davidson, Michael Severance and newborn Shane Severance in September 2004.

Leslie Severance and Brinda Leighton

The Severance family: (l to r) Frank, Leslie, Valerie and Michael.

Leslie Severance and Brinda Leighton

The Peterbilt Mike drove to the prom parked in front of Lee Academy. (l to r) Nichole's friend, Erica, Michael Severance and Nicole Leighton.

Leslie Severance and Brinda Leighton

Michael Severance (l) with his father Leslie and his son Shane.

Leslie Severance and Brinda Leighton

Michael Severance in uniform with his brother Frank by a C-130.

Leslie Severance and Brinda Leighton

Advanced Animal Care Clinic. This building no longer stands. It was demolished to make way for new construction.

Tom Green County District Attorney's Office

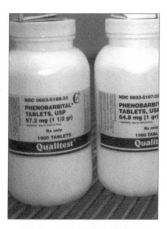

Bottles of Phenobarbital, the drug Wendi Davidson used to make Michael Severance lose consciousness, on the shelf at the Advanced Animal Care Clinic.

Tom Green County District Attorney's Office

An aerial shot of the 7777 Ranch where Wendi Davidson disposed of the body of Michael Severance.

Tom Green County District Attorney's Office

The dock where Wendi Davidson rolled Michael Severance into the water the first time she disposed of the body. This shot was taken in early March when the water level was high.

Tom Green County District Attorney's Office

The receding waters of the stock tank in early July 2006 revealed items dropped by Wendi Davidson when she tried to weigh down Michael Severance's body. The formerly submerged fence is now well above the water line.

Tom Green County District Attorney's Office

The search for Michael Severance ended here as state troopers on the dive team found his body under the water of the stock tank on the 7777 Ranch.

Tom Green County District Attorney's Office

In early July 2006, Terrell Sheen called Texas Ranger Shawn Palmer to report these concrete blocks sunk in the mud on the bank of the stock tank on the 7777 ranch.

Tom Green County District Attorney's Office

Michael Severance with his baby Shane.

Leslie Severance and Brinda Leighton

Shane Severance in Maine in 2008.

Leslie Severance and Brinda Leighton

The community rock on Route 6 between Lee and Lincoln. It is painted with all the important events, birthdays, marriages, return from overseas deployments or anything else significant to the residents in the area. In this picture, the community rock celebrates Shane Michael Severance's first visit to Maine.

Leslie Severance and Brinda Leighton

THIRTY-THREE

Michael's fellow staff sergeant, Randy Pelfrey, served as the official military escort from Dyess Air Force Base when Mike's body made its journey from Texas to Maine on Monday, March 21, 2005. Maine Governor John Baldacci called Leslie Severance to express his condolences to the family.

That same day, Wendi filed a grievance with her jailers. She wrote:

Last week I filled out a non-emergency to Captain Burns + have not received a response, but now I am forced to take further action. I am a model citizen and not a trouble-maker at all. Ever since I have been here, I have been treated poorly by some guards + denied certain privileges.

First of all, I was placed on suicide watch for no reason whatsoever. I was told because the arresting officer requested it. I assure you I was not suicidal + he had no reason, other than to degrade me. So I was stripped of all privacy, including my panties. It took 4 days before I was allowed to brush my teeth. It took 8 days before I was allowed my contact case + saline so I could remove my contacts—in the meantime, my eyes got infected. (My parents brought new solution + case two days after I came in.) It took 11 days before I got my glasses, which I brought with me to jail! It took MHMR 6 days to get here + "clear me." During this time, I spent in "suicide watch", a trustee dropped my tray as I was trying to get it through the bars—the guard saw it and would not bring me another one. So I ate what I could off the floor.

Second, the whole 2 weeks I have been locked up in J-Block, even after being cleared. I think y'all may have me in there for "my protection." There are a lot of problems w/ J-Block. There is no TV and mentally incapacitated people in there. They rant + rave + threaten each other + the firewatchers all the time. It is dangerous. I do nothing to be in "lockdown" or be on "suicide watch" + am being denied TV + being placed in danger.

Third, today I got moved to I-Block which is even worse. The reason being that another inmate was supposed to move to barracks, but she threw a big fit + refused. So they decided to move her to I Block. They don't want her to be by herself because she goes crazy— starts beating her head on the wall—threatening to kick people's ass. So they moved me with her to babysit her. I don't remember being moved to trustee position and getting trustee privileges. I dang sure ain't receiving a salary for this. I don't care if she beats her head—she can beat it until she's unconscious + until I am a trustee I will not do anything about it. And if she beats the snot out of me—that's an easy lawsuit. And still I want to reiterate that there is no TV in here. Other prisoners have TV privileges—why do I not?

I am requesting to either be moved into population or a TV be placed in here immediately.

I am not a trouble-maker and feel bad that I am having to write this but in my experience here, if you let people run over you, they will. This is silly to be here—we have no incentive to be nice—what can be done? TV privileges taken away and locked down? Please! Please help me in this matter.

On Tuesday, Wendi wrote a letter to both her parents and her brother.

I finally got paper and envelopes so I can write y'all. I am being careful what I say, knowing they may read my mail and know 100% that they will read incoming mail b/c they open it and do not let us have envelopes or stickers. I am very sorry for all this mess. I am trying to be patient, but sometimes all I can see is 4 concrete walls + floor + ceiling. I don't even know if it is day or night, cold or hot, sunny or rainy. I know y'all are probably doing all y'all can for me + the kids but I can't see it or hear it—all I can do is have faith + believe it.

I know Daddy is saying I'm in a lot of trouble, that I didn't just run a stop sign, but I honestly do not feel like I did that horrible of a thing. But maybe that is because I can understand what my state of mind was and my reasons. I guess I understand me. I love Mike, still to this day and if he could speak, I know he would not be mad or angry at me—he would understand.

She wrote about different tax statements that needed to be prepared or paid, asked them to cancel her gym membership at the Community Health Club. The final item on her to-do list:

7. Please try to find out what kind + where Mike's services are—I know I probably can't go but it is eating me up not to know where my husband is, what is happening to him or where he is going. Y'all may have to have the attorney to call and ask.

She ended the letter with:

Kiss both of my kids for me and tell them I love them and will be home as soon as the good Lord allows me.
    I love y'all forever + always,
    Wendi

She also enclosed a separate letter to Tristan. In the background, she'd drawn an outline of her hand. The letter read:

Tristan,
  I love you very very much with all my heart. I am sorry I can't be there right now but I will soon. Please take care of Baby Shane for me—kiss him on the head and hum to him for me. I miss you very much. Eat a lot so you will be strong. Take care of Deedee + Pa + Marshall. Tristan, remember how you say your prayers. You can pray for Mommie to come home soon. Just put your hands together close your eyes + say—dear God—please let mommie come home soon. I think that would help a lot—try to pray every night—for everybody. Please draw me a picture especially of yours and Shane's hands.
  Love you lots,
  Mommie.

She also composed letters to Nannie and Emmett Eggemeyer and to her cousin Pete Walker. To Pete, she wrote:

They still have me in a lockdown cell but today I moved to a worse place. I was in the block with all the crazy people that want to kill themselves, but they had a girl they needed to move because she keeps banging her head on the wall + trying to get in fights with everyone. So they moved her to a very strict lock down tank and decided I would be in the same tank next to her. They expect me to babysit her + keep her from hurting herself. So I wrote a grievance today stating that my inmate privileges were being unfairly denied b/c I am not in trouble, but the whole time, have been in lockdown + that I would not babysit that girl without a salary + I didn't care if she beat her head bloody that I would not stop her or call for help.

On Tuesday, she wrote to her family again:

About the insurance—I thought that [the attorney] *was making sure of our benefits before we released Mike's body. I was thinking the benefits may include life insurance policy in my name, social security for Shane until he was 18, social security for me until/if I remarry, TRICOR insurance for Shane + possibly me. Poor Tristan—I guess he doesn't get squat. Not Really! You know that boy will always have as much or more than Shane.*

> *I have learned many lessons in here.*
>
> *1. Don't be so angry + temperamental—life is short and things could always be worse.*
> *2. Try to be patient*
> *3. Don't take anything for granite* [sic]*—not y'all's help, not my kids, not even a mountain dew.*
> *4. Think before I act. Think, think, think or call mom, dad.*
> *5. Trust Mom, Dad + Marshall with anything + everything*
> *6. Cages are cruel*
> *7. If a dog wants kibbles + bits, feed him kibbles + bits*
>
> *I'm sure there are many others, but these are the most important.*

She enclosed the lyrics of a song for her family to the tune of Ponchielli's "Dance of the Hours"—better known as Allan Sherman's "Hello Muddah, Hello Faddah." She wrote kind words to everyone but Marshall:

Hello Marshall . . . My dear brother
You are such . . . a butthole
Even more so . . . Than most others
But I love you . . . And forgive you
Just try to think . . . Before you speak.
Just as you have . . . Told me to do.

She also drafted a letter to her clients to inform them of the situation and announce the re-opening of her clinic, and to apologize for the inconvenience.

> *On March 7, we were forced to close the clinic due to some slight legal issues I found myself in. It has been highly publicized by the press that Advanced Animal Care had closed and that I, Dr. Wendi Davidson, was in legal trouble. While this information is true, there were many lies told and blatant slander as well. At present, I am not at liberty to discuss details but I urge you not to believe everything the news media releases.*

In her next letter home, Wendi complained about not being able to get through to their phone for two hours because the line had been busy.

> *I am considering to just quit calling because there is never any news, y'all get mad at me and I cry + cry and feel even worse than before I called. I always want to talk to Tristan + see how y'all are doing, but I don't seem to have the time. It always turns into "We don't know anything and you are the one that did this to yourself—not us." I know I am really upset right now but I'm so tired of all this crap and all these crazy people.*

She told her parents to sell everything she owned to get her out on bond.

> *I will live in a halfway house w/ the kids or on the streets—I don't care anymore—anything is better than this—as long as I have my kids, I will do anything the police want—trials—courts. In a few days I will lower myself to false testimony if they will let me out.*

She enclosed a note to Tristan:

I cry all the time. Do you still love me or would you rather have a new mommy by now? I hope not. Baby, I am trying so hard to come to you soon but there are a lot of very bad, mean people in the world + they don't like me. They won't let me come home to you yet.

On Wednesday, Wendi received the official written response to her grievance signed by Sergeant Bryan Miears:

You were placed on suicide watch per the arresting officer and while on suicide watch you are not permitted to have anything with you in your cell block. I talked to the Sgt. on dayshift and is going to look into you not being able to brush your teeth while you were on suicide watch. If there is a problem with your food, then you need to notify a guard at that time. You will remain in lockdown until further notice. We are not required to provide a TV in every cell.

Wendi was not pleased with that response. She expected special treatment even though she was charged with murder.

THIRTY-FOUR

Governor Baldacci directed that the flags of the United States and the state of Maine be flown at half-staff in the towns of Lee, Lincoln and Carroll Plantation from sunrise to sunset on the day of Mike's funeral. At 1 P.M. on Thursday, more than 200 people showed up for the memorial service at Clay Funeral Home in Lincoln. The governor was among their number, as were several fellow airmen from Texas.

Mike's brother Frank was the only one to step before the audience and mention the murder, and he only touched on it. "We do not know and may never learn why Michael died, but God does not give us anything we can't handle. It seems really hard right now, but if we remember Mike for the joyous stories we can tell, we can get through this." He shared some of his happy memories of his brother and wrapped up his comments with a message of hope. "The last thing I would want to say is that no matter what we're going through right now, we know that Mike is in a better place, and that we will see him again."

Governor Baldacci presented Leslie with a state flag that had flown at half-mast over the Maine capitol building in Mike's honor. He said, "Michael is part of a long line of Maine soldiers who served their country well in times of strife—including Army Master Sergeant and Medal of Honor winner Gary Gordon of Lincoln, and stretching back to Civil War hero Colonel Joshua Chamberlain. It's important to let the Severance family know that we're there for them."

Major William Walker, Mike's commanding officer with the 317th Aircraft Maintenance Squadron, presented Leslie with Michael's posthumous Commendation Medal for meritorious service. "When we needed a flying crew chief to go on a mission, he was always ready to step up and take care of business."

The Reverend Mark W. York recalled the close and gentle but teasing relationship between the grieving father and the deceased son. He talked about the times that Leslie had been quietly concerned but outwardly supportive of Mike's more adventurous pursuits.

After the service, the funeral procession traveled out to Stevens Cemetery in Carroll Plantation where Michael was laid to rest with full military honors.

Mike's stepsister lingered long at the grave. Her mother Brinda had to urge her to leave. Nicole returned twice every week, standing vigil over the man she'd admired and the stepbrother she'd adored. Her tear-filled, faithful devotion stood in sharp contrast to the cold attitude of the new widow sitting behind bars in Texas.

THIRTY-FIVE

In a letter written to her parents on the day of Michael's funeral, Wendi relayed information she'd received from her visit with one of her attorneys.

> She said they didn't even have a cause of death and they were fixing to bury Mike. And she said they wanted to have it open casket to show off his uniform but not show his face. My God, these people are truly insane and insensitive. He is in no condition, I am sure, to be displayed like some trophy for the damn military. He hated the military and they act like he was part of their family. I only hope Mike forgives me for this because if I could be out + handle this myself, they would not lay a freaking finger on him + let him be buried in peace without all this cruelty.

She whined out a mournful litany, depicting herself as a helpless victim of fate and circumstance:

> Does destruction occur every place I go? And yes, maybe I did this to myself but in my mind I had reasons + y'all were a big part of those reasons. So for once, believe that I would do almost anything to help y'all + second I wish y'all had never made me think like that. I am sorry I am being vague but I have to be right now.

She placed a telephone call to her grandmother, Jessie Mae Eggemeyer. Jessie Mae's condition had deteriorated so much that she wasn't able to have a conversation with her granddaughter. In a matter of days, she was moved to Meadow Creek Nursing Center. The family was told that she had less than two weeks to live.

On March 27, Easter Sunday, chaos erupted in Wendi's unit of the Tom Green County Jail. Veronica, the woman next to Wendi, was cleaning her cell. She grew angry when she believed the guard had brought her a dirty mop. She screamed and pushed the emergency button. Rushing out of her cell with a broom, she banged it against walls and doors as she yelled. She ranted and raved until the broom broke in two. She stuffed one end into a trash can and hid the other half. She went into Wendi's cell and threatened her, "You better not say anything."

Thirty minutes after her tirade began, the guards arrived, put everyone in their cells and locked down the unit. The prisoners were stuck in their cells with no access to a shower.

Wendi thought that one broken end of the broom had been stashed in her cell, and was worried that Veronica might stab her with it. She slipped a note to a guard. A team returned, removing both Wendi and Veronica from their cells while they searched both of their living areas without finding anything.

After they left, Veronica told Wendi that she had hidden the broom in the shower just outside of Wendi's cell. Wendi reached through the bars and pulled back the curtain. When she saw the broken broom, she contacted a guard again.

That night, she wrote to her step-grandfather, Emmett Eggemeyer:

I still want Mike and I need him but I know I can never touch him again. He really did treat me good, despite what mom may say. He loved both the boys + they both loved and adored him.

The next day, Judy wrote to her daughter to warn her about the dangers of a loose tongue:

"She [the attorney] *said you were the <u>Big Cheese</u> in jail + everyone wanted to be your friend so you would tell them something to make it easier for them. Please don't say anything to anyone.*

Wendi responded to her mother's letter with venom:

I've been thinking about all the crap that has occurred to me in the past few years + inevitably to y'all. I guess it makes a person stronger but I don't want to be any stronger—I'm a girl + I feel I am strong enough. It makes you tougher but I don't want to be. Nobody likes steaks tough do they? It makes you meaner, more bitter—I don't want to be—nobody likes hateful people. I just want to be me—caring, sweet, compassionate—do you think I will ever be able to be that way again?

. . . I CANNOT STAY HERE MUCH LONGER! I am fixing to be in real lockdown b/c I'm fixing to start being very mean + ugly + throwing things. I WILL NOT BE NICE IF I AM NOT TREATED THE SAME WAY! I am sorry for being this way, but I am very very very frustrated. Check on the life insurance money—surely $100,000 can do something about this crap.

. . . My back and knees ache constantly because of the metal bed. We have a mat about ½ inch thick, but it doesn't help too much.

She wrote of her worries for Shane:

If someone snatched him + they crossed state lines we would have a real hard time finding him + getting him back. I don't want to worry y'all but it's just a nasty feeling I have. And you know desperate people do desperate things. (Mike's Dad)

She wrote a separate letter to her brother that same day:

*It seems that no matter what I hurt everyone around me +
bring sorrow + grief. And all I try to do is be nice and
loving. It is like I am a hurricane and destroy all in my
path. I don't know if you remember watching* Legends of
the Fall *but if you do then you will understand the character Tristan. Tristan means bold in Welch and sad in
French. I am like that character. So I gave my first son that
name in honor of who I am.*

*I cannot never promise to never break anymore hearts
or never to cause grief but I will certainly try not to and
take y'all's advice to heart. Please know that although you
at first frustrated me, I know you did the right thing for
everyone. I am so sorry I drug you into this mess. I am so
thankful + blessed to have a family so supportive and
caring as y'all. Most inmates don't even have any visitors
on visitation day, but y'all always come twice. Thank you
for everything and know I would do the same for you.*

Two days later, Wendi mailed two letters dripping with
self-pity. To Tristan, she wrote:

*I was so glad to see you two days ago. I am here at this
workplace and they won't let me go home yet because they
are not nice people. I am trying to be nice because I am a
nice person, but they are all making me very mad + sad
because all I want is to be with you + Shane they won't let
me. I will keep praying to God for everything to be OK, you
keeping praying, too. OK, Tiger?*

The theme continued in her letter to her parents:

*Daddy, I am sorry that I am interfering w/ your work
schedule by you having to come up here on Mondays, but I
really really appreciate it—I hope you don't have to much
longer.*

She suggested that her mom put a note on the clinic door saying that they will be reopening soon and if they need a refill on medication, heartworm or flea or tick products, to put Judy's number up so that she could meet people at the clinic once or twice a week.

I kind of wish the attorneys would not come by unless they actually have news to report. Because although I enjoy the chitchat, Saturday when Brad came, I got strip-searched by one of the Lesbian whore guards. I had to take all of my clothes off including panties in a little room by myself. She said, she didn't know, but he could have slipped me something through the crack in the window. So tell Tom + Brad this: "If that bitch makes me take off my clothes again so she can see my naked body, they will probably have to be defending me for more charges."

She complained about her dental problems and then wrote:

I just got one of the very nice guards to finally look + tell me why I was in isolation. Well, we all suspected, but get this—the investigators requested it. They want me in here until the investigation is complete so I can stew on it. That was exactly what the guard said + said sorry there was nothing they could do about it—they just had to do what they were told. This is an awful, awful, horrible place to be. What are the police doing—are they really trying to solve a possible crime or is just easier to try + blame everything on me? At first, I thought I didn't really want to know everything that happened. But now, I do. I wish I did know—good, bad—no matter how bad it hurt me because I would tell those jerk-offs so they would get off my back and I could get out of here.

At the end of the letter, she laid the maudlin approach on even thicker:

Take all my pictures off the wall + just forget I ever existed. That's the only way I know to help y'all is for y'all to just move on.

As if they could. She'd caused so much destruction to her own family, to the Severance family and most particularly to her two young sons. And she was not finished yet.

THIRTY-SIX

Wendi called home on April 1 to complain about the funeral for her grandmother. Jessie Mae was still alive, but her life expectancy was now being measured in hours. "I don't want to get out for the funeral," Wendi said, "because I'm not going to go in jail clothes and handcuffs . . ."

"You don't have to," her mother said.

"Yes, you do. Maybe I could change clothes, but I'd be handcuffed the whole time and I'm probably not going to be allowed to talk to y'all."

"That's stupid. Who told you that? . . . They are not going to do that to you at a funeral. They're not."

"Oh, they probably will . . . I guess I can talk to the attorney, if he ever comes up here, and find out what's going on, but there's going to . . . have to be a guard there. We're going to have to pay them a hundred dollars just to get me out of there. They're going to be there baby-sitting my every little hand [sic], which is the most ridiculous thing. I know for sure I'm going to be handcuffed, and I'm not going to go to a funeral in front of my entire family.

"I didn't get to go to Mike's funeral. Funerals are— All they're cracked up to be is to make everybody that's alive feel better, but dead people, they don't care if they even have a funeral . . . It would have made me feel a whole lot better if I could have gone to Mike's funeral and it would make me feel a lot better if I could go to Nanny's funeral, but I'm not going to go when I'm sitting there being told that I can't talk to y'all, that I can't hold my kids, that I can't do anything.

"You know, I'm not going to go in a freaking police car to a church or a grave or anything else and be like that in front of everybody. You know, everybody already knows that I'm in trouble. I don't want anybody to see me like that, especially like at a funeral. You know, I love Nanny and I want to see her alive. I don't want to see her, you know, in . . ."

"Well, that's your choice . . . You can go see her now or you can go to the funeral. They left it open for you to make that decision."

"What do you mean? I can go see her now?"

"Well, I don't know. As soon as I get the letter to the attorney, then they're going to take it and see if they can't do something."

"Well, I'd rather see her now than at the funeral if I . . . could."

"Well, then Monday we'll see what they can get done. I don't know. They may not let you go to either one, but I'm going to try."

". . . I just can't believe I can't get out of here . . . I know y'all obviously understand better than I do, but I think it's silly that everybody is just, you know, clowning around just because it's, you know, a process. Well, fuck the process. I'm the one in here, not them. So . . ."

"Well, Wendi, I know that and I am so sorry . . . If there were anything I could do, I would do it," Judy said.

Wendi acknowledged what her mother said, then voiced an eerie opinion about Jessie Mae's medical care that echoed her own actions in January: "Personally, I think that if she's not doing good, it would be kinder just to drug her up and not even let her wake up."

When Judy turned the phone over to Lloyd, Wendi repeated all her complaints. Lloyd was growing weary of listening. "You keep going off the handle and you're mad at us and everything else, and we're trying our best to do everything we know how."

"Daddy, I'm not mad at y'all. I promise I'm not mad at y'all. It's just I'm not in control of myself. I'm not. I mean, one minute I'm fine. The next minute I'm crazy . . ."

Lloyd interrupted. "Well, we're not in control of our world anymore. It's just in a big spin right now, and that's what I mean. We're trying to work with that we've got and that's the best we can do."

"I know," Wendi muttered.

"You know, we're going to have to all stick together and work this out."

"I know. I know, Daddy."

"You know, we tell you . . . you've just got to do the best you can, because obviously they're not going to listen to you or me or Mom or anybody else. So you just have to work with what you've got. You've got to accept that you're there and do the best you can, because we can't get you out right now . . . and obviously they won't do a thing we say or they won't even answer questions . . . You have to just accept it . . . What can you do?"

"Nothing. I'm doing the best I can, Daddy. I am."

"Okay," Lloyd said. "Getting all blowed up at—I know you're frustrated and I would be, too. Any probably normal person would be, but, like I say, what can you do? Not a darn thing except for work with what you've got . . . We're hearing all these different rumors going around."

". . . Is it anything to do with me and Mike?" Wendi asked.

Lloyd grew exasperated with his daughter again. "Well, I wouldn't be telling you there's rumors about somebody in Hawaii on a vacation. I mean, obviously it's about what's going on." Lloyd turned the conversation to the veterinary business. "Terrell said that he's going to take somebody by the clinic from Midland and look at it."

"That wants to buy it?"

"Yeah. He said he knows we don't want to give it up yet, but just . . . down the road . . . if it doesn't pan out . . . whoever this is had already looked at it and knows what he's talking about. I said, 'Well, that's fine . . . show it to people if you want and . . . if worst comes to worst and it doesn't pan out, then . . . at least people have seen it,' " Lloyd explained.

"I don't know what I would do if I lost the clinic. I think I would probably move to another country and just start a whole new life or something with the kids, because I don't think I could face y'all or face San Angelo ever again if it came to that."

"Well, it's not us that caused all this, and it's not San Angelo . . . It's you that put yourself in this position, but it just so happens that there's a bunch of jerks doing the investigation and everything. So . . ."

"Well, I know," Wendi said. "But if I can't be a veterinarian, I mean, there's— You know, that's why I moved to San Angelo, to be a vet and be close to y'all, and if I can't do that, I don't know."

"Well, obviously one of the reasons you did, because you had the kids and you couldn't take care of them by yourself. So that was the main reason," her father snapped back.

"I can take care of the kids just fine. I mean, I was doing— Me and Mike were doing just fine, and I was even doing fine after he was gone. I can do that now."

"Well, it didn't seem like you was doing fine with the kids, because you were having such a hard time with them."

"Well, I can do it," Wendi rebutted. "Everything will be just fine if I can just keep the clinic . . . And I should be able to because, I mean, from my understanding, Brad said they could even lower the charge from tampering with evidence to abuse of a corpse, which is a Class C misdemeanor, and that wouldn't even be a felony."

"Well, you know, we just have to take everything a day at a time, because I still feel like they're going to try to press more charges. They might not, but . . . I feel they're going to . . . Take everything a day at a time and hope for the best."

Two days later, on Sunday, April 3—one day before the lawyers were going to try to get Wendi out of jail for a visit

with her grandmother—Jessie Mae Eggemeyer lost her
battle with cancer. She died without seeing her only
granddaughter—without one final squeeze of her hand.
The pain Wendi had caused by her murderous actions on
January 15 continued to grow unabated.

THIRTY-SEVEN

The day after Wendi's grandmother passed away, Officer Carrie Poyner received a call from one of the guards about Wendi. "There may be a needle of some type in inmate Davidson's property."

Poyner and four other guards moved into J-Block for a shakedown. When they searched through Wendi's cell, they found prohibited items: several pieces of string, an extra pair of shoes and two pieces of paper hidden in a sanitary napkin box. On the paper was a list of people she had known, with a description of her relationships with them. The contraband was confiscated.

That night at 7, Johnson's Funeral Home Chapel hosted a rosary for Jessie Mae Elliott Eggemeyer. The family gathered for her graveside service in the tiny Grape Creek Cemetery on Tuesday, April 5, at 4 P.M. Wendi was not allowed to attend either event.

Wendi indulged in a verbal rampage in her letter to her parents dated April 6, 2005:

> *All I know is that the police + DA are probably just trying to do their job and they don't care about anything else. If they destroy innocent people, break families + crush children that is just a by-product of their so-called duty. It's not their lives + families that are being torn completely apart.*

I just want y'all to prioritize everything. My kids have to be y'all's top priority. Y'all cannot worry about me anymore. Do not spend any more money on me. Save it for my kids. They need it far more than me. There apparently is nothing more that y'all can do for me. And I am trying to make peace with that. But don't go telling the attorneys that y'all are worried about me, then he comes up here to lecture me on being patient, it's just a process, to hang, ok.

FUCK! I DON'T SEE ANYBODY IN HERE BUT ME. So unless he has been here, he doesn't have a clue. Not a teeny tiny idea. So then he calls y'all to tell y'all everything is ok. It is not ok. I am not ok. He knows I am not ok. So let him do what y'all are supposedly paying him for. They already are full of lies, don't make him lie more. Just take care of my kids + fight tooth + nail for them. I am in a tank of sharks— the only way to save me would be for y'all to climb in with me. Then, no one would have a chance.

Two days later, Wendi got her wish. Court convened and her bail was dropped to $50,000. She was finally able to go home.

In response to this development, the Lubbock Medical Examiner's Chief Investigator Robert Byers told the *Bangor Daily News*: "Judges tend to not want people sitting in jail for a long, long time. We're waiting for the results from the autopsy for the final definition of what Mr. Severance died of. Because it had taken so long, we thought her attorney would contest it and she might get her bond reduced. She is in jail for tampering with evidence and it was a high bond for that charge. They weren't going to wait forever for us."

That same day, Texas Ranger Shawn Palmer contacted Dr. Sridhar Natarajan at the Lubbock County Medical Examiner's Office. The doctor delivered the results of the toxicology analysis. The lab found Phenobarbital and high levels of pentobarbital in the cavity fluid, gastric contents and tissue from the liver taken from Michael Severance's body.

Palmer pulled out the photographs taken during the consent search conducted by the San Angelo Police Department in January and verified his recollection of what he'd observed in the clinic in March. Bottles of phenobarbital tablets were present at the clinic as well as bottles of Beuthanasia-D Special, containing pentobarbital as the active ingredient. To Palmer, the method used to murder Michael Severance was clear.

San Angelo Police Department spokesman Lieutenant Curtis Milbourn spread the net wider when he spoke to media. "She felt a family member had done it, and that's got to be looked into. She may have done it, and that's got to be looked into. He may have done it himself, and that's got to be looked into."

Up in Maine, the family recoiled at the suggestion of suicide. "It's not a possibility at all," Nicole Leighton responded. "He was a very happy person. He never once complained about his life in general. He was so happy. He had no reason to take drugs. Anyone that would have known Michael would have known that's not a possibility.

"It tears us apart. We don't want anything like that said about him. I guess we can't get frustrated because the police can only tell us so much, so we do our best to handle it."

Palmer reached into his file and pulled out the controlled substances log seized during his search of the clinic. He found the records that documented the administration of Beuthanasia-D to twenty-one different animals. The list also indicated that Wendi had given phenobarbital to Wheezie, a Chihuahua owned by Samantha Norfleet. It was time for a second search of the clinic. Palmer prepared another affidavit. In his request, he reiterated all of the arguments in the previous one and added information about the toxicology results. Then he added:

the suspected person was released from the Tom Green County Jail. It is the belief of your affiant that the suspected person is currently in control of the suspected place and has access to the items sought as evidence.

District Judge Tom Gossett signed the search warrant authorizing another foray into the property at 4240 Sherwood Way on the afternoon of April 12. The next morning, Texas Ranger Shawn Palmer pulled into the clinic parking lot at 9:25. As he did so, he saw Terrell Sheen driving away in a white pick-up truck. He glanced up at the billboard, which now read: "Things aren't always what they seem."

When he entered the building, Judy Davidson was behind the desk in the reception area. Palmer asked for Wendi. Judy walked to the back, returning with a message. "She says that you need to speak to her attorney."

Palmer moved toward the door to the back as Wendi stepped out front. He showed her the search warrant. Wendi picked up the telephone. When she put the receiver down, Palmer told the two women that they were free to leave the premises.

"We'll stay here," Wendi said.

"You'll need to step outside during the search," he said.

Wendi and Judy stood by the front entrance watching technicians and officers come in and out of the building.

Using a *Physicians' Desk Reference* as his guide, Palmer collected drugs: sealed and open bottles of phenobarbital tablets, a box containing Beuthanasia-D and a file with records relating to the purchase of medications and equipment, as well as several containers of medicine prescribed by physicians at Dyess Air Force Base for Michael Severance. San Angelo Police Department Detective McGuire gathered up the twenty-one manila folders for the pets who had been euthanized by Wendi Davidson. He could not find the file for Wheezie, the Chihuahua that the controlled substance log indicated Wendi had treated with phenobarbital. Other officers collected invoices, notepads and unlabeled pill bottles.

One of the most provocative items found during the search was discovered by McGuire in a trash receptacle in the reception area. Across the top of a yellow sheet of paper, someone had written "Wheezie" in blue ink. In the margin, also in blue, was the date 1/1/05. In that same color, there were two other notations: "No Rx meds @ this time" and "Counseled on Epilepsy."

Black ink scratched through the medication notation and replaced it with: "Rx 1½ gr phenobarb and Rx 10 mg valium." The importance of the missing file for this pet was evident. Palmer asked Judy Davidson about it. She looked, but was unable to locate it. Palmer asked her about the office policy for purging files.

Judy tried to avoid answering the question and then cut off the conversation. "I have been told not to talk to you."

At 2:15, Palmer explained the list of seized items to Judy and Wendi. Judy signed the inventory, and law enforcement left the building. But they wouldn't stay away for long.

THIRTY-EIGHT

The day after the search, Palmer met with Samantha Norfleet to question her about Wheezie's treatment. She told him that her 4-and-a-half-pound dog had had a seizure on January 1, 2005, and Samantha immediately drove her pet to Advanced Animal Care. When she arrived, the business was closed because of the holiday.

She'd called the emergency number listed on the front door. She left a message and ten minutes later, Wendi returned the call. Fifteen minutes after that, Wendi came out from the right side of the building and unlocked the front door. They all went inside.

Wendi examined Wheezie, took a blood sample and gave the tiny dog a shot of valium, saying, "Phenobarbital is usually used to treat seizures, but I don't recommend it in this case."

Samantha wrote a check for $196 and left the clinic with Wheezie. Wendi did not provide any additional medication. Palmer drafted a new affidavit—this time for a search warrant and an arrest warrant.

At 10:38 A.M. on April 15, the Texas Ranger pulled into the clinic parking lot again with four other law enforcement officers and a crime-scene technician. Wendi and Judy were outside in front of the building. When they spotted the arriving vehicles, they went inside. Palmer followed them through the door.

He told Wendi that she was under arrest and informed Judy of the new search warrant. Wendi was cuffed and removed from the premises. She was transported to the Tom Green County Jail, where she was booked on a second charge of tampering with evidence for doctoring the controlled substance log and altering the medical records of Wheezie's treatment. The information about the toxicology report had not yet been released. When Wendi had adjusted the records regarding the phenobarbital and pentobarbital, she'd proven that she knew the identity and quantities of the pharmaceuticals used to kill her husband.

Meanwhile, at the clinic, gravel flew as Lloyd Davidson sped his truck into the parking lot and skidded to a stop. He was agitated as he questioned Palmer about the search and arrest warrants. Palmer said, "You can remain here during the search if you quiet down." Palmer then resumed his inspection of the clinic. He and the other officers recovered a large number of documents, including 363 patient files along with one sealed and one open bottle of diazepam—the generic name for Valium.

When Palmer exited the building, Lloyd approached him to share information about a black transvestite named Tu Tu. Lloyd said he'd heard that Michael Severance and Tu Tu had been involved in an altercation on the night of Mike's disappearance. Although Palmer doubted that Tu Tu had been involved in Michael's death, it was a lead that he needed to follow.

Just before 3 o'clock, Palmer took Wendi in front of District Judge Gossett. The judge set a bond of $100,000 on each charge. Jenkins Action Bail Bond issued a property bond and Wendi was released.

Mid-month, Marshall Davidson called Michael Newberry, Mike's friend who'd bought the race car from Wendi while Mike was still missing. Marshall wanted to know if Newberry was interested in buying the two Mustangs at the clinic, and left the Davidsons' home phone number if he decided he was. A few days later, Wendi called him asking about the cars again. "I just want to stay out of the middle of things," Newberry said.

"There is nothing to be in the middle of," Wendi said.

"I think there's a hold on selling Mike's cars."

"There is no such hold. Our mailman is interested in buying them if you aren't."

Wendi took a private polygraph examination. Her attorney, Tom Davidson (no relation to Wendi), told the media she'd passed the test which included the questions "Did you kill your husband?" and "Do you know who did?" He said, "She didn't kill anybody, and doesn't know who did."

The San Angelo Police Department still would not publicly discuss the results of the earlier examination. When asked, Lieutenant Milbourn told the media, "It gives us an idea of where and how to pursue an investigation because of the questions that were asked of what to look for, not to look for, what to concentrate on first, but it's not definitive. Part of it is that polygraphs can be defeated. To totally discount somebody because they passed a poly or to assume that they didn't commit a crime would be a mistake. It's one other tool that we could use."

Nicole Leighton again responded for the family. "I don't even know what to think anymore. I knew they had administered the polygraph in the beginning, in the very beginning, but they can't tell us the results, obviously. She has admitted to dumping his body, filing a missing persons report and filing for a divorce, the whole time knowing where he was, so obviously she has lied before. There's a ton of things she lied about. I guess it depends upon what questions they asked her. I hope we find out who did it, if she didn't."

Palmer and McGuire drove over to Lubbock on April 27, 2005, to interview the people who'd worked with Wendi at the Animal Hospital of Lubbock. Dr. Jay Jones told them that he'd hired Wendi. "She resisted conforming to the procedures to order medications that were not maintained or used by other doctors." Jones also complained that Wendi had not told him she was pregnant when she took the job.

He recalled Michael visiting Wendi on a couple of occasions, but they did not appear very close. In her seven months at the facility, Wendi did not live up to expectations. "If she hadn't quit, I would have fired her."

Dr. Laurel Linn Jones told the investigators that in addition to the fact that Wendi did not follow the policies and procedures at the hospital, it was difficult to get along with Wendi. In contrast, veterinary technician Frank Saiz described Wendi as "pleasant and calm." He said that she'd seemed very nonchalant about her pregnancy but had been seriously upset when Michael went to a car race in Dallas instead of coming to Lubbock to visit her.

Technician Kimberley Rufener had a different read on Wendi. She called her "young and flaky." Wendi had told her about plans to get an abortion, which Michael had promised her anything she wanted to prevent.

Dr. Kerry Blanton found Wendi disagreeable as a coworker, saying that Wendi spoke openly about her sex life and blamed others for her problems and mistakes. "She could lie very well." What bothered Blanton the most were Wendi's discussions about what she would do to keep Michael from getting custody of her new baby. Wendi wondered aloud if she could place a bag over Tristan's head, punch him in the face and then tell police that Michael had hit the little boy. The investigators were revolted by this revelation. They had two felony charges filed against Wendi Davidson—they were looking forward to adding homicide to the list.

THIRTY-NINE

The grand jury convened on Tuesday, May 24, 2005, to consider the charges against Wendi Davidson. They did not have the full autopsy report to review, but they did know the toxicology results. When reporters asked prosecutor Alison Palmer why she didn't wait until that report was in, she explained, "The grand jury's term was nearing a close. We did need to finish."

The panel confirmed the two tampering with evidence charges and added one more. They wrote in their homicide indictment that Wendi Mae Davidson had

> intentionally and knowingly caused the death of an individual, namely Michael Severance by introducing toxic levels of a substance or substances into the body of Michael Severance.

Wendi surrendered herself to Sergeant Ron Sanders at the Tom Green County Sheriff's Office the next day at 1:06 in the afternoon. She was booked and presented with an order to provide handwriting exemplars. Sanders collected two samples. A little after 2, Palmer arrived with a Texas Department of Safety Laboratory Handwriting Specimen form. Wendi complied with the document's instructions, writing out the list of letters and words provided, as well as additional words dictated by Palmer.

While she was being processed, Wendi started a conversation with Lillie Lucio, arrested on a misdemeanor marijuana charge. Lillie told the *Bangor Daily News* that Wendi seemed disassociated with what was happening and declared her innocence several times. "It did not seem like she was going down for murder. I asked her about her husband's body being dumped in the pond, and she's like, 'Yeah, me, I'm supposed to move this body myself.' She said it sarcastically. She's like, 'Come on now. I would not be able to move him because he's so heavy.' She freaked me out. I did not expect to hear that coming from her."

Wendi was released on bond that same day. She went home to her parents' house and stirred up additional outrage in Maine. Leslie Severance told the *Bangor Daily News*: "I cannot for the life of me understand how come he [Michael's son Shane] can be allowed to stay in the same house as her. I just don't see how that can be allowed to happen. We're trying to get Shane—that's my main focus. Nothing is going to bring Michael back. So there's Shane. I don't believe he should be where he's at."

Leslie's custody attorney Thomas Goff, the former county attorney from 1992 through 2000, echoed his client's sentiments. "It's a tragic, tragic situation. He wants custody of the child. It's his son that was killed. I'm a grandparent. I would want custody of my grandchild in that situation."

Judy and Lloyd Davidson wouldn't comment on Shane's living situation. When Leslie requested to visit his grandson, they told him he could see Shane for an hour at a local McDonald's if he came to Texas.

Goff responded to that offer bluntly. "That was cold. This is his deceased son's only child."

Leslie told the *Bangor Daily News*: "That was totally ridiculous, but I was not surprised. It was actually probably more than I figured they would say. I feel temporary custody was given to Judy Davidson, but that doesn't make her lord and master. She's a grandparent just like I am."

Despite the brevity of the promised visit, Leslie vowed to make the trip to Texas if he could scrape together the money to do so. "I told people we come from a logging family. My grandfather was a woodsman, my father was a woodsman. It's like being in the cut. You're in the cut and there's no stopping. It's just a straight-ahead battle. There's no time to grieve or sit back and feel sorry for yourself 'cause you're still in the cut. You're still busy. You still have work to do. You just have to keep working."

The newspaper asked the San Angelo Police Department why they were not doing anything. Lieutenant Milbourn said, "Unless there is a reason to believe the child is in danger, then we would have no reason to act. The murder charge against Davidson gives police little legal grounds to believe she is a threat to her son."

On May 28, a frustrated Texas Ranger Palmer composed a letter to the Air Force OSI headquarters at Langley Air Force Base in Virginia, complaining about his difficulties in getting information from Special Agent McCormick:

> I fully support the task force or team concept when conducting major criminal investigations. This allows numerous resources and numerous years of experience to be utilized to get the job done. This is helpful in both the investigation phase and the prosecution phase of a criminal case. For me, this investigation continues and the prosecution phase has begun. The problem with the task force or team concept is that it involves various individuals and there is sometimes conflict. We as professionals must overcome that conflict and remember what is important in these investigations and that is bringing justice to the victim. I suspect that delicate egos and personality conflicts have already affected the investigative phase of this case. My goal is to prevent these problems from now affecting the prosecution phase of this case.
>
> Any assistance you can provide in resolving this matter would be greatly appreciated . . . I am not in the habit of contacting an investigator's supervisor to resolve matters that arise during an investigation.

The problem is that this particular situation has gotten out of hand.

It was not clear if McCormick was simply a poor communicator or if he deliberately delayed the delivery of information to Palmer, but the Ranger was clearly frustrated with the Air Force investigator.

The OSI office responded, placing the blame on the San Angelo Police Department. They wrote that

the friction arose primarily because our agents perceived a lack of enthusiasm and cooperation from other law enforcement personnel in pursuing this investigation . . . Their perception was that there did not seem to be a sense of urgency by others to help locate an active duty Air Force member who was missing under suspicious circumstances.

The airman's body had been found. His wife was charged with his murder. Now, the task force needed to pull together to help the prosecution team secure justice for the family of Michael Severance.

FORTY

The question of the custody of Shane Severance stepped to center stage in the summer of 2005. On June 16, Thomas Goff, attorney for Leslie Severance, conducted the deposition of Judy Davidson.

Goff asked about the relationship that Judy had with her son-in-law. "You said you didn't like him from the start?"

"No, I didn't. It's not that I disliked him, I just had no reason to like him."

"Had you ever met somebody from Maine before?"

"Not— I'm sure I have, but not that I'm aware of, no."

"Was there some cultural differences, do you think, between the way he was raised and . . ."

Judy interrupted and managed to contradict herself in the span of a sentence. "He had been in Texas for years, so I'm sure there were some differences."

". . . What did you find out about his family just talking to him?"

"I found out that his brother had a car wreck. I found out that his mother had passed away. And other than that, nothing."

"Did you ever just sit down with him and engage him and try to drag this out of him?"

"Why would I?" Judy asked. "I mean, that was his personal life. If he didn't want to talk about it, I felt, you know, give him that much respect."

"Do you know what interests he had or what he enjoyed doing?" Goff asked.

"He had a race car, and that's all he ever wanted to do, as far as I'm aware of."

"Okay. So did you have some conversations with Wendi about the marriage, for instance? Did you approve of the marriage?"

"No, I didn't."

"Did you tell her that you didn't approve of the marriage?"

"Certainly."

"Did you and Mike maintain a cordial relationship or try to maintain a cordial relationship?"

"We tried not to argue for Wendi and the baby's sake. We stayed away from each other."

Goff took Judy to the events of January 15. "She, as far as you know, was going to the . . . clinic where she lived . . . with Mike?" he asked.

"Yes," Judy answered.

"And you further testified that she was in a good mood."

"Yes."

"And you didn't—nothing out of the ordinary. You didn't see anything that would have made you think something was wrong? Nothing was wrong?" Goff pressed.

"Not that I was aware of, no."

"Okay. Now, and further, the statement that Wendi made to your son—and this was in March . . . that she arrived home . . . and found Mike's body, is that correct?"

"From what I understand, yes."

"Okay. So both of the children were with her when she found Mike's body?"

"I assume so."

"Including Tristan, of course. Tristan and Shane, is that right?"

"As far as I know. I don't— I don't know."

"What other explanation could there be? Or do you know of any other explanation other than the children were with her? She left with the children."

"Right," Judy admitted.

"Okay."

"But I don't know, because I wasn't there."

"Right. And Tristan is—was three, right?"

"Exactly."

"Has Tristan ever told you he saw Mike's body?" Goff asked.

"Never."

"Was Tristan traumatized?"

"He was traumatized by the police."

"Okay," Goff said and repeated the question. "Was he traumatized from arriving home and Mike being dead?"

"Not that I know of, because I had no idea."

"The police talked to Tristan?"

"They talked to him, 'Hi,' and, you know—"

"How was he traumatized by the police?"

"Because they were in and out of there several times a day for several months."

"Are you unhappy about that?"

"No, I'm not unhappy," Judy denied.

"Okay. So they didn't interrogate Tristan?"

"Of course not."

"Have you taken Tristan to a counselor?"

"Of course not."

"Why 'Of course not'?" Goff probed.

"Because there's nothing wrong with Tristan. He's happy. He's healthy."

"To see if he was traumatized by seeing his dead step-father?"

"He's not traumatized," Judy insisted, and then she contradicted herself again. "How do I know that he's not anything?"

"That's my question. How could he have not seen Mike?"

"I have no idea . . . but he is fine. He's healthy. He's happy. Why send him to someone that's going to traumatize him?"

"To see what he saw, perhaps?" Goff suggested.

"To confuse him, to traumatize him, to hurt him? To ask him questions he doesn't know anything about? No, sir."

"Wendi further told the police that she transported Mike's body to the Sheen Ranch on Sutton Road. Where were the children when she did all this?"

"I have no idea," Judy stated.

"Have you asked Wendi?"

"I'm not supposed to talk to Wendi about any of this, and we haven't," she snapped. "So, no, sir, I don't know."

"Who told you not to talk to Wendi about this?"

"Marshall said to begin with, you know, 'Y'all do not talk about it' . . . The attorneys have said, 'Do not talk about it.' The grand jury said, 'Do not talk about anything that was discussed in the grand jury.' So, yes, sir, I'm just trying to do what is right."

"Okay. Well, I'm trying to figure out where the children were when Wendi took Mike's body to the ranch."

"Well, I'm sure everybody would like to know that question, but you're asking the wrong person, because I don't know."

"You have no knowledge?" Goff pushed.

"I have no knowledge. All I know is, they're both fine. They're both safe. They're both happy. And they're both healthy."

"Okay. I assume that a three-year-old, if he were along on that ride, would have known what was going on?"

"I have no idea."

"But he's not been traumatized?"

"No, sir."

"Okay. But you still believe that what Wendi is saying is true? Or what she said was true?"

"I don't have any reason to disbelieve it."

". . . She stated that she took Michael's body to the ranch after she found him dead in the clinic. As far as you know, that's true?"

"I have no reason to disbelieve that."

"No reason at all?" Goff prodded.

Judy shook her head from side to side.

"Okay. Why did Wendi tell the police, or make the statement, that she knew members of her family hated him and that she believed a family member had killed him? What basis did she have to say that?"

"Because I very much so disliked Mike, and I told her that daily. And I'm sure, you know, that after a while it probably would get to you. I do not know. You would have to ask Wendi."

"Did you have anything to do with Michael's death?"

"No, sir, I did not."

"So what family member do you think Wendi was talking about—that would have killed Mike?"

"I have no idea."

"No idea. And you've never asked her?"

"No," Judy said. "We don't talk about that."

Judy's bitterness and lack of empathy became more apparent when Goff turned his questions to Mike's family. She spoke of the care and protection she and her husband provided for Shane.

"And, Mr. Severance is concerned about Shane's future," Goff added.

"Mr. Severance doesn't have to be concerned about Shane's future. We have provided very well for our children, and we will provide very well for the next two if it has to be that way."

"Well, what type of contact do you think is appropriate for Shane and his father's family?"

"If Mr. Severance wants to see Shane, he can come to San Angelo."

"He is coming to San Angelo tomorrow," Goff informed her.

"Well, he can see him."

"Okay. When?" Goff asked.

"What . . ." she began and then shifted, "After his deposition."

"Well, he'll be here this weekend. Can he see him this weekend?"

"He can see him after his deposition."

"Why at the deposition? What good does that do?"

"It matters to me," Judy insisted.

"Why?"

"Because you have put us through a lot, today, or me especially. And I think that Mr. Severance needs to have the hot seat as well. He has not been in the hot seat at all over any of this. We have nothing to do with any of this."

"How should Mr. Severance be in the hot seat?"

"I don't know. I just think that, you know, he should be aware of what's going on also, not be calling names about anyone."

"His son's dead and your daughter is . . ."

Judy cut him off. "My daughter has been in jail. She has been scrutinized. We have been scrutinized by him as well as his family. So, you know, I think— And for him— You know, I just think he needs to answer some questions also."

"What questions specifically do you have?"

". . . I don't have anything to say to Mr. Severance at this point. Our attorney will handle that."

"So you are hostile to Mr. Severance?"

"No, sir, I am not hostile. I just . . ."

"Angry at him?"

"No, I'm not angry. I just— You know, right now I just think things need to be cleared, and maybe then after his deposition."

Tim Edwards, the Davidsons' custody attorney, interrupted the questioning to say that he would be available later to talk with Goff about the timing of Leslie's visit with his grandson. Goff continued the interview, asking, "Do you feel that Mr. Severance shouldn't see Shane for any reason?"

"Shane is at the age right now that he is very alert and wants to be with whom he knows. And putting Shane with Mr. Severance, whom he doesn't know— He's a total stranger. He has never been around him— Yeah, it's going to be . . . very hard and very detrimental to Shane. So, yeah, I have some concerns."

"You took Shane to a day care, is that right?"

"Yes," Judy admitted.

"The people at the day care were total strangers?"

"No. I took Shane there and I took Tristan there and I stayed with them for hours and let them get acquainted with those people. They were my children's day-care providers."

"You understand that Mr. Severance is not wanting to take Shane back to Maine right now; he just wants to see him? . . . I'm really interested in your attitude about it and . . ."

"Well, I feel very bad for Mr. Severance; I do, in the fact that he's lost his son. I feel empathy and sympathy, and I am so sorry. But at the same time, he needs to realize that Shane is a member of our family. He has been here with us since he was born. Shane doesn't know him or his family at all.

"So that is going to be hard enough for me and Lloyd and Wendi to put him in the arms of someone that he doesn't know and walk away, and he may cry. So, yes, sir, it's going to be kind of hard."

". . . But you're not opposed to Mr. Severance seeing the child while he's here?"

"No," Judy said, but then added, "A supervised visit."

". . . Why does it need to be supervised?"

"Because he doesn't know the child, sir. The child doesn't know him. So, therefore, it has to be someone that knows the child."

"No, when I hear 'supervised,' it's like there's some problem with Mr. Severance or there's some threat or danger," Goff said. "You're not saying that?"

"I'm not saying that, no. It's just that he doesn't know him, and Shane doesn't know him. So why would we want to just let him have him and walk away?"

"You're very protective of the children, is that right?" Goff asked.

"I'm very protective of my family. I am."

"I'm getting the sense, and so I want to ask you if my opinion or what I'm hearing is correct, that you don't think what Wendi's admitted to, that is, dumping the body in the pond, is serious."

"I did never," Judy objected. "I've never said that, sir."

". . . So that's why I'm asking you to clarify . . . Do you believe it's serious?"

"I believe it's very serious. I do. And nothing has ever happened in our family to traumatize a family like this."

"Right."

"So, I take it very seriously."

"Okay . . . Do you believe, aside from who killed Mike, which will be determined later, do you believe that what Wendi did was wrong?"

"It was not right."

"And I haven't really asked this question. Do you think Mike was killed by another person, or do you think that there might be other possibilities?"

"There could be other possibilities," Judy said.

"And what would those be?"

"Probably suicide. He could have done it to himself. He could have overdosed. I mean, there's many other possibilities. I don't know."

"But you don't know of any reason that Wendi had to hide his body, is that correct?"

"Not other than her really believing that maybe we did something, or I did something, and she was trying to protect her family."

Goff deposed Lloyd, who repeated most of what Judy had already said without any real distinction until he came to the question of why Leslie Severance would have to have supervised visits with his grandson. Lloyd theorized that Les might be a "child molester or criminal." Many in the room were shocked that such a vicious, unfounded and unnecessary comment was being made about a father who was still grieving the death of his son.

Judy and Lloyd made it clear that the family—their family—was of primary importance. How Wendi's actions impacted the Severance family paled in comparison. They would stand behind their daughter, no matter what.

FORTY-ONE

The next day, Leslie and Frank Severance arrived in West Texas. On Saturday, June 18, Leslie got a one-hour visit with his grandson at McDonald's. Nine-month-old Shane seemed to instinctively recognize his grandfather. Leslie noticed family traits: the thin, reddish-blonde hair that bleaches to a deeper color in the summer sun, the shy smile and the occasional mournful frown.

"He actually sat in my lap the whole time," Leslie said. "Can you imagine an infant just sitting in your lap all peaceful for an hour?"

On Sunday, Father's Day, Leslie got the pleasure of one more hour with Shane, this time in a local park. Throughout both visits, Judy hovered within inches of them. Leslie complained to reporters, "It would have been better if they had someone else bring the baby to me. I don't want to see these people or be forced to look at them. The whole thing is so cruel. So cruel."

That week, Les and Frank drove up to Abilene, meeting with a couple dozen members of Mike's unit. They also went to the race track, where more than twenty cars carried a Severance memorial bumper sticker or wore No. 4, the number of Michael's car. His parking space still sat vacant.

Both sides of the custody battle crowded into the courtroom of State District Judge Barbara Walther on June 24. Angela Voss with the Texas Department of Family and Protective Services testified that her agency's investigation found no evidence of abuse or neglect in Davidson's home.

When criminal investigators testified to the possibility that Wendi had had the children with her when she disposed of Michael's body, Leslie's attorney Thomas Goff was visibly shocked. He told the judge, "It was significantly bad judgment" to allow Davidson to stay in the same house as her son. "Not just by the Davidsons, but by CPS." In another case, Goff noted, CPS had removed four children from a parent's custody on the suspicion that the parent was using drugs. "They can remove four children in that case, but see no danger for the children here?"

Goff grew increasingly frustrated that the relevance of the murder was not given weight in determining whether or not the child should be in the custody of Wendi's parents. Davidson's attorney, Tim Edwards, accused Goff of trying a murder case in custody court.

The judge rebuked Goff at one point, saying, "Just because someone has been indicted, this court has not reached any conclusions about guilt. In the state of Texas, we continue to engage in the presumption of innocence until guilt is proven, and you, as an attorney, should be aware of that."

Other witnesses included a day-care worker and a pediatric nurse who said that Shane and his 3-year-old half-brother were close to each other, and to their grandparents, and were happy.

Lloyd testified that moving Shane to Maine would devastate the child. "It's the only home he's ever known. We love him, he loves us, he loves his brother. He's part of our family."

When Judy Davidson took the stand, Goff asked, "Do you hate Michael Severance?"

After a pause and an overruled objection from Edwards, Judy said, "Yes, I did."

In his testimony, Leslie expressed his fear that the Davidsons were party to the homicide. "I came to Texas to protect my grandson and stop the lies about my son and family. I have been totally ignored by authorities since I came to San

Angelo. I fear that with Wendi being charged with murder, she may commit a murder–suicide, harm the child, take off to Mexico, any of those things."

He said that he had a deep bond with Shane, but on cross, admitted that he'd only spent about two weeks total with Shane since his son married Wendi in September.

In the end, Judge Walther awarded joint custody of Shane Severance to Wendi's parents and Michael's father, Leslie. The judge granted a sixty-day period for Leslie to take his grandson back to Maine.

She also restricted Wendi's access to her son, allowing her only supervised visitations every Saturday for two hours at a neutral site. She ordered Wendi to move out of her parents' home. Walther requested home studies by social workers of both homes, and psychological evaluations for both parties.

She ordered that an attorney be appointed to represent the child and allowed the Davidsons to retain their right to determine where Shane would ultimately live when sixty days had elapsed. The Davidsons were granted permission to visit Shane in Maine if they chose to do so during the time he was out of state.

Leslie wanted primary custody of his grandson, but he told reporters, "We're thrilled. We're thrilled with everything, pretty much. We're on the right track and we're making a little bit of headway, especially compared to everything we have been up against. It's still a total nightmare, but we're getting there."

Judy and Lloyd Davidson said they would not appeal the ruling. Their attorney Tim Edwards spoke on their behalf: "That's what the court decided, and we respect that and we'll stand by it."

At 6 P.M., Leslie and his son Frank took custody of Shane for the next sixty days. The next day, they went up to Abilene to the race track to spend time with Mike's friends.

Diane Slater, one of Wendi's clients, who had visited the clinic shortly after the custody hearing, told the San Angelo *Standard-Times* that Wendi's pain had been obvious. Wendi, she said, was very distressed by the court's decision. "I could tell by looking at her eyes. And her mother was devastated. Her parents' attorney said that it would be better if Wendi didn't go to the hearing." Wendi, she said, was regretting that decision.

On June 27, Frank and Leslie flew back to Maine with Shane, landing at Bangor International Airport a little after 10 P.M. They were greeted at the airport by a large group of family and friends who smothered them all in hugs, kisses and cheers. They approached Leslie and Shane a few at a time in order not to frighten the little boy.

A weary Frank told reporters on the scene, "This has been a very long, mentally, physically tiring ten days. I'm kind of speechless. We knew there would be people here, but we didn't expect this."

They all formed a caravan to make the fifty-mile, late-night drive from Bangor to Lee. The next day, Shane was already making himself at home, crawling freely across the living room floor in his grandfather's home, gravitating to the enlarged portrait of his late father propped on the floor. When Shane reached up and touched the picture of his dad's face, the emotional impact of that gesture hit Leslie hard. He had to leave the room to avoid breaking down in tears. When Shane wasn't exploring the environment down on all fours, he was relaxing in his grandfather's arms.

That afternoon, the family took Shane out to the cemetery. Along the way, they spotted several stores in Lee and Lincoln sporting signs that read "Welcome home, Shane," and neighbors out driving honked at them to draw their attention to the words "We love you, Shane," written on the sides of their cars.

At the foot of Michael's grave, Leslie held Shane and said, "I've got him, Michael." The family stood behind Leslie, weeping.

As they left the cemetery, Leslie promised Shane, "Someday we'll have a big long talk about this."

FORTY-TWO

At some point, Wendi became less concerned about the Severance family taking Shane than she did that her parents might not allow her to have either of the children back after her legal troubles were over. She concealed a tape recorder when she went to her parents' home, hoping to catch one of them in an ugly moment. She succeeded.

Lloyd badgered Wendi in front of Tristan. Lloyd played off the littlest member of his audience when he chanted, "'Cause you wanna be mean. 'Cause you wanna be mean." He repeated the phrase ten more times, causing Tristan to giggle.

Egged on by his grandson's amusement, Lloyd's voice turned sing-song. "Her hates her family, She hates her family, Her hates her family, Her hates her whole family." He repeated the last sentence six more times, then started singing to some unknown tune. "Her hates everybody in her family. She despises her mom, she wishes her dead. She hates her pa, she wishes him dead. She hates her brother, she wishes him dead. She hates Cissy [the nickname for Wendi's Aunt Yvonne, her mother's sister], she wishes her dead. Why does this girl hate her whole family and wishes her whole family dead? Her wishes her family dead. Why does this girl hate her whole family and wishes her whole family dead? She wishes her family dead. She wishes her mommy dead. She wishes her family dead, dead, dead. She wishes her family dead."

After a couple of minutes of additional repetition, Lloyd

added: "And she hates her children, too. She wishes her children would get run over . . . flatten them flatter than a pancake, so she has no more children to worry with.

"She told me, she told me she hates everyone in the whole world, including her two children. She hates her whole family. She hates her kid, especially. She despises the ground her family walks on, even though they loved her through everything, thick and thin. But she loves Leslie, her first boyfriend. She's in love with Leslie." he sang mocking reference to Mike's father, made in an attempt to bait Wendi into an angry response.

Wendi maintained her cool. This behavior was exactly what she'd wanted to capture on audiotape.

Tristan said, "I wanna go outside, Mommy."

Wendi tried to soothe him, but ignored his wishes. She was too caught up in her personal mission to give any consideration to Tristan's best interests.

Lloyd resumed a sing-song delivery more suitable for a school yard than a conversation with another adult and a child. "She's in love with Leslie. She's in love with Leslie. Leslie is her boyfriend. Wendi has a boyfriend. Wendi has a boyfriend. Wendi has a boyfriend," he chanted and then broke again into song. "Wendy has a boyfriend and she's in love. She also has a sugar daddy named Goff [a reference to Leslie's custody attorney]. She has a sugar daddy."

Throughout this melody, Wendi tried to ignore her father and talk to Tristan, but Lloyd's voice drowned her out. Lloyd zeroed in on his grandson. "Your mommy's got a boyfriend and a sugar daddy." After droning on a bit more, he switched his focus back to his daughter. "So how's your boyfriend doing? Did you give them plenty of hugs and kisses today?" he said, making kissy noises with his mouth. "Your lips got together. What I want to know is, since y'all are a—a trio, does Leslie and Goff smooch together, too, or do you just smooch them?"

He ragged on Wendi about that and then broke into a new song to the tune of the spiritual "He's Got the Whole World in His Hands." "Wendi hates the whole world. Wendi hates the whole world. Wendi hates the whole world, even the little kids. Wendi hates her family. Wendi hates her brother. Wendy hates her Mom and Dad. Wendi hates Tristan. Wendi hates baby Shane. Wendy's so full of hate. She's so full of hate because all she loves is her sugar daddy and boyfriend."

Lloyd switched to a talking voice and continued on. "But she hates the whole world and wishes the whole world dead, especially her parents and her brother and her aunts, who have tried so hard for her. She wishes they would die immediately. Why is that? Nobody knows. It's just that Wendy is so full of hate."

While little Tristan listened, Lloyd broke again into song. "Wendi's so full of hate that she hates everybody. She hates her mom especially, because her mom has done so much for her. Her mom has loved her since she was born. She had to . . . help her get her ass out of the crack a million times, and continues to do so, that Wendi says, 'I want to repay you. I would like you to jump in front of a train. I wish a truck would run over you. I wish you'd just go out and die under a tree.' That's the thanks Wendi gave Mom. And she's dedicated to her poor ma and her poor pa because she knows he's right and that she's also wrong. Because they're not full of hate like she is, she thinks they're wrong.

"And she hates her brother because he did not get his ass in a crack like her from making such a poor choice, a poor judgment. She hates. She hates. She hates. . . . She hates that stuffed toy because it resembles life. She hates. She's so full of hate. She hates—she even hates herself so much because she tries to dig herself in deeper. Why would anybody that has their ass in such a crack that it's pinching their cheeks off would want to get in deeper?"

He stopped singing and talked directly to his grandson. "Watch it, Poppy! Watch it! Watch it. She'll try to strangle you. She's gonna try to kill you like she kills all them animals up at the clinic. You'll be next. Don't trust her. She'll put you up on that table and kill ya. She's done many of them that way. They go in and expect to come out alive and"—Lloyd made a choking noise—"she kills them dead.

Better watch it. She hates them pets just like she does every—
even every— She hates every animal in the world except her
sugar daddy and her boyfriend. Hates them.

"Watch it! You're fixing to get it. She'll rip your heart
right out. She's already ripped Mom's out and stomped it as
much as she could and continues to do so. She thinks if she
rips her heart out, it will just kill her dead, and she's trying.
And it probably will kill her. And when she's dead, Wendi
will be so happy. She'll be at Mom's grave, sitting on it, saying, 'I'm so happy you're dead.' And then I'll die and she'll
say, 'Pa, God, I'm happy you're dead.' "

Lloyd continued his tirade in front of innocent little
Tristan, his voice building in its power of delivery to a crescendo reminiscent of a fire-and-brimstone revival preacher.
"And then perhaps her brother would be in some kind of
accident and be killed and she'd say, 'Man, am I happy now.'
And then Cissy died for some unknown reason and she'll say,
'I don't know what to do with you, but I'm so happy.' Wendi
would be the happiest person alive, because people would be
dying and it makes her feel happy to see them die. Except her
sugar daddy and her boyfriend will not die. They will be
there with her forever. They will be like"—Lloyd made a
series of kissy noises—"until after her family is dead.

"She'll move to other families, wishing they were dead.
'I wish every family on earth dead,' she says. 'Please die.
Please die. All dogs die. All cats die. I,' she says, 'I hate every
living thing except for my boyfriend and my sugar daddy.
Why couldn't every living thing on earth die except for my
sugar daddy and my boyfriend? Why, oh, why?'

"Why would anyone hate so many living organisms? . . .
How could there be that much hate? . . . It couldn't be hu-
manly possible, so it must be some kind of evil spell that
was cast on Wendi to make her hate her entire family and
wish her entire family would drop dead right this second.
And if I should drop dead right this second, I would always
hope that a big grin come on her face, because maybe that
would be a sign that there was a glimmer of hope." Without
warning, Lloyd returned to his normal talking voice as if a

spell had passed—as if the whole crazy rant had not happened at all. "Baby, I've got to go," he said. "It's going to take a bulldozer to clean that thing out. What's all those toys up there?" Lloyd started humming, and again he launched into sing-song, "Watch it, she'll kill you dead. Watch it. Watch it. She's about to kill that one there . . ."

"Mommy," Tristan asked, "did you kill somebody?"

"No, baby," Wendi said. ". . . No, Pa's brainwashing you, that's all."

". . . I'm not trying to brainwash you. I'm talking to your mom," Lloyd argued.

"Why don't you go play? You don't need to be around all that," Wendi urged Tristan.

"That's right, he don't. I don't know why his mama inflicted that."

"I don't know why Pa's acting ugly on you. That's terrible. Sorry," Wendi said. "Don't listen to anything he says, baby."

"Yeah, don't listen to anything your mom says, because she does tell you awful ugly things . . . she just comes out here to be mean." Lloyd ranted on again—this time, the keyword was "ugly." Poor little Tristan took it all in with no comprehension of the complexities beneath the words. And he walked away bearing the scars of their battle.

FORTY-THREE

Sergeant Randy Pelfrey traveled from Dyess Air Force Base to Lee, Maine, toting the door of Michael Severance's race car. It bore the signatures of sixteen of Mike's Abilene friends. He presented this remembrance of Mike's life to Les Severance at his home.

In West Texas, additional artifacts from Mike's death surfaced in the remote pond at the desolate ranch. On July 11 at 4:50 in the afternoon, Terrell Sheen called Ranger Shawn Palmer. The dry spell had caused the water to recede at the stock tank, exposing cinder blocks. Sheen granted permission for law enforcement to access his property.

Palmer, Detective McGuire and a crime-scene technician drove out to the 7777 Ranch. The blocks were on the northwest edge of the pond, partially submerged in mud. They collected two blocks, tied together with monofilament line. They pulled a third one and a plastic zip tie out of the muck.

Palmer reviewed the controlled substance logs seized during a search of Advanced Animal Care. He'd done his homework and knew the proper dosage of Beuthanasia-D Special that a veterinarian needed to administer to put a pet to sleep: one milliliter for every ten pounds of body weight.

When he added up the excessive amounts recorded as being administered by Wendi Davidson between October 5,

2004, and February 21, 2005, he got 10.85 milliliters—enough to euthanize a 108-pound dog. Then he turned to Patience, an animal owned by Daina Schwartz.

According to Wendi's veterinary tech, Jamie Crouch, this dog had died while being moved for x-rays on February 16, 2005. But Wendi had called Daina and informed her that Patience needed to be euthanized. The bill for services included a charge for this service. The controlled substance log documented that six milliliters of Beuthanasia-D was administered to Patience.

Since the dog had died without receiving that procedure, Palmer added that amount to the excess dosages noted on the paperwork, and there was enough to euthanize a 168-pound human being. Michael Severance weighed 155 pounds.

Perhaps that excess use was not significant. Many veterinarians deliberately used a small amount of Beuthanasia-D above what was necessary, particularly when the pet's owner was present for the procedure—others under-dosed unless they weren't alone. Authorities do not know what Wendi normally did. They also knew that during Wendi's initial six months of practice, she traveled with her father to Zapata to visit Marshall and, on more than one occasion, went into Mexico to purchase veterinary pharmaceuticals for her practice. Investigators did not know what she'd bought on her trips out of the country. Beuthanasia-D is a controlled substance across the border, too, but it might be easy to find someone willing to ignore the law for the right price.

Judy Davidson's stepfather, Emmett Eggemeyer, widowed in April, tried to pick up the pieces of his life that summer in the midst of all the family turmoil. He answered the questions posed to him by law enforcement, provided an unflattering view of the Davidson family in the child custody deposition and battled Judy over his deceased wife's estate.

On July 14, he called Ranger Palmer. Someone had placed roofing nails in the driveway, causing damage to the tires of his truck. He'd reported the incident to the Tom

Green County Sheriff's Office, but thought Palmer should know about it in case there was a connection to the investigation of Michael Severance's death.

Friends of Michael's family donated more than 500 household items to a yard sale to benefit the custody fight for Shane on July 15 and 16. Sporting goods, clothes, furniture, exercise equipment and more filled a two-bay garage at Mount Jefferson Junior High School in Lee, Maine.

Terrell Sheen called Palmer again on July 17. There were more revelations at the pond as the water continued to recede. Palmer returned to the 7777 Ranch with a crime-scene tech. The fence that ran north and south across the stock tank, which was completely submerged in March, was now fully visible. On the east side of the fence, they found a brake drum resting in the mud, and at the spot where they'd recovered Mike's body, they seized a cinder block tied with a yellow rope.

In Maine, the Severance family made the most of their interlude with Shane. The little boy spent a lot of time with Nicole Leighton, who had a son just a few months older. The family choked on their grief as the day that would have been Mike's twenty-fifth birthday approached. On that day, July 20, 2005, the state of Texas issued an amendment to Michael's death certificate, adding the cause of his death:

> acute combined Pentobarbital, Phenytoin and Phenobarbital drug intoxication.

In addition, in the box for a description of how the injury had occurred, they wrote:

> *Deceased was administered lethal amounts of drugs by someone unknown to this certifier, against the health and safety of the Decedent causing death.*

The mournful day was made even more difficult by the crass insensitivity of Wendi Davidson. First she sent flowers with a request that Les put them on Michael's grave in Carroll Plantation. Then, a package arrived with gifts for Shane. Enclosed was a birthday card. On it, Wendi had written:

> *Mike,*
> *Happy Birthday,*
> *Love,*
> *Wendi.*

She also included a note to Les and Brinda:

> *"Please know how much I am thinking of y'all during these times of trite [sic]. I know how much Mike loved y'all and that is how much I love y'all as well. I believe family is so very important and after all of this turmoil is over, we will still be family and I will be happy to say so.*
>
> *Here are some new toys + clothes for baby Shane. Tell him how much I love him. Tristan says he misses him very much. Maybe next time, Tristan can come visit, too.*
> *Love Always,*
> *Wendi.*

Nick Sambides, Jr., a reporter for the *Bangor Daily News*, was at the Severance home when Les opened the mail. On reading the note, Les shouted, "I just don't know what to make of this. Goddamn it! She dumped him in a pond and stabbed him forty-one times, and now she wishes him a happy birthday!" He continued in a calmer voice. "It's vicious and revolting. Maybe we should respond by saying, 'Wendi, please take these flowers out to the pond where you buried him.'"

At 8 that evening, family and friends gathered on the front lawn of the Lee Academy for a candlelight vigil.

Wendi sent another note that arrived in Maine less than two weeks after Mike's birth date:

I am so full of grief these days. I love and miss Mike so much—it hurts so very bad. I want to talk to you, but the attorneys all told me not to. They said you are angry and it would only hurt me. But I know if you are angry, it is because of all the nonsense that people have told you—the police, your attorney and the news people. All of those people have their personal agendas—money and fame to gain. All I want is my family to love and support me, the way I love + support them. I cannot have my husband here on earth, but he is in my heart and mind now and forever. He will always be a part of my children's lives. If you want to tear this family apart, that is your prerogative, but I want to keep it together. I think the attorneys, news media and police want to pit everyone against each other because it just helps to add fuel to their fire.

Les, once this mess is all cleared up, I want to have a good relationship with you and the rest of the family—I want this for me, for y'all, for the kids, and most of all, because Mike would want this. I know Mike would not want the boys split apart like they are right now. He would not want it anymore than I do. It is very important to keep them together. They are so very close to each other. Tristan asks for his brother daily and when Shane gets a little older, he will do the same. I am asking you—begging you to please call and talk to me. I am so angry at all the attorneys. If they can keep making their money, they are happy.

But none of this is right—none of it. My parents just want what is best for the children (for them to be to-gether.) I want this and for all my family to get along. As soon as I possibly can, I would like to come up to Maine for a couple of weeks with both of the kids. I would like to meet your family up there and visit the cemetery. I hope you got the flowers I sent for Mike and took them to him.

Les please call me—I can't talk about a bunch of

*specifics, but I can tell you the news media has fabricated
a whole story so they can sell papers.*

*Also, I would be glad to see you and my parents drop
the whole custody issue—the boys need to be together—
here and when they visit in Maine. I will gladly work out
visitation for y'all to see them if everyone will be civil and
act like a family should.*

Love Always,
Wendi.

She included her phone numbers beneath her signature.
Then she added:

*If you feel more comfortable writing right now, that is fine,
too.*

Beneath that note she jotted down both her address at the
clinic and the address at her parents' home.

To the Severance family, it seemed as if they and Wendi
were living in separate worlds where the reality of Michael's
death had starkly differing meanings.

FORTY-FOUR

On Wednesday, August 3, Savvy, Incorporated of Portland, Maine, launched a new website, keepshaneinmaine.com, to raise money to help the Severance family with their custody battle for Shane. The firm agreed to take only 10 percent of the proceeds to cover expenses, a rate much lower than what was normally charged.

Wendi filed a request that Les Severance be ordered to pay for the attorney she'd hired to represent her in the custody battle for Shane. The audacity of this maneuver baffled both Les and his attorney Thomas Goff.

The next day, Les, with his grandson, left Bangor International Airport on a 6:20 A.M. flight back to Texas. He flew back with a heavy heart, but high hopes about the outcome of his day in court in San Angelo to make his case in the best interests of his grandson.

Judge Jay Weatherby passed down his ruling on Friday, August 19. The attorneys for the Davidson family heaped criticism on Les's head for using his grandson as a fundraising tool. Les explained that he needed community support to get funds to travel to Texas. It wasn't a good enough excuse for the judge. He rejected the Severance petition to gain sole custody of Shane from December 1 through Wendi's trial, scheduled to begin on March 20, 2006.

He granted custody to Judy and Lloyd Davidson, allowing Wendi weekly two-hour supervised visitation with her

son. The judge gave Les permission to visit Shane from 9
A.M. to 6 P.M. on Saturdays and Sundays up to three times
per month—not very practical for a grandfather of limited
means who lived so far away. He also left open the possibility that Shane could visit Maine for four days around
Christmas.

Les was crushed. He transferred custody of his grandson
to Judy and Lloyd on Sunday, August 21, at 8 P.M. He still
had a difficult time believing that any judge in any court
would not see the injustice of this decision.

Les walked into a small San Angelo lunch counter with
just four stools. He'd been a pretty thin guy before January
15, 2005—now he was twenty pounds lighter, and appeared
emaciated. Sorrow stretched his long face a bit closer to the
ground than it had just a few months before.

The lone man seated on one of the stools, turned toward
him when he entered and asked, "Are you Mr. Severance?"

Still skittish from his recent encounter with the Davidson
family, Les paused a moment before saying, "Yes, I am."

"Sorry to hear the news about your grandson, Mr. Severance. I'm a retired Border Patrol agent. I've spent most of
my career in San Angelo. You're not from around here. You
never had a chance."

FORTY-FIVE

Ranger Shawn Palmer had a theory about Michael's murder and the disposal and mutilation of his body. Now he was going to put it to the test.

He gathered up San Angelo Police Officer Kara Jeffcoat and a training dummy from the fire department. Kara weighed 148 pounds and was 5'4" tall—a couple of pounds under Wendi's weight, and a couple of inches over her height.

Jeffcoat loaded the 167-pound dummy—heavier than Mike—into the back of a four-wheel-drive Dodge pick-up. At the pond, she pulled it out of the truck bed and dragged it over to the dock. She had no problem shoving it from there into the water. Then, they tried it from the boat. Jeffcoat could dump the dummy into the water from on board without capsizing.

There had been weights attached to Michael, making him heavier than the stand-in Jeffcoat used. But it wasn't essential that Wendi lift all that weight. Although difficult, she could have secured the body to the boat and used the natural buoyancy of the water to make the job easier, and explain why cinder blocks and a brake drum were found buried in the mud—she'd dropped them as she tried to attach them.

Lloyd had said that Wendi hated Marshall because he didn't get his ass in a crack like she did. That was about to change. Marshall's family was in turmoil and now his job was on the line.

Back in March, Internal Affairs for Texas Parks and Wildlife had begun an investigation. They met with Major Steve
Whiteaker, in the San Angelo office of their agency. Next,
they interviewed Ranger Shawn Palmer, who told them that
Marshall had lied to law enforcement, was refusing to cooperate with an ongoing criminal investigation and had possibly tampered with evidence. "I have enough evidence to file
on Davidson for making a false report to a peace officer," he
said. Subsequent statements from San Angelo Police Department Detective Dennis McGuire and Tom Green County
Sheriff's Office Detective Ron Sanders backed Palmer's
claim. But Marshall sent a memo telling a different story
and denying all the allegations.

At the agency's request, Palmer put his comments in
writing at the end of July. On September 13, Internal Affairs
Investigator Joe Carter interviewed Marshall. The contra-
dictions between his statements and the other members of
law enforcement piled up.

One week later, Marshall received notification from
Lieutenant Colonel Craig Hunter of Parks and Wildlife that
he was being considered for formal corrective action, "up to
and including termination." Marshall hired attorney Rae
Leifeste to file a reply to the agency.

The lawyer prepared a lengthy response. In it, Marshall
denied: that he'd ever heard his sister say she'd found the
body "in the bed deceased"; that he'd attempted to mislead
Palmer about Michael's clothing; that he'd had any knowledge of his father removing items from Wendi's car; that he'd
made a false statement about the reason for his hardship
transfer; that he had been dishonest about seeking custody of
his sister's children; and that he'd lied about his location on
January 18, 2005. Attachments included eight letters in support of Marshall as a valuable law enforcement officer from
officers with the Zapata County and Starr County Sheriff's
Offices, U.S. Border Patrol, DPS Narcotics Service and a
game warden with the Texas Parks and Wildlife Department.

The next day, Marshall sat down on a different hot seat.

FORTY-SIX

On September 14, Marshall finally submitted to a deposition that Thomas Goff had requested for months in the child custody case. After Goff took him through a series of questions about the men in Wendi's life, he asked, "Do you think that your sister was promiscuous?"

"As in . . . ?" Marshall hedged.

"Was that an opinion you held of her, that she was promiscuous?"

"I guess you'd have to define 'promiscuous.'"

"Sexually promiscuous," Goff said.

"No . . . I don't think she was just out and about doing her thing and trying to get pregnant or trying to create a problem. Yeah, she had had some boyfriends."

"She wasn't out in bars picking up men?"

"No," Marshall insisted. "That's not something she did."

"So do you believe that she had relationship problems? You've already mentioned that she kind of picked up losers, in your opinion. I don't want to . . . put words in your mouth."

"Well . . . some of the people she dated, I mean—most of the people she dated, she had went to school with or worked with or, you know, whatever. But no, she wasn't one to go out to bars and just pick up . . . guys on the street and take them home."

Midway through the questioning, Goff asked him how

he'd learned about the mutilation of Michael's body and if he believed Wendi was responsible for that.

"I'm assuming, yeah, if she moved the body, then she probably would have been the one that did that."

"Logical," Goff agreed. "Have you thought about the fact that she did this to her—even if he was dead—her child's father, her husband? And this wasn't just an animal. This was a human being that she was married to. Does that not trouble you?"

"It does trouble me if she was able to do that, but, again, I don't know what was taking place in her mind . . . when she discovered the body. You know, in my situation, would I do that? No. Would most people? I don't believe so. But, you know, like I said, I don't know what went through her mind. And yeah, it is troubling why she would, you know, do that."

"Do you think she was temporarily insane?" Goff asked.

"I don't know. I wasn't there. You know, the temporary insanity defense is used for everything. So, I mean, I don't know this case. I don't think she was in her right mind at the time, No. I mean, anybody that does that, freaks out that bad, you know, obviously, she's not thinking rationally."

"And do you believe she could have . . . gotten him into a boat without tipping it over in the middle of the night in January, gone out to wherever it was dropped, gotten out of the boat without tipping the boat? And you've spent a lot of time in a boat. So professionally, do you think that's plausible?" Goff asked.

"It's plausible, but I don't know how it was done, no. You know, I've had an investigator also question me on the deal . . . His understanding is, yeah, she did it by herself . . . Of course, she's not going to tell me anything of what happened."

"A police investigator?"

"Yes . . . he wouldn't tell me of what all happened, but he said, 'Yeah, trust me, it could be done.' So, you know, leaving it at that, I guess it could be done."

Later in the deposition, Goff asked Marshall, "Is it your testimony, then, that you don't know who murdered Mike?"

"No, I do not know."

"No one's told you?"

"No. The only person that has told me anything about this murder is my sister, and that she didn't do it."

"And that somebody in the family—she suspects somebody in the family?"

"She's assuming, yeah," Marshall said. "She's assuming somebody in the family."

"And that the family hated Mike?"

"Right. Not the entire family, but, yeah, there was a lot of dislike towards him."

"Do you know if Wendi told anyone else, at the same time, in your family on March third, fourth, fifth, what was going on? Anybody she would be close to? I guess her grandmother was too far gone at that time to talk to?"

"Well, no . . . My grandmother . . . wasn't up and about . . . but . . . she was able to talk to you and stuff . . . My sister didn't talk to anybody about it until that breakdown."

"Okay. Not your grandmother? Not your aunt?" Goff pressed.

"No, I mean, nobody knew anything. I mean, everybody was in shock. I'm the one that told my grandmother . . . about the deal. And, of course, that's the last thing she needed to hear . . . at that stage in her life, you know."

"That was difficult, I'm sure."

"Right. I guarantee you it's been real difficult since March for the most part."

Goff switched gears and asked, "Have you ever considered the fact that you might have to end up raising one or any of Wendi's children?"

"Yeah, I've thought about that seriously, and . . . I guess a person's got to do what they got to do. I love them to death, both of them to death, and if that's the case, you know . . . if something happens to my parents, Lord forbid, they die in a car accident tomorrow . . . I have no problems raising those kids."

". . . Have you ever made derogatory comments in the past about your sister or your family?"

"Derogatory as in what? I mean, me and my sister have had fights, you know."

"Have you called her 'goofy'?"

"Called her 'goofy'?" Marshall asked.

"Yeah."

"Yeah, she's goofy sometimes."

"So you think she's acted goofy in the past?"

"I mean, yeah. I mean, I guess, you know, depending on your definition of 'goofy' and my definition of 'goofy.' Yeah, I mean, she's done goofy things before."

"The body disposed of, the mutilation, would you say that would be out of character for Wendi, a surprise, or . . ."

Marshall interrupted. "That's, you know, that's what I'm saying. That's way out of character. I mean, obviously she's never done anything like that before, you know. She's a vet. She takes care of animals. She doesn't kill them, even if she finds one that should be put down, she doesn't even kill it.

"So, yeah, I mean, to find out she moves . . . a dead person's body, and now if she did all the rest of that stuff, you know, then, yeah, I mean, that's severely out of character."

Toward the end of the questioning, Goff asked, "What type of relationship would you like to see your family and the Severance family have?"

"Well, I think everybody just needs, you know, to work something out. I mean, it's not like everybody's going to be buddies over this whole thing. I mean, obviously, you know, whether—whether my sister, you know, killed Mike or not, if she moved the body and I'm on the Severance family's side, obviously I'm not going to be able to be friends with the family here.

"But I think for Shane's interest, I think everybody needs to work it out and, you know, work out a deal there instead of, you know, just— This kind of fighting and stuff is not helping anybody."

"Do you ever envision a time when Wendi could resume raising both of the children?"

"I think eventually, she'll be able to, I mean, that's her whole deal. I mean, she loves her kids to death, you know.

I–I foresee that once this all plays out, you know, if she gets her punishment or whatever, I'd like to see her resume, I mean, that's her place. The kids love her. You know, I think that would be her place, yeah."

"I guess you're in the same boat as everyone else until you know what happens with the criminal case," Goff said. "Everyone else is depending on that, wouldn't you agree?"

"Oh, I agree totally, I mean, you know. Everybody is kind of . . ."

Goff interrupted. "If she's convicted of murder, it's going to be one . . ."

Marshall stepped on Goff's statement. "Well, I mean, whether she's convicted or not, as far as— As far as I see for the kids, if she's convicted and she does her time like everybody else, whatever punishment she gets, then I still don't think she's a threat to the kids."

". . . If that happens and she's convicted of murder, she's not going to be around the kids for a length of time."

"Yeah, some length of time," Marshall acknowledged.

"Ten years, maybe, at the minimum."

"Right."

"So at that time, Tristan will be thirteen, fourteen. Shane would be ten."

"Right."

"Do you really conceive that . . . Wendi could come back and resume a life with her children and have a normal relationship with Shane after being convicted of murdering his father?" Goff asked.

". . . That's the part I'm saying about the whole deal with the families getting together. If there's always fighting . . . especially from your client's side . . . he's going to know all this. It's not right and this and that, whether it's right or not, you got to do what's best for the kid, you know, I think even if she's convicted.

"But I mean, I've known people that haven't known their family for most of their life, you know—and you can watch it on TV all the time—they get back with somebody, and then they . . . get back to being a successful family."

"If it was your sister that was murdered instead of the way it is now . . . do you think you could have a relationship with . . . his family, the husband's family?"

"I would put it the same way that I put it," Marshall said. "Like, I don't think you're ever going to come down here and spend Christmas together, but I think that, you know, you need to work together . . . and do what's best for this kid."

"If ten years from now, Shane comes to Uncle Marshall and says, 'Tell me about my father, tell me what happened,' what will you say to him?"

"I mean, I guess I'd have to tell him the truth, you know. I don't know a whole lot about his father, you know . . . Depending on how the case goes—I'm going to be honest about the case."

"Just assume now that there's no murder conviction, just what you know now, how would you . . . explain that to Shane?" Goff asked.

"Something happened to his daddy, and, you know, no matter what it is, something happened, and his mom, you know, freaked out, lost control and disposed of the body.

". . . Eventually, he's going to know all the graphic details. Does he need to know all the details at, you know, nine or ten years old? I don't think so. But, you know, eventually he's going to know it. But I mean, I think he ought to— He's going to know that . . . something happened here.

"And, you know, I mean, he's got to know that everybody still loves him, and that's the whole key, is for the kids. I have doubts that until this took place that they had much to do with Shane himself. . . . The only time, like you said, that Leslie come down was on the wedding. It's the only time he saw the baby. To me, that doesn't show a real interest in taking, you know, grandparenting steps towards the baby.

"And, you know, I mean in events that have take place since then, from what I understand, you know, it's been more of a media battle than it has been worrying about the baby. You know, putting it all in the media is not good for the kids. Separating the two kids is not good for the kids.

"So my concern would be that what's good for Shane is

for him—for consistency. He's getting plenty of love here, but I agree that he [Les Severance] needs to show him love. And that's why I'm trying to get them to work together on him, getting to see him, but I don't think that the household that they have up there is based on a loving household for him."

"What do you think it is based on?" Goff asked.

"I think it's more of a, 'My son,' you know, 'is deceased. And I want to replace him.' And that shouldn't be how it is. You shouldn't just replace something, you know, with something new. I think it should have been a loving relationship before and continued on through there."

"Well Shane was only three [sic] months old when his father was killed, so aren't you making a stretch to say that there was no loving relationship? . . ."

"No, I'm saying . . ." Marshall interrupted.

". . . when the child was only three months old?"

"If he only came down here when they got married, he didn't come down here when the baby was born. Right?" Marshall snapped back.

"The baby was born and they were married, what, a week apart?" Goff said in amazement.

"But he didn't come down here when the baby . . . was born, is what I'm saying. I was there when the other child was born. I couldn't be here now, you know, being that far away, because I didn't know what day it was going to be, if, as a grandparent, you know, he knew the baby was coming, he could have come down and been ready for the baby. You know, I was there for Tristan's birth, and I wouldn't have missed it for the world, you know, because my sister didn't have anybody else . . . And to me, you know, he never really showed a whole lot of interest. And then you're right, you know, whatever happened to Mike comes along, and from that point, you know, it's been focused on, you know, getting Shane to Maine, separating the two kids, you know. That's the best thing.

"I don't foresee that. I don't see how separating two kids that love each other, you know— Tristan is old enough to where obviously he has a lot more understanding and love and everything else. And, you know, to put them together and you separate them, I don't see how that's good for Tristan or Shane.

"And then to be in a family, like you're saying that their son has been lost, so they're going to sit up there, and, you know, tell their side of the story, you know, when he's old enough for that to happen. I don't think that's the way it should be."

"When you say the two sides ought to resolve this, how would you suggest—or what are you suggesting to your parents?" Goff asked.

"I'm not suggesting just to my parents, I'm suggesting to both sides that—I mean the way the custody battle is now is— You know, the way it's set up is, you know, my parents get him all the time, but the ways it's set up there is, he gets him all the time.

". . . I don't think so. If he would like to see the kid and everything else, I think he should be allowed to, but I— You know, the biggest problem I've got is, the only people winning in this whole fight is the lawyers. You're the ones that are getting all the money. The kids are not winning this thing. The parents aren't winning this thing."

A few minutes later, Marshall expressed his parents' fear that Les "might just try to take the baby and run."

"You're a law enforcement officer," Goff said. "You know that's not realistic."

"I wouldn't think it was realistic for my sister to move a body, either, and that happened. So, I mean, you know, I guess you got to look, yeah, is it realistic? I don't think realistic . . . he would do it, you know, for the sheer fact that he would get in so much trouble. But I don't . . . know him and I wouldn't put it past anybody."

Goff wrapped up by asking him if, given that his mother hated Shane's father, she would be able to answer his questions about Michael's death. He said that he thought she could and hoped she would. He didn't want Shane to learn about it at school.

FORTY-SEVEN

A tip came in on the Crime Stoppers website on October 5, 2005, that Steven Johnson and Scottie Cook had possession of Mike's racing car, suggesting that the two men may have helped Wendi, and that that was their payment for services rendered.

That lead took Detective McGuire and Ranger Palmer to Michael Newberry, who showed them the cancelled check he'd used to pay Wendi for the race car. He told them that the transmission in the vehicle actually belonged to Scottie Cook, and when he'd picked it up from Wendi, Newberry had had it towed it to Cook for repairs.

While in Abilene, the investigators interviewed additional racing friends of Mike, who talked about Mike meeting Wendi at a night club and taking her home that night. Those who'd seen Mike with Shane, a couple of days before he died, said that Mike hadn't mentioned having a fight with Wendi, or any troubles in his marriage.

In early December 2005, Marshall received the document he did not want to ever see. It read:

> This notice is to inform you that your employment with TPWD is terminated, effective the date this notice is presented to you.

Attached was a report detailing the conclusions of the Internal Affairs section that he had provided untruthful or misleading information, had withheld information and had failed to fully cooperate with other agencies in connection with an ongoing homicide investigation in San Angelo, Texas.

Internal Affairs found the statements of the accusing law enforcement officers credible because they found proof of Marshall's dishonesty in audiotapes of his telephone conversations with his sister while she was in jail. Their conclusion:

> Mr. Davidson's untruthful statements and representations indicate that he lacks the credibility and integrity to continue to function as a peace officer and a Game Warden for the Texas Parks and Wildlife Department.

They cited TPWD policies about standards of performance and ethical behavior that included the expected cooperation with other officers and agencies.

> Police officers will cooperate with all legally authorized agencies and their representatives in the pursuit of justice. An officer or agency may be one among many organizations that may provide law enforcement services to a jurisdiction. It is imperative that a police officer assist colleagues fully and completely with respect and consideration at all times.

Unfortunately for Marshall, there were no loopholes—no exception to the rule if your sister was the perpetrator. By putting the desires of his family before the requirements of his duty as an officer of the law, Marshall had shredded the dream he'd carried for a lifetime.

Shane arrived in Maine to celebrate Christmas. He sniffled from a cold that he shared with everyone in his father's family. Although noses were running, spirits were high.

It was the first Christmas for Les Severance without his son. Shane could not replace Michael, but he did bring many moments of joy tinged with bittersweet regret. In four days, he returned to Lloyd and Judy Davidson.

The investigation into Michael's death continued in Texas as law enforcement followed every lead, no matter how unlikely. A finger of suspicion pointed in the direction of Wendi's cousin, Randy Walker.

Randy told Ranger Palmer that he'd learned of Mike's disappearance from Wendi, who'd told him her husband "had run off and gone AWOL." On the night that Wendi was arrested for tampering with evidence, Marshall had stopped by and let Randy know about the discovery of Mike's body. But no one, he said, had discussed any details of the murder or the disposal of the body.

Palmer then asked Randy about a suspicious conversation he'd had with Wendi while she was in jail. Randy did remember her asking if he was scared, but he'd thought she was asking if he was scared for her. He denied having anything to do with the crime.

Finally, Palmer ran down the elusive black transvestite, Tu Tu. His real name was Donyell Laron White and he was in the Allen Correctional Center in Kinder, Louisiana, on a parole violation. Twenty-eight-year-old Donyell had a criminal record of forgery, theft and escape from custody, but there were no violent offenses on his record.

Although he'd been living in Louisiana since 2000, he acknowledged that he did visit San Angelo and when he did, he frequented Graham Central Station. He said he had not had a confrontation with Michael—in fact, he didn't recognize his photo at all. The only incident at that nightclub, he said, was when a female employee named Teresa threw him out for using the ladies' restroom. Teresa corroborated his statement.

Palmer scratched Tu Tu off of his list. No matter where he looked, every avenue led back to Wendi Davidson.

FORTY-EIGHT

In January 2006, Judy and Lloyd Davidson kicked off a campaign to get their son's job back. Judy wrote a letter to Robert Cook, Executive Director of the Texas Parks and Wildlife Department. In the heading there was a line reading: "Reason for Termination: Unknown."

She wrote of her son's dreams:

> *Marshall has wanted to be a Texas Game Warden since he was a small boy. He has worked extremely hard to reach his goal.*

She highlighted his excellent grades in school and his commendable performance on the job. She defended his actions after Wendi's arrest:

> *Marshall turned his own sister into the police. This is probably the hardest thing that he had to face in his life. He told Texas Ranger Shawn Palmer and San Angelo Detective Dennis McGuire that he would not investigate his sister that was their job. He has fully cooperated with them in every aspect of their investigation. It is my belief that Ranger Palmer got his feathers ruffled and he turned Marshall into Internal Affairs out of vengeance.*
>
> *. . . It is my belief that Marshall has suffered a terrible injustice, and Internal Affairs did not do a complete investigation. I feel they trusted and believed a corrupt*

*Texas Ranger over one of their own. I must ask the
question "WHY?"*

*. . . If you choose to uphold Marshall's termination, it is
my belief that you will truly lose the best game warden
Texas could possibly have. His integrity and honesty are
above reproach.*

*. . . Ranger Palmer and Detective McGuire should be
investigated for Abuse of Power and also lying under oath.
My heart and soul are heavy with grief and sorrow for
Marshall as he has become a victim of a savage, relentless,
and unfounded attack. It is my belief that no one has given
him the benefit of doubt, nor examined the evidence.*

*Should his own department not stand behind him and
do further investigating on these issues? I beg you to give
this your full consideration and reinstate Marshall to the
position of Texas Game Warden. I promise you will not be
disappointed.*

As always, in Judy's mind, her children were right and
the rest of the world wrong. She saw both of her children as
victims of the cruelty of others, and grieved for their suffering. But, she never once shed a tear for the terrible loss of
life suffered by the 24-year-old airman who was the father
of her grandson.

Lloyd's letter was much the same, but he opened with an
attack before launching into the positive attributes of his son:

*I have been reluctant to reflect my thoughts, thinking with
patience, I would see justice and good prevail.*

*Several months ago, I was warned that the investigators
may use several tools. One, break people financially, thus
making it difficult to fight back. Secondly, destroy the
entire family, hoping this would generate a confession.
Third, lie and fabricate evidence, anything goes. It appears
the predictions have all materialized to some degree,
mostly without success.*

*It seems vengeance is a trademark of Shawn Palmer.
Dennis McGuire and Ron Sanders are merely puppets.*

They are no longer investigators seeking the truth. I believe the trio have lied, given false statements, fabricated evidence and manipulated those of authority.

He wrote about the strength of Marshall's character—"as solid as an oak"—and the letters of recommendation included in his son's fight to keep his job.

Marshall has steadfastly worked along the border, where it has become a war zone, approaching that of Iraq. Marshall has given his all; he has put his life on the line every day. Now, Marshall is being repaid with betrayal and hung-out to dry, by those who should be watching his back.

He called the termination a "travesty of justice" and reminded Cook of the promise made to Marshall when he graduated from the academy as a Game Warden:

One of the speakers said to all of the graduates "you have the entire department backing you, you have the entire State of Texas backing you." Now is the time to fulfill this promise.

Lloyd had to have known about Marshall's deception of law enforcement. After all, he had been an integral part of some of it. He did not acknowledge Wendi's role in her brother's downfall. Family was first. Always. He would attack anyone who threatened that unit—most particularly the investigators laboring to bring his daughter to justice.

At the end of the month, Executive Director Robert Cook sent his response—separate yet identical letters to Judy and Lloyd Davidson, written in the stuffy style of a bureaucratic brush-off:

I received your correspondence dated January 10, 2006, regarding your son and former Texas Game Warden Marshall Davidson. Mr. Davidson's com-

plaint concerning his termination is currently pend-
ing. I am forwarding your letter to Human Resources
to be included with that complaint. Your allegations
regarding law enforcement personnel from other
agencies will be provided to those agencies for re-
view.

Throughout the month of January and into February, Palmer continued to run down leads, interviewing anyone who was connected to the case in any way. On February 27, he met Wendi and attorney Jenny Campassi at the Shannon Medical Center in San Angelo.

Wendi agreed to provide a sample of her blood, signing the consent form that made it official. Palmer took two purple-top tubes of her blood into custody as evidence in her murder trial. Her case was on the docket in three weeks— slated to begin on Monday, March 20, 2006.

But jury selection didn't begin that day because of a defense motion. Attorney Tom Davidson had withdrawn from the case in December. Wendi's new defense lawyers, Fred C. Brigman III, Christi Manning and Melvin Gray, explained their need for additional time to prepare their case. District Judge Tom Gossett granted their request.

The trial was postponed until April 17, much to the distress of the Severance family, whose pursuit of justice for Michael had now passed the fourteen-month mark. Palmer took advantage of the extension to continue seeking evidence to strengthen the state's case.

On March 31, Lloyd and Judy jointly signed a letter to Robert Cook at Texas Parks and Wildlife. After thanking him for his response to the previous letters, they attacked "the propaganda that Ranger Shawn Palmer has perpetrated about Warden Marshall Davidson." They provided a bullet-point list of six one-sided arguments in support of their son and five in condemnation of Palmer and the other investigators.

The letter ended:

> *I can easily point out a minimum of twenty-four lies told by the investigators. All facts and evidence lead to the same conclusion, Ranger Palmer created false accusations against Warden Davidson to satisfy his personal need for revenge. Again, I emphasize common sense in this matter. As Marshall has performed in exemplary fashion, it is time to return Marshall back to work as Texas Game Warden Marshall Davidson. As my wife and I were witnesses to many of the events, we look forward to a discussion with you. And again thank you for your time and consideration.*

The Texas Parks and Wildlife Department did not budge. It was clear to the agency that there was dishonesty and revenge at work in this case—but all of it came from the Davidsons' camp.

State District Judge Tom Gossett granted a defense motion to postpone the trial until the week of May 15 to allow Wendi Davidson's new legal team time to get an analysis from their own expert on the DNA evidence in the case. The prosecutor was not pleased.

The biggest hardship caused by the delay fell on the family and friends of deceased victim Michael Severance. Many had to change travel and vacation plans to come to San Angelo from far-flung Maine or nearby Abilene to testify or observe the trial. But worst of all, the fate of the youngest victim, 17-month-old Shane Severance, remained on hold pending the outcome of the criminal trial against his mother.

FORTY-NINE

On May 2, Judge Barbara Walther allowed the defense more time to do additional testing. The trial was moved to August 21. But when that day neared, some of the results were still incomplete. The defense attorneys requested and received yet another postponement until October 16.

Les Severance staggered under the emotional impact of yet another delay. Like most family members of homicide victims, he never expected to get complete closure after losing his son. However, the completion of a trial was an ordeal that hung over his head like the fist of doom. Getting past that necessary obstacle would at least draw a portion of his suffering to a close. The news was heart-wrenching and frustrating.

At 12:10 A.M. on Sunday, August 20, Buffalo Wild Wings customers spotted something strange and alarming in the parking lot. They informed restaurant manager Glacia Bear. She went outside and saw a little boy on a yellow, mini–Suzuki QuadSport four-wheeler circling around cars in the parking lot, crying for his mommy. She brought him inside, where the toddler said he didn't know where his mommy was. She called the police.

The San Angelo Police Department responded, and someone suggested the child might be 4-year-old Tristan Davidson, who lived across the street. Officer Barry Ratcliffe drove over to the veterinary clinic and got a phone number off the sign on the front door. He called and left a message for Tristan's mother with her answering service. Wendi rushed into the restaurant, telling responding officers that she'd left the child sleeping at home while she ran into Wal-Mart Supercenter for fifteen minutes.

On the other side of Sherwood Way, Ratcliffe inspected the clinic and discovered that one of the three doors to the outside was unlocked. It was apparent to him that that was how little Tristan had left the building, and then crossed five lanes of traffic on a busy, highly commercialized thorough-fare late on a Saturday night.

When Wendi arrived, Ratcliffe told her to drop the Wal-Mart story, because police officers in the parking lot had spotted her leaving Graham Central Station. She folded right away, admitted the truth and said, "I made a bad choice. It will never happen again."

Wendi was handcuffed and taken into custody, where she was charged with child endangerment. The arrest affidavit read:

> any reasonable person would believe that due to the Defendant's actions, the child was at great risk of im-minent danger of death, bodily injury, or physical im-pairment.

Lloyd Davidson drove into town and picked up Tristan, bringing him back to his home.

Wendi called her mother from the jail. "Hey, Mama."

"Yes, ma'am," Judy said in a cold tone of voice that made her displeasure clear.

"I know I really screwed up, okay? Don't give me a lecture 'cause I don't need one. Okay? Are Dad and Tristan there now?"

"They just drove up."

"Okay. Well, this is what I think is going to happen. I think as soon as—somewhere between eight and noon— I think a judge is going to show up. I should get a bond and it should be reasonable and I'm going to call David Jenkins and I'll be able to bond myself out. Theoretically, if the bond is reasonable. And so he can come pick me up, he can take me to the clinic, he can do all that. Now, apparently, they're trying to charge me with child endangerment, which is a state jail felony. It's not near as bad as all the rest of that stuff. But another thing that happened is, I know it is a really bad lapse in judgment—a one-hour lapse in judgment. And please, whatever happens, please don't y'all come and take Tristan from me. Will ya please not do that?"

"Wendi, have we ever done that?" Judy answered in an even sharper tone.

"Well, CPS is going to do an investigation and there's nothing real binding or anything. They told me that when this is all cleared up, which it should be by morning, and they told me it's going to take a few days to do their investigation. And that in the meantime, all I have to do is be supervised. But I can't be supervised out at y'all's house because of Shane. Will one of y'all come to the clinic and stay for two or three days? So Tristan won't be away from me? I just can't do this all by myself. That's why I wanted Tristan with me, 'cause I just can't do it all by myself."

Acid etched the next words out of Judy's mouth. "Then you turn around and leave him by himself."

"Please, Mama . . . Obviously. I should pay for this, I should. This is one thing I should be punished for. Okay? So whatever happens to me, happens to me. You don't understand how stupid I was. I'm glad I'm here and I'm glad he's not dead on the road, okay? . . . I'm so glad that I came here and that he didn't get killed and he didn't get kidnapped, okay? I really, really am stupid and sorry. It's just that I'm so lonely," Wendi sniffled through her tears. "I just needed to be around humans for just a little while. And I tried to call several people and everybody had plans, and I'm just so scared you're going to keep Tristan with y'all. I'm just so afraid y'all are going to try to take him away."

"Oh Wendi, puh-lease."

"What? Why?"

"If we were going to do that, we would have done it long ago," Judy said.

"It's so easy for y'all to do 'cause you already got Shane," she sobbed.

"Wendi, we didn't take Shane. How many times do we have to tell you?"

"I didn't . . ."

"We didn't take Shane," Judy repeated.

"You have Shane. All you have to do is say you want Tristan and you will have him. I'm just scared. I just can't do this all by myself."

"Well, we have tried to tell you that from day one. Besides, you know, your call is being taped."

"I know that."

"You know that, right?"

"I know that. I've already talked to the police, too, I mean, you know, they already know what happened, okay? I haven't called Fred. I haven't called David," Wendi said, referring to her criminal attorneys. "There's no point. They can't do anything. They won't do anything. I know I have to wait till morning till I figure out what's going to happen then, okay? I don't know, I mean, will one of y'all please— Will one of y'all please come to the clinic and stay for a couple of days, please?"

Judy sighed. "Wendi, I don't think a couple of days will do it."

"They told me it cannot go on for more than a month. They put a date on there. The guy told me it should just be a few days. It's not a court order or anything. It's just that something that I agreed to by signing it, that Dad agreed to by signing it."

"Agreed to what?" Judy asked.

"That I'd be supervised with Tristan. I signed it and Dad signed it."

"Well, I don't know what we're going to do," Judy said in a weary whine.

"Please, don't take him. I don't see why you can't stay with me for just a couple of days."

"Wendi, a few days is fine. A month is not," Judy snapped.

"Okay. Just a few days. Okay?"

"Well, I don't know. I can't talk for Dad. Because I'm going to have to be the one that takes care of Shane. So if your dad will, that's your dad."

"I can't believe that Shane would be that much trouble or nothing. Shane's at day care during the day and Tristan can be at the clinic during the day, with your assistance. And then at night, Dad could take care of Shane for a couple of hours. I think he could take care of him. Please, Mama, please. I know he's [Tristan] so upset. He's scared and doesn't know what's going on."

"Well, he has a right to be," Judy said.

"Well, I know he does, okay? I know he does. I know how bad I screwed up. I don't need anybody to tell me that, okay? That's not the problem here, okay? I screwed up because of what I did. I screwed up. You know, I should've known. I should've known that it was bad. I should've thought about every single consequence that ever could have happened. But then, no. I thought if I put Tristan to sleep, I could go out for an hour or two and nobody would know the difference. That's what I thought. Okay, I'm sorry. I'm stupid, stupid, stupid . . . Can you please forgive me?"

"Yeah, I can forgive you."

"Will you try to help me?"

"Wendi, we've been trying to help you since day one, and you just keep crappin' on it."

"Mama, I went to the bar because it was a bad day. He was cranky and irritable all day long. I'm sorry . . . I should be home tomorrow. I should be at the clinic tomorrow, and I'll call you when I get to the clinic . . . Okay?"

"Well, just call and let us know, Wendi. You better keep your mouth shut there."

At that, Wendi dropped the sobbing, poor-me approach and turned testy. "Mama, I've already talked to the cops,

okay? . . . I already talked to them. There wasn't any denying anything. I pretty much told it all, you know. So,
anyway . . . But I'll let you go. How's Tristan? Is he crying?"

"No, he's asleep."

"He's already asleep?"

"Um hmmm."

"Well, don't worry about the clinic, 'cause I should be
there before noon, and y'all don't have to do anything, because everybody should have enough food and water until
tomorrow 'cause I took care of them tonight. So, if for
some reason, I'm not out by Monday morning, then you're
going to have to go let Cissy in, 'cause she can take care of
everything . . . Okay?"

"All right," Judy said in an exasperated tone.

"I love you, Mama."

"I love you, too."

"I really do."

"I really love you, too."

"When Tristan wakes up tomorrow, please tell him I love
him and I'm sorry. Okay?"

"All right," Judy sighed, ending the phone call.

When many of Wendi's supporters picked up the newspaper or tuned into the news on the radio and learned of the
arrest, they abandoned their long-held belief in Wendi's innocence. Opinions changed overnight. Loyal clients switched
to someone else to meet the medical needs of their pets.
Wendi marched closer to her day in court—there would be
no further postponements.

FIFTY

In a motion filed on September 25, the defense claimed that Wendi's

> constitutional rights against unreasonable search and seizure under both state and federal law were violated when law enforcement agents illegally installed and used a mobile tracking device on her vehicle on private property and tracked her movement on private land to which she had a reasonable expectation of privacy.

They moved that all the evidence obtained after the installation should be suppressed.

The defense also requested a change of venue. On October 2, the judge ruled against that motion, but set a hearing on the suppression of evidence for October 16, 2006, the day jury selection would begin in the trial of *The State of Texas* versus *Wendi Mae Davidson*.

Exactly twenty-one months from the day Wendi had filed a missing persons report on her husband, Michael Leslie Severance, the day of the trial for his murder finally arrived. The major players took their places in the courtroom. Fred C. Brigman III, Melvin Gray and Christi Manning gathered around the defense table. For the prosecution, 51st District Attorney Steve Lupton and first assistant Alison Palmer prepared to do battle. Behind the bench, Judge Tom Gossett brought the courtroom to order.

The witnesses waited in the wings. The state alone had subpoenaed more than sixty-five people to testify. Among that number were members of Wendi's own family. The witness list for the defense was still clothed in secrecy.

Members of the jury pool passed through the security facilities in the lower floor of the courthouse. The panel of 130 citizens of Tom Green County moved into a courtroom adjoining the trial chamber to go through an initial screening by another judge. District Court Judge Tom Gossett explained that Wendi had a right to be present at that proceeding as disqualifications and exemptions were heard and people were weeded out of the pool. Wendi and her attorneys declined their right to be there.

"All right," the judge began, "since this is a motion-based or a mobile tracking device that was done, I believe, without a search warrant and without authorization of the court, I think in the interest of time, it will probably be best if the state acknowledge that the burden shifts over to the state."

"We are pleased to assume that burden at this point, Your Honor," Assistant District Attorney Alison Palmer acknowledged.

"Are you ready to proceed then?"

"Yes, sir," Alison Palmer said and called her first witness, Air Force Special Agent Arch Harner. "How did you become involved in the investigation?"

"Greg McCormick from my office notified me that we had received a report from our security forces section on Dyess Air Force Base that Michael Severance had been reported missing."

"Who reported him missing?"

"To my understanding, it was his wife."

"Who was his wife?"

"Wendi Davidson."

"Do you know Wendi Davidson?"

"I do."

"Do you see or hear her in the courtroom?" the prosecutor asked.

"Yeah," Harner said, pointing to the defense table. "She's right there."

"May the record reflect that the witness has identified the defendant?"

"Very well," the judge said.

"Agent Harner," Alison Palmer continued, "in the course of looking for Michael Severance, did you all have occasion to apply for permission to use a mobile tracking device?"

"We did."

"Do you do that all the time?"

"Rarely."

"How often have you applied for permission to use a mobile tracking device?"

"In my career, this is the first time."

"All right. What happened that led you to want to apply for this device?"

"We had suspicion to believe that Ms. Davidson or her family may know his whereabouts. And we wanted to use the tracking device to help us focus our search for him."

"Had you exhausted other resources in attempting to find Mr. Severance?"

"We conducted extensive interviews of people that had known him."

"Had you searched various properties?"

"Yes, we had."

"So what did you have to go through to acquire an authorization to place a mobile tracking device?"

"The first step I needed to do was, we had to brief our—my higher headquarters in a field investigations region, and we had to tell them our intention to place these tracking devices. Their advice was to contact our technical services folks—the people who maintain control of the tracking devices, to see if they had any available. In this instance, we found out, there were some available, so the next step would be to brief our OSI staff judge advocate, the OSI legal office, to brief them on the scope of our investigation and our intentions.

"They approved—they approved the scope of what we

wanted to do and then . . . we learned from our region and from the lawyers that we needed the region commander's approval to install these tracking devices. We applied for that approval and received it."

"At this time, you are applying for the mobile tracking device, what sort of investigation is going on?" Alison Palmer asked.

"We had a missing persons operation, and a deserter investigation."

"A deserter investigation?"

"Yes, ma'am," Harner said with a nod.

"So there wasn't a criminal, you know, a state criminal case pending, or really being investigated at that point?"

"No state criminal case, ma'am."

"At that point the only information, the only good hard information you had, was that you had a missing person?"

"That's correct."

Alison Palmer asked, "Who told you about the possibility that Michael Severance was a deserter?"

"Wendi Davidson."

"So Wendi Davidson advised you of what led you to believe that Michael Severance may have deserted his post?"

"She mentioned to investigators that he had mentioned how easy it would be to disappear to Canada, and he may have gone to Canada."

"Did she talk about whether he enjoyed being in the military or not?"

"She said that he did not enjoy it and was not looking forward to deploying, and that he had intended to leave the service."

"In fact, he had an upcoming one scheduled, is that correct?"

"That is."

"So was that some of the things she said to lead you to believe he may have deserted?" Alison Palmer asked.

"Yes, ma'am."

"So the best information you had was that Michael Severance was a missing person?"

"Yes, ma'am."

"Any investigation that foul play may have been, or any belief that foul play may have been involved, would just be— It was speculation, it was a possibility, but no sound evidence to support it, is that correct?"

"That's absolutely correct," Harner confirmed.

Alison Palmer turned her questions to the actual placement of the devices. "What vehicles were you given authorization to place mobile tracking devices on?"

"I was given authorization to place tracking devices on three vehicles: two trucks and a car."

"And who did these belong to?"

"The Davidson family."

"And who had the car?"

"Wendi Davidson."

"Who had the trucks?"

"Lloyd and Judy Davidson."

"Can you describe the car for us?" Alison Palmer asked.

"It was a Chevy Camaro, and it was red."

"Doesn't Wendi Davidson's red Chevy Camaro have on it, at that time at least, any Air Force Base insignia or attachments?"

"To my recollection, yes, it did . . . It had a Dyess Air Force Base sticker . . . on the windshield."

". . . What does that mean, if you have an Air Force base sticker on the car?"

"The sticker identification card allows you access to Dyess Air Force Base, allows that vehicle to access on Dyess Air Force Base," Harner explained.

"And with that you were given— are you able to avail yourself of all the benefits of the Air Force base?"

"Without that sticker on your car or a guest pass, you cannot bring that car onto the base. You cannot drive onto the installation."

"So someone with a sticker can just get onto the installation anytime?"

"That's correct."

". . . Now, off base, does that sticker carry with it any

inhibitions or any agreements of what a person could do because the sticker is on their car? Off base, it doesn't really have a lot of effect?"

"That's correct, ma'am."

"Okay. So let's talk about the placement of the mobile tracking device—just the one on Wendi Davidson's car. Lloyd and Judy Davidson are not complaining about the placement of the devices. Regarding Wendi Davidson's car, was the mobile tracking device placed inside the vehicle? Did y'all have to enter into the vehicle to place the tracking device?"

"No, ma'am."

"Was it placed on the exterior of the vehicle?"

"Yes, ma'am."

"Was the vehicle damaged in any way in the placement of a tracking device?"

"No. No, ma'am."

"Was any of the energy of the car used to generate energy for the tracking device?"

"No, ma'am."

"So it operates independently of the vehicle?"

"That's correct, ma'am."

"And was it attached in such a way that removal would have harmed the car?"

"No, ma'am."

"Okay. When was the tracking device placed on Ms. Davidson's, the defendant's, vehicle?"

"On the twenty-sixth of February, at forty minutes past midnight."

"Okay. And where was the vehicle when the tracking device was placed?"

"It was parked in front of the veterinary clinic."

The prosecutor asked how the device operated, and Harner explained, "First of all, it works with a Global Positioning System. Once the device is placed and turned on, it mans the logging, geo-coordinates of that device. It's not like a real-time tracking. What we do is, at a later point, we have to come in the vicinity of the vehicle and download data from where the tracking device has been."

"So you are not able to turn it on and then go sit in your office and just monitor a computer and watch wherever the tracking device goes?"

"That's correct."

"What all information can you get from this tracking device?"

"You can determine time and location."

"Okay," Alison Palmer said. "Does it tell you who is driving the car?"

"No, it doesn't."

"Does it tell you anything much about the place where the car goes? In other words, there is no video capability?"

"That's correct."

"So it can give you even less information than if you had been able to have the manpower at that point to dedicate someone to follow this car around?"

"That's correct."

"In fact, if you had the manpower to dedicate someone to follow this car around, and that person had a cell phone, you would have more advanced technology and more help . . . than by using this tracking device."

"Yes, ma'am, that would be ideal," Harner said.

On cross-examination, Fred Brigman asked, "And how many deserter cases have you worked on in your career?"

"I don't know the number, sir. Several."

"Well, a lot?"

"I wouldn't say a lot, no, sir, but several cases."

"Of those cases, how many involved a staff sergeant?"

"At Dyess Air Force Base, none. That is, to my recollection. I believe I recall an NCO going AWOL when we were in Japan, but I can't say that specifically."

". . . Let me ask you this: Mike Severance—did he fit the profile of a deserter?"

"Not necessarily," Harner admitted. "But his wife did say that he had been talking about it."

"What did his other family members say?"

"They said it wasn't possible."

"They said it wasn't possible that he deserted?"

"They said it would be uncharacteristic for him."

"Early on, you thought there was foul play, didn't you?" the defense attorney accused.

"It was among the many possibilities that we considered."

"In fact, in just about every report that I have seen between the time that you all got involved, January eighteenth up until this application for a mobile tracking device was filed, you all referred to Mike Severance as a victim in your reports, didn't you?"

"I didn't, not to my recollection," Harner denied. "I mean, I may have speculated in my notes, but I don't recall referring to him as that."

Brigman presented the witness with copies of notes. Some were written by the agents who'd interviewed the Severance family in Maine. The descriptive word "victim" ran throughout their reports. Harner insisted that he could not explain what other people had written.

The defense attorney then turned to Harner's own notes and asked, "You checked to see if he had gotten a cab, is that right? You checked to see if . . ."

Harner cut him off. "What these— I can explain what these notes are, sir. Those notes weren't as if I was going to be interviewing like that. Early on in an investigation, we will come up with an investigative plan and consider all the possibilities, game out different scenarios, different possibilities. We start with everything and then work our way down. We consider all the possibilities and then look at what we do know and try to eliminate the impossible by proving what happened."

"Okay. So you look at everything early on?"

"That's correct, sir."

"And narrow down to what you are doing, is that right?"

"Yes, sir."

"And that's what you did in this case?"

"On those notes, that was really early in the case, and I was just considering every possibility."

"Okay. But in the beginning, you suspected that there was foul play, did you not?"

"It was among a bunch of possibilities, yes, sir."

"Well, you and Agent McCormick both suspected that, didn't you?" Brigman accused.

"We both considered the possibility," Harner admitted.

"You didn't think people were being honest with you in the Davidson family?"

"That's correct, yes, sir."

"And yet— And nobody else believed that Sergeant Severance deserted; is that right?"

". . . We had speculated it was a possibility."

"Okay. Now, going back to your application, your commander signed off on that and approved it, and he is an OSI guy, right?"

"Yes, sir."

"So he is a law enforcement agent?"

"That's correct, sir."

"So he is not a magistrate?"

"No, sir."

Near the end of the examination, Brigman returned to the language found in the reports. "You don't usually refer to deserters as 'victims,' do you?"

"No . . . 'Investigational target' or 'subject' is the typical terminology."

"One other— Maybe just one more question," Brigman said. "In here, in your assumptions, you have a question, and it's 'How do we get the perpetrator to take us to the remains?'"

"Yes, sir."

"And this is on January twenty-fourth, and you are making an assumption that Michael Severance is dead?"

"I was considering the possibility."

"Is it fair to say that that was one of the bigger possibilities throughout this investigation?" Brigman pushed.

"At that point in the investigation, we had no idea where Mike Severance was."

"Okay. I will pass the witness," Brigman said to the judge.

On redirect, Alison Palmer asked, "You wouldn't be a good investigator if you didn't consider every possibility?"

"Yes, ma'am, that's correct."

The prosecutor had the witness reinforce his testimony that the application for the mobile tracking device was based on the Davidson family allegations that Mike had gone AWOL and that Terrell Sheen had granted permission to search the ranch without any knowledge of the existence of tracking device data. He was only the first witness, but already the defense allegation looked weak.

FIFTY-ONE

Alison Palmer called San Angelo Police Department Detective Dennis McGuire to the stand next. "Officer McGuire, is a missing persons investigation a criminal state investigation?"

"It's one that we try to find a missing person if they are reported to us, yes, ma'am."

"You try to help?"

"Yes."

"But is it a crime to be missing as an adult?"

"No."

"As a juvenile, you may be a runaway, is that correct?"

"Yes, ma'am."

"And then you could have some juvenile kinds of charges, but if you are over seventeen, can you go missing?"

"You can be reported missing, but it's not a crime for you to go."

". . . It was kind of a community caretaking function, is that correct?"

"Yes."

"It wasn't really like you were investigating Michael Severance, that he committed a crime or that there was a crime committed, is that right?"

"No, ma'am."

Alison Palmer turned her questions to his knowledge of Terrell Sheen, laying the groundwork for the state's contention that investigators would have searched the 7777 Ranch without any information from the tracking device.

McGuire said, "I actually learned of him on the eighteenth [of January] in my initial interview. He owned the clinic building where the business was housed."

"So early on, you all knew that Terrell Sheen was involved with his family?"

"Yes, ma'am."

"Did you all have any intentions with regard to Mr. Sheen and any property?"

"We were interested in it, of course, because we knew that he had properties," McGuire testified. "Lieutenant Sweet ran a property check to see what property he owned."

". . . You were searching to determine various properties that Terrell Sheen had owned so that you can conduct searches of properties that you felt Michael Severance may have had access to, is that right?"

"Yes, ma'am," McGuire affirmed.

"Did you learn, after those meetings, and with your research on Mr. Sheen's properties trying to find some particular place to search for Mr. Severance, that the military wanted to place a mobile tracking device on the vehicles of Lloyd Davidson, Judy Davidson and Wendi Davidson to assist in their search for Mr. Severance?"

"Yes, ma'am."

"When you heard about it, what was your response?"

"It was something that they were going to do to try to find an AWOL or deserted individual who is missing. My response also was to contact Sergeant Mabe and inquire of him about the tracking device and ask him to check also with the assistant U.S. attorney's office."

"And why did you do that?"

"To make sure everything was done properly, and to make sure that Sergeant Mabe felt that there was proper authorization for that—basically. So we weren't doing anything on a state level that would violate her rights or privileges, or anything just to make sure that everything looked good."

"You all, in addition to the military authorization going

through all the procedures, wanted to preserve her constitutional rights, to make sure from your aspect that you were observing the constitutional rights of anyone who these tracking devices would be placed on?"

"Yes."

"Wendi Davidson and Judy Davidson or Lloyd Davidson?"

"Yes, ma'am."

Alison Palmer next asked him why he'd made the trip to Grape Creek Cemetery.

McGuire said, "Because I was summoned there by Marshall Davidson."

After going through the events of that night, the state turned the witness over to the defense for cross-examination. Fred Brigman asked, "As far as the decision to search the pond on the Four-Sevens Ranch, when y'all went to Terrell Sheen's house earlier on March fifth, was that when it was at your decision to go search the pond, or who had made that decision?"

"Well, there hadn't been a decision made at that point to search the pond. I think because of the information that Special Agent Harner gave us on the fourth, that we were certainly interested in looking at that property, and we went and . . . asked for Mr. Sheen's consent to go look at the property at that time . . . It was a collective decision. Ranger Palmer was actually at this point basically lead investigator, I guess, so it was something that probably several people felt might be beneficial."

"You had some input in it, but it really wasn't your choice to do that?"

"Right. It was outside the city, so it was outside my jurisdiction."

Brigman shifted the questioning to the investigation itself. "When you were working on this case, what were your suspicions or your hunches?"

"Well, I mean, certainly the longer that he was missing, I felt like there was a possibility that something happened, and I think that was probably just about everybody's feeling, that the longer he was missing without contact or without any visible means of supporting himself, that there was a chance that something had happened to him.

"As late as February twenty-sixth, Ranger Palmer and I went and interviewed a gentleman in Hamlin, Texas, and actually searched his house to see if Mr. Severance was there, so we were still looking, hoping, and I had made comments several times throughout that, you know, 'I hope he has gone somewhere, that we find him.' You know, until the comments were made at the cemetery, I wasn't sure if he had gone somewhere or not."

"Well, realistically, and you have been a police officer for twenty years, and worked real hard at it, when you searched the veterinary clinic where they lived, his clothes were still there, is that right?"

"Yes, there were even some clothes that he brought back from a trip."

"His clothes were there, his personal vehicle was there. Did you check to see if he had used credit cards?"

"Yes. Actually, the defendant checked her own records while we were there, computer banking. We ran subpoenas for credit cards to see if anyone had used the credit cards, and they had not. We even talked about contacting some people here locally that had been in contact with someone who had actually deserted and gone off to Canada, and so I think we were looking at a lot of different things," McGuire answered.

"I mean, you checked all that out? You checked out there were no big cash withdrawals from the bank?"

"Yes."

"You checked to see if he had left—checked the airlines to see if he had flown out of town?"

"I checked buses, I checked cab companies."

"Rental cars?"

"There was a rental car that I checked into, but that was based on his vehicle being repaired or something."

Next witness for the state was San Angelo Police Officer Bill Mabe. He corroborated much of McGuire's testimony.

"And what did you do to determine whether or not you felt like everyone's constitutional rights were being observed?" Alison Palmer asked.

"Well, I told him [McGuire] that I felt like that if the military did the installation, that they would be under federal guidelines and I contacted an assistant United States attorney in Lubbock, Texas, and asked her opinion on it . . . She stated that she, after I kind of briefly gave her the scenario of our incident, she stated that she felt like, being's they were military personnel, they would be considered to be federal agents and that they would be under the same guidelines as federal law enforcement agents and that the tracking device could be installed without a court order."

"Without a warrant?" the prosecutor asked.

"Yes, that's correct."

"How come?"

"She said that was the federal guidelines again, and that it was authorized under federal law."

"Is that if the tracking device were in private places or public places?" Alison Palmer probed.

"In public places, if it was installed in a public place."

"And monitored in a public place?"

"Yes."

"And that was the basis that you asked if . . . the authorization was sufficient to just be careful of everyone's constitutional rights?"

"Yes."

"Y'all's intention, then, in seeking this advice was to make sure you weren't violating anyone's rights?"

"That's correct."

After Mabe, Texas Ranger Shawn Palmer took the stand. Alison asked how he'd become involved in the investigation.

"My first involvement was on January, I believe it was the twenty-fourth, 2005, I attended a meeting with other investigators."

"From various agencies?"

"Yes, that's correct."

"And at that meeting did you all discuss trying to find this missing person, perhaps on some properties owned by Terrell Sheen?"

"I don't remember discussing it in that meeting on the twenty-fourth. I think that there were some locations discussed at a later meeting at the second meeting that I attended."

"Do you recall the military was getting authorization to place a mobile tracking device on some vehicles involved in this missing person investigation?"

"Yes I do."

"Do you remember when the tracking devices were placed?"

"I want to say it was on or around the twenty-ninth."

"Was it late February 2005?" Alison Palmer asked.

"Yes, ma'am. It was all on the twenty-fifth of February 2005."

"Were you involved in that placement?"

"I was present at the Advanced Animal Care clinic when I was told that it would be placed on," Shawn Palmer clarified.

"At the time of the placement of the mobile tracking device, what kind of investigation is going on?"

"A missing person investigation as far as law enforcement, and then an AWOL investigation as far as the Air Force."

"So there wasn't really . . . a crime you are investigating? The only crime being investigated was being investigated by the military?"

"Correct."

"You all know that there was a possibility, you know looking at all the possibilities, there was a possibility that foul play was involved?"

"Correct."

"However, you didn't have a whole lot of evidence to support that at that time, is that correct?"

"That's correct."

"In fact, the best evidence you had was that this man had deserted the Army?"

". . . Right," Shawn Palmer said, "there was no evidence that I was aware of that he'd been the victim of any crime, or that any crime was committed other than him not reporting for duty."

"So the only information y'all had, as far as criminal investigations go, was really it was the military's purview to investigate a crime, at that time? And all law enforcement was doing was the community caretaking function to assist with the location of this missing person?"

"Correct, I think the only other offense that may have been involved was, there was a reported theft along with the missing person report."

"Were y'all actively investigating that theft during the course of this investigation?"

"I was not."

Alison Palmer rested her case for the irrelevance of the tracking device in the outcome of the investigation. It was only a hearing on the admissibility of evidence, but the prosecutor knew that the decision on this motion would dictate whether or not justice would be served.

FIFTY-TWO

The courtroom was now in the hands of the defense. They called Air Force Special Agent Greg McCormick to the stand. It seemed odd that Wendi's attorneys would call someone to the stand who'd played a role in their client's current predicament, but the purpose of this witness was clear: The defense hoped his testimony would drive home their theory that the Air Force hadn't really been looking for a deserter when they requested permission to install tracking devices. The defense alleged that the military investigators had concealed their belief that foul play had occurred and hidden their real objective to find the dead body of an airman.

Brigman presented documents to his witness. "These are not in order, but I will show you what starts out as Defendant's Exhibit Number Four. It's titled 'Agent's Notes, Interview with Leslie Severance.' And in your notes, you have a little breakdown of who the players are in it—and the first one is 'victim'?"

"That's correct," McCormick said. "These agent notes are done by two other special agents that we send a lead out to, so this would have been their handwriting instead of mine."

"Okay. But they refer to him as a victim as well?"

"Again, I can only explain why I would have used 'victim' in any of my notes."

Brigman pressed that point and McCormick said, "I used

'victim' on the medication profiles . . . a Bank of America statement. Again, my explanation is that I use that quite frequently in my case reports, and to use it on a cover sheet for [this report] would be something of a habit."

The defense turned to questions about the investigation itself. "Did you bring in a bus load of Air Force personnel to conduct a ground search?"

"Yes, sir, I did."

"What day was that?"

"That was on the twenty-eighth of January, oh-five."

"And where was that ground search located?"

"That search was located mainly around the veterinary clinic itself. We tried to cover a two-mile-square radius. Again, this is my guess to how the radius was, a two-mile radius. We covered possible areas that Michael could have walked off to, or might have led to a way to try to find where he went off to at any point, so that is just one of the areas that we eliminated."

"And you didn't find anything?"

"No, we did not."

"Was there an aerial search conducted as well?"

"No," McCormick said. "No, I could never get a helicopter, for some reason."

"Are you familiar with— that the DPS conducted an aerial search?"

"I do recall them saying something about an aerial search, but I don't know the— I cannot recall exactly what was said about it. I never saw any photos or anything like that."

"When you installed the device on Ms. Davidson's vehicle, you said that was at twelve forty A.M.?

"Yes, sir."

"And that was in the parking lot of her clinic?"

"That is correct."

"Are you familiar that there is an ordinance in San Angelo that you can't be present in the parking lot of a business during these hours that it's not open to the public?" Brigman asked with "Gotcha" written all over his face.

"No. I am not aware of an ordinance. There were vehicles driving through that parking lot all through that time period."

An incredulous defense attorney asked, "There were vehicles driving through there all during that time period?"

"Yes, that's correct."

"So there were people driving through there while y'all were putting this on the vehicle?"

"That's correct," McCormick repeated.

On cross-examination, Alison Palmer asked, "So those vehicles that were driving through there weren't being stopped and ticketed for being in that public parking lot?"

"Oh, no, ma'am, they weren't."

As soon as Alison Palmer finished with the witness, the judge got right to his decision. "I am going to make the following findings: I first find there is no violation of the Fourth Amendment to the United States Constitution." He cited case law and said, "There is no expectation of privacy in traveling in an automobile on a public thoroughfare, therefore, there was no search and no seizure."

He also found that the U.S. military were not bound by legal restraints imposed by the state of Texas, as state and local law enforcement were, and that military rules of evidence were not violated. "Lastly, even if any of these findings were incorrect, I find there is sufficient attenuation. Law enforcement were directed to this pond by Ms. Davidson and by her brother. At that point in time, that's when they were able to discover the body, so I am going to deny the Motion to Suppress evidence. Now are we ready to proceed?"

Fred Brigman rose to his feet behind the defense table. "Your Honor, if we could have about ten minutes, we will be ready."

The judge nodded. "We are in recess for ten minutes."

Wendi collapsed, lying on the floor of the courtroom sobbing while her attorney attempted to comfort her. With this hurdle crossed, the prosecution's case looked more and more like a slam dunk—and the defense knew it.

FIFTY-THREE

The defense team had made a decision on the previous Friday night: If their motion was denied, there was only one possibility remaining—their client had to plead no contest. If she went to trial, Wendi would face a sentence ranging from 9 to 99 years. They had to improve the odds. A no contest plea allowed her to not admit guilt, preserved her ability to appeal and locked in a period of incarceration far more tolerable than the maximum she faced. According to Lloyd Davidson, the attorneys assured Wendi that if she entered this plea, she'd never serve a day in jail and she would not lose her license to practice veterinary medicine.

In minutes, the plea agreement was ready. Both sides agreed in open court to forgo a jury trial and submit the case to the judge. The defendant waived the reading of the indictment. Wendi sobbed and shook when she choked out "No contest." She then admitted her guilt in the unrelated child endangerment case.

District Judge Tom Gossett warned her, "You will be found guilty, and you will be convicted of the offenses just as if a jury found you guilty."

Wendi acknowledged her understanding of the outcome.

The judge announced that it appeared to him that the defendant was competent to stand trial, was not influenced by any consideration or fear, and that her statement was free and voluntary. After hearing arguments from both sides,

Judge Gossett stated there was sufficient evidence to support the no contest plea and announced his ruling of "Guilty."

He asked Wendi if she had anything to say about why sentence should not be pronounced. Wendi did not respond. The judge read out the sentence: 25 years on the murder conviction and 10 years each on the two tampering charges, to be served concurrently. Judy cried as the judge intoned her daughter's fate. Her father sat stock-still without a trace of emotion on his face.

In the hallway outside of the courtroom, Leslie Severance spoke on the phone to a reporter in Maine, telling the *Bangor Daily News* that he felt neither joy nor satisfaction. "We all kind of realized that this isn't going to bring Mike back. We're kind of glad it's over, this part of it. Surprisingly, it doesn't do anything for the pain. I think we got robbed again. She is in jail right now because she is guilty of murder, but she has never admitted to anything. I guess we didn't get a whole lot of answers we were hoping we would get."

Melvin Gray, one of Wendi's lawyers, said, "By going this route, we've limited the exposure to our client. There are real issues as to who committed the murder."

After being assessed nearly $2,500 in court costs and fees on the three felony charges, Wendi signed the Waiver and Stipulation of Evidence form. She was then handcuffed and escorted from the courtroom. She waited in the Tom Green County Jail for her transfer to a state prison facility.

Doctor Wendi Mae Davidson would be eligible for parole in thirteen years.

FIFTY-FOUR

In November, Fred Brigman filed a notice of intent to appeal the verdict in the case. Wendi spent the month in the Tom Green County Jail.

After Thanksgiving, Les Severance flew down to Texas once again. On December 1, he petitioned the Tom Green County Civil Court for extra visitation rights with his grandson, and met with attorney Tom Goff to plan the battle for full custody of Shane Severance.

By mid-December, Wendi was in a state of panic. She wrote letters to two judges—the one who'd presided over her criminal case and the one still holding the reins on the custody case. To District Judge Tom Gossett, she wrote:

My name is Wendi Davidson. I am sure you remember who I am. I am writing you this letter out of fear and desperation.

In mid-October, I was in your courtroom and pled no contest to charges I am perfectly innocent of with the absolute assurance of my attorneys that an appeal would be the safest, quickest route to end this horrible nightmare I have been in for almost two years. They assured me that an expedited appeal would take 3 months to 9 months, maximum.

Well, it has been over 2 months now and I am trying to be patient and strong while the wheels of justice slowly turn. But, I was given the impression I would remain in

Tom Green County Jail while we waited for the appeal. My mother has recently found out that I will probably be going to TDC [Texas Department of Criminal Justice] in 1–2 months.

I know my opinion means very little at this particular place and time but I am definitely opposed to going to TDC for several reasons. First, this appeal process should be finished w/in 1–7 months. Second, I have child custody issues I am dealing with right now in Judge Walther's court. It seems questionable if I could be bench warranted back for these. Sir, my small boys are the reason for my existence—I have to be in court when it concerns them. One more reason, I do not want to go to TDC is that I just found out I am pregnant. I am concerned for this child's safety and feel much safer here than in a dangerous prison.

So, I am begging you, on my hands and knees to please have mercy on me. Please be just and fair. Please place a hold or bench warrant on me so I can remain here where I can attend court hearings and keep in contact with my attorneys, until the appeal is finished.

In her letter to Judge Barbara Walther, she claimed her innocence once again, but didn't repeat the lie about being pregnant:

The custody suit involving Shane has resided in your court for the past, almost two years. And we may be requesting hearings involving Tristan soon. So, this is why I write you . . . I am begging you to please, please do something—anything to hold me here. . . . Please can you do this, not for me, but for the well being of two little boys?

She enclosed a 14-stanza poem, "Angels" in which she anguished about her sons.

In documents Fred Brigman presented to the Texas Third Circuit Court of Appeals in Austin, the defense alleged:

The actions of the Major Crimes Task Force and Air Force Special Agents were unreasonable and prohibited by the Fourth Amendment to the United States Constitution and Article I, Section 9 of the Texas Constitution. The trial court erred in denying Ms. Davidson's motion to suppress.

On December 29, Shane flew into Maine. The Severance family had delayed the celebration of Christmas until his arrival. They hoped for snow so Shane could go sledding. They cherished the time they had with Michael's only son.

At one point, Shane very nearly broke Nicole's heart. "My daddy is in Heaven," Shane said. "Is my mommy in Heaven, too?"

Nicole couldn't spew the truth at this small child. Instead she said, "No, Shane. But she doesn't live around here. When you're older, you will get to know her."

Wendi was transferred out of the jail and into the custody of the Texas Department of Criminal Justice on January 9, 2007. One month later, the Texas Board of Veterinary Medical Examiners revoked Wendi's license to practice veterinary medicine. They did leave open the option that she could apply for re-licensure upon her discharge from prison.

FIFTY-FIVE

Wendi Davidson moved to Gatesville, in Central Texas, home of the largest spur collection in the world, and one of the last fully operational, full-time drive-in movie theaters in Texas. It was also where the state had planted four prison facilities for women on 1,317 acres of land.

Tom Goff traveled to meet with Wendi in her new home and to finally get her deposition for the child custody case. Wendi took the Fifth on all questions pertaining to Michael's death, including if she knew who killed him, but insisted she was innocent of the charges. Finally she answered one of his questions, saying, "I did not kill my husband, no."

"Do you think that your family is—any member of your family, your brother, your mother, your father, was capable of killing Michael?" Goff asked.

"I don't know."

"Do you believe that they did—were involved at the time? Did you believe that?"

"I'd like to plead the Fifth on that," Wendi said.

After that comment, lawyers for both sides engaged in a lively discussion over whether or not the Fifth would apply. Finally, Goff said, "Let me rephrase the question. At the time, March fifth of 2005, did you believe that your family was involved in either the killing of your husband or the disposal of the body?"

"I don't know."

"Were you involved in the selling of drugs from your veterinary clinic?"

"I would like to plead the Fifth on that."

When Goff asked about the father of her oldest son, Tristan, Wendi said, "I don't know who his father is for sure. I was dating several people then. I do not know."

"You were having sex with several people?"

"I had slept with several people, yes," Wendi admitted.

When they talked about life insurance, Wendi said she didn't believe in it and didn't want it, not even for Shane. She said making money off of someone's death is wrong.

Goff asked Wendi about sheep or goats that were alleged to have been found dead at her parents' ranch. He asked if she'd killed them. His question was in response to a rumor running around San Angelo that Wendi had slit the throat of an animal and left it on her parents' porch with the knife protruding from its body and a note that read, "I cleaned up your mess, now clean up mine."

Wendi said she'd euthanized two of her "sheep that were severely sick" out at her parents' place " 'cause that's where the sheep lived." She denied slitting their throats, saying she'd used euthanizing solution.

Goff asked if she'd left the dead sheep on the porch. She said, "I left them there for my dad to bury, yes."

"Did you leave any notes with the sheep?"

"I asked my dad to bury the sheep."

"And that's all that was in the note?"

"That's all I recall."

Goff asked for copies of the letters Wendi had received. Wendi said that when she'd read them and re-read them, she flushed them down the toilet.

"I requested copies and you've destroyed them?" Goff asked.

She said, "I didn't receive anything about that."

"You are on notice now," he snapped. He then asked if she'd talked to her family on the telephone and she said no.

"Have you ever made any—any kind of recordings of any family member, audio or video?"

"You mean like ever?"

"Since Michael's death," Goff clarified.

"I think I made one audiotape maybe, and that's all I can recall."

"When was that?"

"A year ago maybe. I don't recall."

"An audiotape of what?"

"My dad talking to me."

"Okay. And why did you make that tape?"

"Because I was just interested to see what he was going to say to me when I was asking him some questions or something that I don't even remember what that conversation was," Wendi explained.

Goff was stunned. This was the first he'd ever heard of an audiotape. "Where is that tape?"

"I don't know. I don't know where the original is."

"A copy? Where are the copies of the tape?"

Wendi said that she'd given her lawyer "a copy at some point in time."

This tape was never produced in discovery. Goff was outraged that it had been concealed from him against court orders, but he suppressed his indignation until after the deposition was over. He asked about the situation with Tristan in the Buffalo Wild Wings parking lot and Wendi took the Fifth again.

Next Goff turned to her spotty employment record after graduation from veterinary school. He asked her how long she'd worked at the clinic in Abilene.

"About a year-and-a-half."

"Why did you leave?"

When Wendi answered, she shed no tears nor offered a word about the animals that had died because of her actions. Instead she brushed away any personal responsibility and pointed an accusatory finger at her employers. "Because Dr. Ellis and his wife were very immoral people."

" 'Immoral'?"

"Yes."

"In what regard?"

Wendi dredged up a litany of her own sins from her stint as a clinic operator in San Angelo and threw it on the couple in Abilene. "They lied to clients, they charged people for services they didn't do, they were very rude to every employee they had. They—they were just very awful people, in my opinion."

"So that's the reason you left, then, because of the way he conducted his practice?"

"Yes, sir," Wendi said, and then responded to the series of questions about her employment in Lubbock with a total denial of her sub-par job performance there.

On another front, Goff asked, "Did you tell the police that you thought Michael was AWOL?"

"I'd like to plead the Fifth on that."

Goff countered with another touchy question. "Why did you file for divorce?"

"I'd like to plead the Fifth on that," Wendi said again.

Goff demanded and, in a little over a week, finally received a poor copy of the audiotape of the recorded conversation between Wendi and her father. The original was nowhere to be found. After listening to it, Goff copied the tape to CD and sent that copy to attorney John Caldwell, following up with a note on March 13:

As I understand . . . you are not inclined to take any action in response to this new information. I hope that you have listened to the recording. My name is mentioned three (3) times, as is my client, Leslie Severance. The recording lasts 22 minutes and raises serious concerns about Mr. Davidson's mental stability. [We] are concerned for the safety of the children, as well as our own safety.

As an amicus attorney, you have the legal right to take these concerns to the court. I request you do so. In the meantime, I am going forward with a motion for additional temporary orders, asking the court to remove the children from the Davidson household.

In an immediate faxed response, Caldwell wrote that he'd been unable to reach the psychiatrist who was evaluating the custody situation, so

> I decided to take the CD to Angie Voss with CPS. I left the CD with her. She said she was not aware of any other reports to CPS . . . Ms. Voss said that it would be helpful if others made reports concerning Shane.
> I chose to report this matter to CPS not only because of my concern for Shane's welfare but also Tristan's.

Up in Maine, plans were afoot for another fundraising dance to help defray travel expenses to San Angelo to fight for the custody of Shane. Even after that battle was over, the Severance family planned to make the dance an annual event in Michael's memory, raising money for organizations and scholarships.

FIFTY-SIX

From prison, Wendi wrote repeatedly to Les Severance. She referred to Severance custody attorney Tom Goff as "the devil." She discussed the paternity of her son Tristan, writing:

> *They'll never figure out who the father is. They are so stupid. They can't see who is right under their nose.*

Wendi desperately wanted to talk to her former father-in-law, but she was adamant on one condition—she had to meet with him alone, without anyone else in the room. Les wanted to hear what she had to say. The warden, however, would not cooperate. A prisoner could not meet with a family member alone.

On June 21, 2007, Wendi was served with a bench warrant and moved back to Tom Green County Jail. She would remain there for five months.

The small town of Lee had gathered behind the family of Michael Severance, holding them up in their time of loss, mourning the death of one of their own at another's hand. More pain ripped through their hearts in 2007.

On June 23, a roadside bomb tore through a humvee in Taji, Iraq, stealing the life of another native son and Lee Academy graduate, 22-year-old Army specialist Joel House, the brother of Michael's best friend. The tears did not have time to dry before they were invoked anew on November 30. Blair Emery, a 24-year-old Army corporal was felled by another roadside bomb in Baghdad. He'd been scheduled to return home in early November, but like many fighting that war, his deployment had been extended. Blair was Frank Severance's best friend.

Frank staggered under the blow. Only in his early twenties, Frank's life had been a litany of sudden loss—first his mother, then his brother and now his dearest schoolmate. He told the *Portland Press Herald*, "It feels like I'm losing a brother all over again."

The folks in Lee bowed under their sorrow. Joel had planned to be a game warden when he left the military, Blair a police officer. Now, both of their dreams were gone, their contributions to their community unfulfilled.

Lee, like other rural areas across the United States, carried a disproportionate burden during this war. A study by the Carsey Institute at the University of New Hampshire found that although

> rural areas account for only 19 percent of the adult population in the United States [they] have suffered 27 percent of the casualties . . . the death rate for rural soldiers is 60 percent higher than the death rate for those soldiers from cities and urban areas.

The institute believed that the enlistment rate was higher out in the countryside because of the more limited employment opportunities present in rural areas.

Although deeply touched by the losses of these two young men in their community, the Severance family had a reason to celebrate that Christmas. Shane was coming to visit for a full month. It was a time filled with happiness and new fond memories.

Back in Texas, bad news was brewing. The audiotape of Lloyd Davidson's disturbing conversation didn't prompt

CPS to investigate. Angie Voss, the same CPS employee who, in the spring of 2008, would pull hundreds of children out of the FLDS compound in Eldorado, took no action after hearing Lloyd's rant. People aware of the tape couldn't understand how she'd ignored such a blatant example of verbal abuse.

Tom Goff had argued for months for the inclusion of the audiotape in court for the custody hearing. Judge Jay Weatherby resisted until finally admitting, "How come everyone else can hear this and I can't?"

"Judge, have you tried headphones?" Goff asked. The judge plugged in a pair, listened and agreed to admit the audiotape. Goff was jubilant. He believed, with that item in evidence, Les Severance's victory was a slam dunk. He didn't, however, count on local politics.

Throughout the hearings, dozens of people testified on behalf of the Severance family. No one did so for the Davidsons. Shane's *ad litem* attorney produced a report demonstrating that the environment at the Davidson household was poor, at best. The one at the Severance home was excellent. Psychologist Johnny Burkhalter, however, disregarded all the reasons for awarding custody to Les. He was focused on one thing: it was detrimental, he believed, to separate Tristan and Shane. The counselor hired by the Severance side disagreed, saying that that rationale "defied common sense." Judge Weatherby, however, agreed with Burkhalter's assessment, awarding custody to Judy and Lloyd Davidson.

Tom Goff lashed out. "This custody case was a no-brainer. The entire system failed the Severance family from Maine—the criminal justice system, the child protection system and the legal system. They failed Michael. They failed Les. They failed Shane. I am very disappointed in the system."

Goff appealed the decision to the same judge who'd issued the ruling. He noted that Judy and Lloyd Davidson received more than $2,000 monthly from an Air Force benefit and Social Security to care for the two boys, as well as a $500,000 life insurance policy.

> It is shocking that the family of Wendi Mae Davidson will benefit financially from the murder of Shane Michael Severance's father by his mother. This fact alone should convince any trier of fact that it is not in the best interest of the child to be with and be in the custody of [Lloyd and Judy Davidson].

Weatherby rejected the Severance claim. The only recourse now was to appeal it to a higher court outside of San Angelo. That required money and resources that the Severance family simply did not have. It was a bitter pill for them to swallow. They still suspected that someone in the Davidson family had helped Wendi with the disposal of Michael's body, and now Michael's son was going to live in their midst. Les would have gladly taken Tristan into their home as well, because they knew that Michael had loved Tristan and the fatherless little boy had loved Les's son.

On February 18, 2008, Lloyd wrote another letter to Texas Parks and Wildlife—this time to the new executive director, Carter Smith.

> *I would like to introduce myself and my wife and congratulate you on your new job with TPWD. My name is Lloyd Davidson and my wife is Judy Davidson. We are the proud parents of Marshall Davidson, who was a Texas Game Warden before he was wrongfully terminated from your department.*

Lloyd detailed his outrage once again and wrapped up his letter with questions:

> *Please let me know if your department has started an investigation of Ranger Palmer and notified the District Attorney. Also are steps being taken to get Marshall Davidson back in the field as a Texas Game Warden?*

Lloyd definitely was a tenacious man. And Ranger Palmer was not the only person in his sights. He placed blame on all but the one person who really deserved it—his daughter, Wendi Davidson. "They never had proof. No motive. No time frame. They really have nothing." But by 2008, he was no longer mentioning the possibility of her innocence.

On March 13, 2008, the Texas Third Circuit Court of Appeals denied Wendi's appeal, upholding her conviction. Justice Jan Patterson wrote:

> *Because AFOSI agents had an independent military purpose for their investigation, they did not violate the* Posse Comitatus *Act and were authorized to and did comply with their rules and regulations to install and monitor the tracking device. The record does not show that the trial court abused its discretion in determining that the police did not violate appellant's reasonable expectation of privacy by monitoring the tracking device on Sheen's property and the evidence obtained through use of the device was properly admitted. Having overruled the appellant's sole issue, we affirm the trial court's order denying appellant's motion to suppress and the judgments of conviction.*

The defense took their case to the Texas Criminal Court of Appeals. On September 3, 2008, they denied a rehearing of the case. Wendi had exhausted her line of appeals in the state court system.

In between the two decisions, Wendi wrote a letter pleading her case:

> *I swear, I did not murder my husband. I did not interview with the police, I did not go to trial, and never, ever have I told my version of anything. Basically, upon poor advice, I plead "no contest," assuming*

> *upon more bad advice, I would be freed within a few*
> *short months on appeal.*

Despite the fact that her license had been revoked, she signed the letter: "Wendi Davidson, DVM."

AFTERWORD

Lloyd Davidson urged me: "Do your best to sift lies from the truth." I believe I've honored that request.

I traveled a long and circuitous route to reach this point. I now believe, with reasonable certainty, that Wendi was the sole perpetrator in the murder and disposal of the body of her husband Michael Severance. Do I think there are others who bear some moral culpability for contributing to this crime and the cover-up? Yes, I do. But I think that Wendi acted alone.

There are many who will disagree with that conclusion. Some have said that the wrong person is in prison. Despite evidence to the contrary, some still believe that Judy Davidson committed the murder. Others have said that Wendi should not be the only one behind the bars. They think that a member of Wendi's family—Judy, Lloyd, Marshall or one of her cousins—helped her dispose of the body. Some even suggested that the person who helped her with that gruesome task was the hired hand at 7777 Ranch.

What happened in the courtroom played a huge role in creating an environment where multiple scenarios flourished. Wendi did not plead guilty; she pled no contest, owning up to none of her actions. The judge warned her that that plea meant the court would find her guilty of murder, yet she went ahead with it anyway. The end result was no trial, no open forum for the public release of documents, evidence and the giving of testimony from those who'd uncovered the crime.

That complication made it difficult and time-consuming for court watchers to do a complete analysis of the crime. Throughout the city, a crazy quilt patchwork of impressions, theories and conflicting stories created confusion for area residents and out-of-town media alike. In many ways, Wendi's case defies expectations. A rural upbringing is usually envisioned as a wholesome one, producing All-American kids with old-fashioned values. On top of that, the image of a professional woman is hard to reconcile with the kinds of responses to problems that Wendi demonstrated. But once those obstacles are overcome, the path of logic and evidence made her culpability clear.

The next question was, how did she get here? What influences molded her into a woman with sociopathic intent?

She was raised in a place that was isolated from the rest of the world in a household where no one had ever traveled outside of the state of Texas. There seemed to be an underlying hostility toward outsiders in that home, as evidenced by the lack of social interaction in their community and their refusal to extend hospitality to Les Severance on his first visit. But surely that was not sufficient to shape a criminal mind.

Other contributing factors were at play. When Wendi got pregnant, her parents stepped up to take charge of the problem, disparaging the other half of the relationship as they did. When she lost two jobs in a row, they set her up with her own clinic. Her parents rode to her rescue at every sign of trouble, teaching her not to accept responsibility for her own actions, and to blame others for the problems in her life while, at the same time, pushing her to excellence.

Judy's negative attitude toward and constant criticism of the men in her daughter's life, with Michael in particular, had to have an impact on Wendi's view of others. Judy's constant expression of hostility, disdain and paranoid thinking toward her son-in-law and his family had to have insidious, water torture–like effect on Wendi's thought processes.

Lloyd was not blameless, either, in the molding of his daughter. Listening to the audiotape Wendi recorded, it was obvious that this was not the first rant of this nature he'd directed toward one of his children. It sounded like a practiced, lifelong habit of emotional abuse.

But was there more? Drifting through San Angelo was a meandering stream of rumor and innuendo that suggested childhood sexual abuse in Wendi's past. Psychologists saw evidence of that in her promiscuity and poor social skills, among other things. Criminal behaviorists, however, looked at it differently, seeing her sexual impulsiveness and lack of discrimination as a sociopath's quest for power and control.

Without full and honest disclosure from Wendi and her family, there will be no way to know, without doubt, all that contributed to the creation of this killer. These revelations are not likely to happen.

How much did the environment of the area itself contribute to the shaping of Wendi Davidson? The potential for loneliness out in the vastness of West Texas is apparent to anyone traveling the byways. It is easy to wander for miles without seeing another person or a single vehicle on the road, making small towns like Junction, with a population under 3,000, feel like major metropolitan areas in comparison. But many friendly and delightful people live in West Texas. They chose the area because they love the solitude, the wide open spaces and the freedom of living far from governmental and corporate power. They still hold the pioneer spirit close to their hearts.

It is a place that breeds rugged individualism, self-sufficiency and a can-do attitude. It is also an environment where people who want total control over others find it easy to isolate themselves and their subjects from the rest of the world. It is no surprise that the secretive and cloistered FLDS chose nearby Eldorado to built their most elaborate compound. Controlling leaders, parents and spouses find an ally in this environment, one that makes it easier for them to restrict the boundaries of those under their power.

The isolation of West Texas, and the Davidson family's reaction to it, played a role in the making of their daughter, but it doesn't answer all questions. Many were stunned and bewildered by the total lack of empathy and the complete absence of sensitivity that the Davidson family displayed toward the grief of the Severance family in Maine. No matter how they looked at it, they could not understand it at all.

Thomas Goff and many others were equally baffled by the decision of Judge Jay Weatherby in granting custody of Shane to Lloyd and Judy Davidson. In fact, after hearing the audiotape and the testimony of the Davidsons' behavior, they do not comprehend why Child Protective Services did not remove both Shane and Tristan from that home. The poison in the atmosphere of that household was more than apparent.

Many told me the reason for that is San Angelo itself. The city is controlled by a select few, and they always get what they want. The Davidsons were not part of this power structure, but they did have an influential ally in Terrell Sheen. More important, they were area natives, while the Severance family was from distant Maine.

Whatever forces created these people and this situation, the end result is the same. Michael Severance, a young man who'd served his country well and grabbed life with both hands is dead. A family in Maine staggers under the loss. Tristan, a sweet little boy, lost the only father he had ever known and now has to grow up without a mother. And Shane, the most innocent victim of them all, will never clutch his father's hand in his own, will never hear his words of encouragement and praise, and will never grow and mature in the light of his guidance. Instead, he is spending much of his life in the home of people who despise his father and make excuses for his father's killer.

That, by any measure, is not justice.